KT-472-427

N 0096798 X

ROOTS OF THE RIGHT

READINGS IN FASCIST, RACIST AND ELITIST IDEOLOGY

General Editor: GEORGE STEINER

Fellow of Churchill College, Cambridge

ITALIAN FASCISMS

ITALIAN FASCISMS

FROM PARETO TO GENTILE

Edited and Introduced by

ADRIAN LYTTELTON

Senior Research Fellow at
St Antony's College, Oxford

Translated from the Italian,
unless otherwise indicated, by

DOUGLAS PARMÉE

JONATHAN CAPE
THIRTY BEDFORD SQUARE
LONDON

FIRST PUBLISHED 1973

JONATHAN CAPE LTD, 30 BEDFORD SQUARE, LONDON WC1

Hardback edition ISBN 0 224 00833 1
Paperback edition ISBN 0 224 00899 4

PRINTED IN GREAT BRITAIN
BY EBENEZER BAYLIS AND SON LIMITED
THE TRINITY PRESS, WORCESTER, AND LONDON
BOUND BY G. & J. KITCAT LTD, LONDON

GENERAL EDITOR'S PREFACE

Reliable estimates put at about seventy million the figure of those dead through war, revolution and famine in Europe and Russia between 1914 and 1945. To all but a few visionaries and pessimistic thinkers of the nineteenth century, the image of such an apocalypse, of a return to barbarism, torture and mass extermination in the heartlands of civilized life, would have seemed a macabre fantasy. Much of the crisis of identity and society that has overshadowed twentieth-century history comes from an impulse towards totalitarian politics. The theory of man as a rational animal, entitled to a wide exercise of political and economic decision, of man as a being equally endowed whatever his race, has been attacked at its religious, moral and philosophic roots. The most 'radical' attack—'radical' in that it demands a total re-valuation of man's place in society and of the status of different races in the general scheme of power and human dignity—has come from the Right.

Using the concept of the Fall of Man, of man as an instinctual savage requiring total leadership and repeated blood-letting, a number of elitist, racist and totalitarian dreamers and publicists have offered an alternative statement of the human condition. Fascism, Nazism, the programme of the Falange or the *Croix de Feu*, represent different variants of a related vision. Although this vision is often lunatic and nakedly barbaric, it can provide acute, tragic insights into the myths and taboos that underlie democracy.

Because the political and philosophical programme of the Right has come so near to destroying our civilization and is so alive still, it must be studied. Hence this series of source-readings in elitist, racist and fascist theory as it was articulated in France, Germany, Italy, Spain and other national communities between the 1860s and the Second World War. These 'black books' fill an almost complete gap in the source material available to any serious student of modern history, psychology, politics and sociology (most of the texts have never been available in English and several have all but disappeared in their original language). But these books also touch on the intractable puzzle of the co-existence in the same mind of profound inhumanity and obvious philosophic and literary importance.

GEORGE STEINER

CONTENTS

ACKNOWLEDGMENTS AND SOURCES

The editor and publishers are grateful to the following for permission to reproduce extracts in this collection:

Cambridge University Press, for 'The Doctrine of Fascism' by Benito Mussolini, from *Social and Political Doctrines of Contemporary Europe* by Michael Oakeshott; La Fenice, for 'Which Way is the World Going?' by Benito Mussolini, from *Opera Omnia* edited by E. and D. Susmel; Dr Federico Gentile, for an extract from *Origini e dottrina del fascismo* by Giovanni Gentile; Giuffré Editore, for five extracts from *Scritti e discorsi politici* by Alfredo Rocco; Signora Vittoria Piazzoni Marinetti, for 'Futurism and Fascism' by Filippo Tommaso Marinetti, from *L'Ardito*; Arnaldo Mondadori Editore and Il Vittoriale degli Italiani, for 'Letter to the Dalmations' from *Prose di ricerca* by Gabriele D'Annunzio; The Pall Mall Press, for an extract from *Vilfredo Pareto: Sociological Writings* Introduced by S. E. Finer; Vallecchi Editore, for extracts from *L'Europa vivente* by Curzio Malaparte and *Lemmonio Boreo* by Ardengo Soffici; Volpe Editore, for 'A Nationalist Programme', from *Vecchio e nuovo nazionalismo* by Giovanni Papini; George Weidenfeld & Nicolson, for 'The Futurist Manifesto' by Filippo Tommaso Marinetti, from *Intellectuals in Politics* by James Joll.

Corradini: Article from *Il Regno*: from *La cultura italiana del' 900 attraverso le reviste*, vol. 1, ed. D. Frigesi (Turin, 1960). 'The Principles of Nationalism', 'The Proletarian Nations and Nationalism', 'Nationalism and Democracy', 'The Cult of a Warrior Morality' and 'Nationalism and the Syndicates': all from *Discorsi politici* (Florence, 1923).

D'Annunzio: 'Letter to the Dalmatians': from *Prose di ricerca* (Verona, 1947).

Malaparte: 'Mussolini and National Syndicalism': from *L'Europa vivente ed altri saggi politici* (Florence 1961).

Marinetti: 'The Futurist Manifesto': translation from James Joll, *Intellectuals in Politics* (London, 1960).
'Old Ideas which always go hand in hand and must be separated': from *Opere*, vol. 2, ed. L. De Maria (Milan, 1968).

Mussolini: 'The Doctrine of Fascism' and 'The Nature of Fascism': translation from Michael Oakeshott, *Social and Political Doctrines of Contemporary Europe* (Cambridge, 1939).
'Which Way is the World Going?': from *Opera Omnia*, vol. 18, ed. E. and D. Susmel (Florence, 1923).

Papini and Prezzolini: 'A Nationalist Programme', 'An Aristocracy of Brigands' and 'Can the Bourgeoisie Revive?': from *Vecchio e nuovo nazionalismo* (Milan, 1914).

Pareto: 'From *Les Systèmes Socialistes*' and 'From *Trasformazioni della democrazia*': translation by D. Mirfin, from *Vilfredo Pareto: Sociological Writings*, edited and introduced by S. E. Finer (London, 1966).

Rocco: 'The Critical Objections to Nationalism', 'The *Politica* Manifesto', 'The Syndicates and the Crisis within the State', 'The Law on the Defence of the State', 'The Formation and Functions of the Corporations': all from *Scritti e discorsi politici*, vols. 1–3, (Milan, 1938).

INTRODUCTION

Anyone who produces a collection of writings devoted to the ideological roots of Italian Fascism must try to answer two sorts of objection:

1. That Fascism was an anti-intellectual movement which had little relationship to any intellectual theory.
2. That the intellectuals and writers whose texts are chosen were not Fascists.

Both objections contain a partial truth. In relation to the first point, it must certainly be admitted that there is no exact correspondence between practice and doctrine. In passing from literature to politics the concept degenerates into a slogan. This is obviously true to some extent of the relationship of political ideas to any organized movement, but it is also true that in a movement like Fascism, based on irrationalist premises, the role of precisely formulated ideas in guiding political action will tend to be small. It can be legitimately argued that one of the weaknesses of Fascism was the lack of a coherent and reasonably stable ideology. None the less, Fascism as a movement and a regime was prepared, interpreted and shaped by ideas formed in a generation of anti-democratic thought. These ideas were not all compatible. They came from men of different intellectual traditions, and their influence was discontinuous; different phases of Fascism required different ideological justifications. And this leads me to the second objection. Every one of the writers represented in this collection, except Mussolini himself, had serious reservations about some aspect of Fascism. Early Fascists like Lanzillo and Malaparte were not at home in the atmosphere of the later regime: conversely the nationalists Rocco and Corradini disapproved of many of the features of the movement. Gentile, the regime's official philosopher, only adhered to Fascism in 1923, after the March on Rome; Pareto, though he approved of the Fascists taking power, would probably have been critical of the full dictatorship established after 1925. However, in the case of all these writers it is possible to see how some of their ideas became current within Fascism, very often through the agency of Mussolini. The Duce was a voracious if superficial reader, and popularized many of the ideas examined here.

Some of the texts I have included (Soffici, D'Annunzio) are important for their style and imagery rather than for their content. One would be neglecting a valuable clue provided by the Fascists themselves if one did not pay attention to their definition of Fascism as more a 'style of life' than a philosophy. Unfortunately, a history of Fascist imagery and ritual had yet to be written. This anthology cannot claim to be a substitute, and the reader must be warned that a collection of texts of this kind inevitably stresses argument at the expense of rhetoric and emotional incitement.

Fascism, reduced to its essentials, is the ideology of permanent conflict. It is misleading in the extreme, in my belief, to refer to Fascist ideology as 'Utopian', as some writers have done. It is possible to describe the racial community of National-Socialist visionaries as a Utopia; but at this point National Socialism can be held to have diverged from or 'transcended' Fascism. One might object: but is not liberalism also an ideology of conflict? It could be argued that this is a description of all anti-Utopian schools of thought, since they believe that the suppression of social conflict and the achievement of a steady state either in domestic or international politics is impossible. Moreover, pluralist liberalism is also in some sense committed to a belief that conflict and competition are not only inevitable but beneficial. Truth and progress are seen as the result of the clash of opposites. However, the liberal does not seek to maximize conflict. He does not believe that the most extreme forms of conflict, organized violence and war, should be the paradigm. He seeks on the contrary to limit and regulate conflict and to establish rules of fairness which will be accepted by the contestants.

There is a closer kinship between Fascism and certain forms of existentialism. The idea that the true value of a man's character and beliefs can only be discovered in extreme situations, and especially in the face of death, is certainly not the property of Fascism. However, it is none the less the ethical underpinning for the Fascist belief in war. War, and other forms of conflict, are ennobling because they force man to reveal the nature and efficacy of his ultimate commitments. 'All other trials are substitutes, which never really put a man in front of himself in the alternative of life and death.' (Mussolini.) However, Fascism, at least in its mature form, rejected totally the idea that man's ends were of his own making and free choice. Instead, the individual was required to acknowledge the prior and absolute claim to obedience of the particular historical entity, the nation, of which he formed a part. What was left, therefore, of the militant existentialist ethic was the cult of sacrifice divorced from the idea of responsibility; the nihilistic violence of the Fascist (*Me ne frego ...*) would resemble the *acte gratuit* of the existentialists were its direction not predetermined.

The unity of Fascist doctrine, even in its mature phase, was always precarious. The structure of 'The Doctrine of Fascism' reveals this fact. The first half of the article was the work of Giovanni Gentile; only the second half was Mussolini's own work, though the whole article appeared under his name. The difference of tone and style could be explained away: 'fundamental ideas' needed different treatment from 'political and social doctrine'. However, this difference did not merely reflect the distinction, drawn by Gentile, between 'the contingent forms of politics' and 'the higher level of the history of thought'. What Eugen Weber calls 'the original mystique' of the Italian Fascist movement had sources of inspiration which were not identical with those of Gentile. The political philosophy of Gentile was elaborated after the Fascists had come to power. It was an attempt to explain the regime in terms which would give it a historical and philosophical legitimacy. For many Fascists, on the other hand, Fascism was an anti-philosophy. The systematic nature of Gentile's thought automatically made it an object of derision to the typical spokesman of the violent *squadrismo* of Fascism's early years. Benedetto Croce, admittedly inspired by a subtle malice at the expense of his one-time collaborator Gentile, remarked in 1923 that Fascism had more in common with the Futurists' 'thirst for the new' and their 'exaltation of youth' than with those apologists who were attempting to place the movement in the context of the Risorgimento or of idealist philosophy.

There was more to the Fascist opposition to 'philosophy' than mere philistinism, although no one should wish to deny that the latter was a typical Fascist trait. There was an anti-intellectualism among the intellectuals, which had identifiable cultural roots. The dislike of the coherent, the systematic and the formal owed something to the Nietzschean exaltation of the aphorism and to modern critics of metaphysics. Similarly, belief in the primacy of action and the irrelevance of argument received nourishment from the sociologists and psychologists who had 'unmasked' moral and political theory as mere rationalization of interest or sentiment. The 'style' of the Fascist, his self-image as a man impervious to rational conviction who would cut short 'sterile' discussion by a command or a blow, had been prefigured by those writers who called for a new, virile elite to restore vigour to Italy's flagging polity and culture.

If Fascism was an 'anti-philosophy', however, it none the less had, or acquired during its history, precise aims. These were first and foremost of a negative or defensive kind. One can, of course, argue that there is nothing negative about a sincere commitment to the preservation and greatness of the nation. It is a positive value, and Fascism would be inexplicable without the force of simple patriotic sentiment. However, not all patriots are Fascists and even the reverse is true. For patriotism to be converted into Fascism, love of country had to be transmuted into hatred of the 'internal enemy'.

The circumstances of Italy's participation in the Great War explain the widespread extent of this conversion, this turning-inwards of patriotic feeling. Italy's entry into the war in 1915 was opposed by the Socialists, by many Catholics, and by her leading pre-war statesman, Giolitti. The suspicion that Italy would be betrayed to the foreigner by the forces of 'neutralism' was in these circumstances understandable. It reached hysterical pitch during 1917, after the Bolshevik revolution and the disaster at Caporetto, which was attributed to the influence of subversive propaganda among the troops.

However, the theme of the internal enemy was not invented during the war. If one goes back to the beginnings of the Italian nationalist movement, one finds already that they are characterized not merely by the cult of national greatness but by the reaction against socialism. In Papini's *Programme*, the need for a 'national policy' is quite frankly stated in terms of the maintenance of the power of the bourgeoisie: 'if we middle-class monarchists want to maintain our position as the ruling class and leading caste, those who own the property and give the orders, we must follow above all a national policy.' The defeat which Italian troops suffered at the hands of the Abyssinians at Adowa in 1896 and the subsequent fall of the prime minister Crispi were the critical events which inspired the new nationalism. It also fed on the more diffuse disillusionment with parliamentary corruption and the failure of successive governments to realize the ideals of the Risorgimento. The nationalists attributed the humiliation of Italy's imperial ambitions to the cowardice and irresolution of the bourgeoisie and to the influence of the small but resolute socialist opposition. When in the early years of the century Giolitti came to power, he inaugurated a new policy of tolerance towards the socialists. This marked the recognition that the attempt to suppress the working-class movement by orthodox police methods had failed. In reality, Italian socialism was still a far from irresistible force. However, it had won an important moral victory. Many intellectuals in the 1890s had shown sympathy for socialist doctrines; this was the decade during which the *socialismo della cattedra* (*Kathedersozialismus*) flourished. The mental climate fostered by positivist scientism and an optimistic belief in progress, the peaceful advance of democracy, and class harmony seemed to the young nationalists so to have enfeebled the bourgeoisie's will to resist that the ultimate victory of socialism was probable unless a new spirit of resistance could be evoked. Enrico Corradini's outcry 'against the cowardice of the present hour' was prompted in the first instance by a consciousness of the internal threat posed by 'ignoble socialism'. In 1903 Corradini founded the review *Il Regno* together with the two Florentine intellectuals, Papini and Prezzolini. Of these three, only Corradini remained a nationalist. The volatile Florentines had both left the movement by the time it had crystallized into a definite form with the foundation of the Nationalist Association in 1910. However, at the outset it was they rather than Corradini who did most to provide nationalism with a new, fashionable doctrine and idiom.

The imperialism of the Italian nationalists clearly had much in common with that of German, French and English writers of the time. But nationalists do not like to be reminded of foreign sources, and this is one reason why Prezzolini emphasized his debt to the Italian theorists of the elite, Mosca and Pareto. This acknowledgement at first sight looks suspect. Neither Mosca nor Pareto could be called a nationalist; Pareto frequently exercised his corrosive sarcasm at the expense of chauvinists, and during the 1880s and 1890s he had been a leading opponent of Crispi's programme of imperialism and high military expenditure. However, elite theory must none the less be accounted a central feature of nationalist and Fascist criticisms of socialism and democracy.

At this point another objection can be raised. Most political scientists would agree that Mosca and Pareto had made a valuable contribution to the understanding of democracy. The importance of competition between rival organized groups; the phenomenon, described by Roberto Michels, of the formation of stable and only imperfectly accountable oligarchies of leaders and bureaucrats within the democratic parties themselves: these are among the aspects of politics to which elite theory has drawn attention. Both Mosca and Pareto regarded themselves as objective political scientists whose purpose was to discover valid laws of political behaviour. However, it would be somewhat naive to accept these claims without examination. In spite of a genuine preoccupation with scientific method (more marked in Pareto than in Mosca) neither author could really disguise his *parti pris* as a critic of democracy.

The essence of the theory of the elite, which is common to both writers, is in the assertion that political power is always exercised by an organized minority and never in reality by the majority of the members of a society. From this it followed that the prime agent of historical conflict and change was no longer to be seen in the class struggle, but in the competition between rival elites. The ideological uses of this theory are fairly clear. First of all, it could be used to deny that the principles of democracy had any particular validity; the rule of the many, like the rule of the one, is in reality a disguise for the rule of the few. Secondly, the theory provided an answer to the Marxist teleology. Instead of bringing about the end of history, the victory of the proletariat, or rather of its representatives, would merely mean the supersession of one elite by another. Marxism itself would therefore have to be treated not as a philosophy radically different from all previous class-based ideologies, but as simply a new 'formula', used by the counter-elite of the leaders of the working-class movement to support their claim to power.

Mosca's standpoint was that of a conservative liberal, and both his temperament and theoretical concerns were far removed from the universe of the twentieth-century radical Right. His ideal was of a dynamic hierarchy something like the English ruling class, aristocratic but open to recruitment from below. His later writings show an increasing concern with the problem of making the government of the few responsible, protecting legal rights and limiting the arbitrary exercise of power. He disliked and opposed Fascism. The new Right borrowed from him, but their debt was severely circumscribed.

The case of Pareto is different. It is true that too much should not be made of Pareto's support for the Fascist government in 1922–3. It has been pointed out that at that time Croce was also a supporter of Mussolini. If Pareto approved of early Fascism, he retained an old-fashioned liberal belief in the freedom of opinion and was critical of its limitation. One imagines that many features of the regime after 1925 would have been distasteful to him: the enforced uniformity and the increasing trend towards state intervention in the economy violated the two main precepts which he had urged on Mussolini. However, if Pareto also remained in some respects a liberal, this does not exclude the possibility that his theories influenced Fascism, and in a far more profound and far-reaching way than those of Mosca. We must recognize that there was a powerful strain in Italian Fascism which originated in an exasperated and disillusioned liberalism.

The accent of Pareto's theory falls far more than that of Mosca on the debunking of ideological and theoretical pretensions. There is a strange paradox at the heart of his book on *Les systèmes socialistes*—politically though not theoretically the most important of his works. While seeking to show the fallacies or lack of empirical foundation in socialist theory, he rejected the idea that such an enterprise could have any practical relevance. For the truth or falsity of a theory was irrelevant to the question of its social effects. From the standpoint of the sociologist, it did not matter whether a theory employed in politics was 'from a certain point of view, false, provided the emotions it inspires are useful'. The falsity of socialist theory was not in itself a reason for absolute condemnation. No doubt Pareto is right that in the short term most men are more easily moved by sentiment than by reason in evaluating political theories. But isn't Pareto's dichotomy too absolute? The truth of a theory, in the sense of its capacity to explain historical conditions and predict future possibilities, is surely not irrelevant to its survival. Should one not see the decline of anarchism, or the disappearance of Utopian socialism before Marxism, as in part a consequence of their inadequacy as explanations?

The social scientist, in Pareto's view, is necessarily a cynic in possession of arcane knowledge which cannot be revealed to the multitude. As Schumpeter caustically remarked, Pareto's approval of 'derivations' (his name for rationalizations of sentiment) with positive effects is like the attitude of a psychoanalyst who recommends belief in God because, though an illusion, it is psychologically beneficial. A politician who read Pareto could justifiably conclude that the art of politics consisted in the clear-sighted manipulation of mass passions; once Pareto had unveiled the truth, the way was open for the technicians of collective psychology. On the other hand, as critics of Pareto and Sorel (among them Mussolini) have observed, once the irrational nature of a derivation or myth has been exposed, it loses its effect. The manipulative attitude of Mussolini towards his own movement after 1919 and the insufficient commitment of many Fascists to the myths which they used to mobilize the masses were a critical weakness in the movement. This Pareto himself perceived; it led him to doubt whether Fascism would become one of 'the great factors of social evolution'.

Pareto was a more radical and more pessimistic thinker than Mosca. He emphasized more strongly the part played by force in maintaining the rule of the elite, and less that of shared values and the creation of an effective consensus. Like his friend on the other side of the barricades, Georges Sorel, he admired heroic qualities and greatly preferred revolutionary socialists to reformists. One of his most withering phrases describes the reason for the failure of 'the Liberal Utopia' of free trade and free enterprise; its defenders, he wrote, had been 'satisfied men of tepid convictions'. Pareto's appreciation of the virtues of conflict was rooted not only in a Machiavellian appreciation of the realities of power but in social Darwinism. Humanitarian pity for the weak or the criminal not only impaired the elite's resolution but weakened the whole society through inhibiting selection. The demographic vitality of the peasantry, maintained by their traditionalism about sex and the family, was indispensable if the elite were to be renewed.

It is true, as Professor Finer has pointed out, that Pareto's condemnation of humanitarianism is not absolute. He accepts that 'humanity', or altruism, is a natural sentiment without which society could not subsist, and he rejects the cruder forms of eugenic selection (murder, prohibitions on reproduction), on the grounds that they would be too offensive to this basic sentiment. Pareto is merely arguing that justice, in the punitive sense, and therefore coercion, is also necessary if society is to subsist. However, consider now Pareto's specific historical diagnosis. He regarded contemporary France and Italy as countries which were sick with the malady of excessive humanitarianism. The function of these humanitarian sentiments when preached by socialists is 'uniquely to break the resistance of the elite in power'; bourgeois humanitarianism is more peculiar, but even less admirable. It reflects the cowardice of those who have no desire to fight, and who believe that a theory of gradual pacific evolution and the practice of social reform will avoid their violent dispossession. They are however mistaken, because the prevalence of humanitarianism will lead to progressive social disintegration and decadence. When either of the two basic 'residues' has prevailed almost totally over the other, then it is safe to predict that the tendency will be reversed and a new phase of the cycle of the decadence and renewal of elites will begin. The most probable solution is that the bourgeois humanitarians will be swept aside by a forceful counter-elite from the lower classes. However, if this solution is avoided the ultimate fate of bourgeois society will be no better. For humanitarianism will continue to 'inhibit selection', and the process of decadence will continue until halted by external conquest.

Pareto's tone is not that of cool prediction but of prophecy. Bourgeois society will be destroyed for its sins by a kind of barbarian conquest at the hands of the socialist or syndicalist elite. The prospect fills him with grim satisfaction. However, Pareto rejected collectivist economics and believed that state socialism would lead to economic decadence, as it had done in the late Roman Empire. What, then, if one took Pareto's diagnosis seriously, could be the alternative solution? Only the advent of a new non-socialist elite, without humanitarian scruples, and capable of using force. Such an elite would have to draw heavily on healthy, unspoilt plebeian elements, rich in the right conservative residues. Fascism, guided as it was by an elite of 'combatants' and plebeian ex-revolutionaries, filled the bill. It combined the positive features of revolutionary determination with a rejection of the collectivist myth, which to Pareto was the most objectionable aspect of socialism. Pareto protested to his nationalist disciples that he did not take sides; he was a detached scientific observer. But the sociologist is always potentially an actor as well as an observer, since he may alter men's beliefs about the situation in which they live and thereby alter the situation itself. If humanitarianism and reluctance to use force were the sure signs of an elite in decline and only war could arrest the progress of socialism, it was hardly illegitimate for the nationalists to cite Pareto in support of their programme. As Prezzolini wrote to Pareto, 'You see in the theory of aristocracies a scientific theory: I see in it instead a scientific justification of my present political needs.' In the columns of *Il Regno* Pareto himself wrote in terms which can only be read as a direct incitement to the nationalists to organize: 'If there were a frankly reactionary party in Italy, I would say that there are only two parties which might hope for a prosperous future, i.e. that one and the other of the revolutionary socialists ... '

Before 1900 Pareto's main energies as a controversialist had gone into the free trade campaign. Although he recognized that free trade was not always beneficial, the protectionist industries in Italy were to him mere bands of robbers united to despoil the consumer. The diffused interests of the consumer or the ordinary investor were no match for the powerful pressures of the organized groups of producers. Protectionism and socialism were similar phenomena: both entailed the destruction of wealth and its redistribution by political means in favour of a particular group. After 1900 Pareto developed this analysis further. He christened democracy the regime of 'demagogic plutocracy'; there was a common interest in the short term shared by protectionist plutocrats and socialist agitators in the spoliation of the middle class and the peasantry. These two blocs of interests he christened the 'speculators', and the 'rentiers'; they coincided approximately with the two main types of 'residue', 'the instinct for combinations' (innovatory and consensual) and 'the persistence of aggregates' (traditionalist and coercive). Pareto's attack on 'demagogic plutocracy' had something in common with the denunciation by the *meridionalisti* (Southern experts) of the *de facto* collusion between the Northern trades unions and the capitalists in favour of higher wages and higher prices, which worked to the detriment of the backward South. In the post-war period, Pareto's theory became a perfect expression for the resentments of the middle class, which felt itself to have been despoiled of its savings by arms profiteers and which was at the same time threatened with expropriation by the working class. It is a characteristic of classic middle-class Fascism that it posits some form of conspiracy between financiers and demagogues; one could say that if Pareto's theory had not existed, Fascism would have had to invent it.

Pareto has frequently been criticized for his tendency to

explain social facts in terms of individual biological or psychological constants. Papini and Corradini followed him in treating the theories of democracy and socialism as the expressions of a state of mind. As activists, their task was to evoke new passions; it was only by acting directly on the passions that 'formulas and ideas' could really be changed. This assumption of the primacy of psychology and of the capacity of affective states to determine judgment, political choice and even the forms of political action needs constantly to be borne in mind in considering the genesis of the Fascist way of thought. When some revolutionary syndicalists interpreted their syndicalism as above all 'a state of mind', they were confessing a kinship with nationalism that was to prove decisive. Later on, Fascism was also to be defined by Mussolini and others as a 'state of mind', rather than a theory.

Nationalist and pre-Fascist propaganda made much use of appeals to the aesthetic sense. Sorel's myth was defined as a 'body of images'; the contrasted physical images of the New Man—young, virile and athletic—and of the old representative of the democratic order—paunched, short-sighted, slow-moving—were highly effective. The aesthetic and the biological views of politics reinforced each other. It is characteristic of Fascism that the attention is focused on the man rather than on what he says. Soffici's hero Lemmonio Boreo sees no reason to prefer anarchist doctrine to socialist, but 'what interested him were the men preaching these doctrines' ... 'In a speech basically the words count for much less than we think.' In Weberian terms, this is a magical as opposed to an ethical conception. Vitality is the supreme good, and life has its highest expression in the active, decisive individual. The influence of Nietzsche is here apparent: the vogue for his thought, admittedly often known only at second hand or in popular vulgarized versions, was at its height in Italy during the period 1900–1915. Chief among the mediators between Nietzsche and Italy was D'Annunzio. In his novels, starting with *Le vergini delle rocce* (1895), D'Annunzio explored the idea of the superman in his various guises as aesthete, lover and man of action. The counterpoint to the superman is provided by the description of the baseness and corruption of post-Risorgimento Italy. The destruction of the villas and parks of Rome by building speculators was for D'Annunzio a paradigm of the vulgarity of the new plutocratic and democratic age. The yearning for heroic leadership, for a politics of glory and adventure, was already widely diffused. D'Annunzio immensely heightened the psychological appeal of such dreams by his successful fusion of the sexual, the religious and the political. D'Annunzian politics are linked to sex because both are seen as the manifestations of a single will to power and dominion, and to religion through the imagery of sacrifice. Indeed, in his later political writings and speeches D'Annunzio elaborated a whole liturgy for his patriotic religion.

Nietzschean conceptions can also be seen in the work of Papini; in the condemnation of the respect for human life as the basis of the democratic mentality, in the idea that the development of higher forms of life requires the sacrifice of the mass, or of the little man. More important still was the conception of the new intellectual as the man who would bring about the 'transvaluation of values', the eternal seeker never satisfied and always endeavouring to overcome himself as well as the world, the breaker of the tablets of the law. This was the self-image of Papini and other intellectuals, and it was one which was, consciously or unconsciously, exploited by Mussolini. Mussolini's restlessness, his scepticism about programmes and doctrines, his faith in action, could be interpreted as marks of the new man.

One could claim that this Nietzschean nationalism is beset by a major contradiction. On the one hand, the nationalist insists on the need for unity; on the other hand, the contempt for human life violates the minimum conditions or principles on which community is possible. The prophets of a heroic elite of superior individuals could not with consistency also claim to be propagating a 'national consciousness' which would effectively unify the Italian people.

The influence of Nietzsche was not confined to the Right. Some socialists and anarchists found his dislike of Christianity and his contempt for bourgeois mentality sympathetic, and even tried to give a revolutionary interpretation to the image of the superman. The morality of Nietzsche (see *The French Right*, edited by J. S. McClelland, in this series) was adopted by Sorel, and Sorel's influence was probably greater in Italy than in France. The revolutionary syndicalists conceived of themselves as a new aristocracy, a kind of heroic war-band waging civil conflict. Mussolini, though he rejected syndicalist ideas about political organization, shared their basic *Weltanschauung*. Like theirs, his Marxism had been modified by the influence of Nietzsche and Pareto. The concept of the elite, and the importance of heroism, dynamism and faith in Mussolini's vocabulary involved what Nolte has described as a 'tension' within Mussolini's early Marxism. He was also in touch with Papini and Prezzolini, and shared, at least at a superficial level, in the revolt against positivist scientism. He saw in the new voluntarist and pragmatist philosophies, which asserted the influence of the will or the imagination on the process of cognition, an arsenal of slogans which he could use to fight the complacent optimism of evolutionary social democracy. As Lichtheim has pointed out, Engels transformed the Marxist idea of the dialectic as the process by which men make their own history into a mechanical determinist conception, in which the dialectic becomes a law exactly analogous to those of physical science. The reaction against this on the part of Sorel, the syndicalists and Mussolini was to go to the other extreme and to put the accent on the creative force by which individuals can transform the given historical situation. The revolutionary impulse is divorced from the consciousness of historical development and becomes a matter of will and faith.

The crisis of 1914–15 transformed an intellectual heresy into a political schism. The failure of the Second International to prevent war exploded social-democratic orthodoxy. Both Communism and Fascism were the children of this crisis. In Italy the crisis was particularly acute; pacifist forces were stronger than elsewhere, and the long debate between interventionists and neutralists produced a clear-cut ideological conflict. The conversion of Mussolini and many of the syndicalist leaders to the cause of intervention in war can at least partly be explained by their feeling that the revolutionary must be on the side of action. Aside from this generic psychological preference, the outbreak of war did furnish cogent arguments to justify a conversion to nationalism. It exposed the weakness of international class solidarity and the strength of national ties. The belief that class consciousness would be the most effective form of group solidarity in the future was shattered. The test of the effectiveness of a myth was in its capacity to inspire heroic action, to create a religious frame of mind which would accept sacrifice and martyrdom for collective values. Now it was evident that it was still easier to get men to die for their country than for their class. It was therefore possible to argue that the nation, and not the class, could alone inspire an effective ethic which would counteract the decadence of hedonist individualism and restore the tragic sense of life.

The revolutionaries who supported intervention formed a loose grouping known as the *fasci di azione rivoluzionaria*. These first *fasci* were the direct ancestors of those of 1919. Like them, they were an 'anti-party' composed of activists in revolt against organization and systematic doctrine. The situation of the interventionist intellectuals gave a new edge to the polemic against rationality and the belief in gradual progress. Both the syndicalist intellectuals and the noisy group of Futurists led by Marinetti shared what may be called a Heraclitean vision of social reality. All was flux; Bergson's metaphysical conception of ultimate reality as a continuous, unpredictable process of creation which could not be grasped by the intellect but only intuited and lived, had its influence on political and social thought. 'Social Bergsonism' was hostile to law, institutions and other stabilizing forces; the spontaneous, irrational creative act was the highest value and the motive force of history. This political metaphysic was admirably adapted to the needs of a group of 'marginal men' who saw their opportunity in the bewildering rapidity with which events disrupted established patterns of thought and organization. For Lanzillo, war was a creative as well as a destructive force, because 'modern society was about to crystallize into fixed forms', and war had prevented this. The socialist and democratic ideologies had failed because they were too rationalistic and war, the irrational phenomenon *par excellence*, had been the instrument for showing up their deficiencies. The Europe of 1918–19 gave little sign of a return to stability, either internal or international. The pessimistic prediction of a new age of conflict, requiring an ideology of conflict, was in these circumstances persuasive. Nationalists and proto-Fascists like Lanzillo agreed that the democracies had won the war in spite of, and not because of, their ideology. Alfredo Rocco spoke of a 'a contradiction between the reality of the war and its ideology'. Even in the hour of victory, he felt able to affirm that 'the ideology of democracy is by definition an ideology of defeat'. Later, democrats like Salvemini who were willing to renounce excessive territorial claims were blamed for Italy's disappointments at the Peace Conference.

Early Fascism thrived on a mythology of improvisation and audacity. The spirit which its leaders liked to believe they possessed is typified by the exclamation of a character in one of Marinetti's experimental novels: 'Everything can be improvised, even God! I am the leader of that crowd!' Fascism appealed to youth by appearing to side with modernity and change. It offered liberation from the stuffiness of paternal values and from the cloying oppressiveness of maternal sentimentality. Talcott Parsons has suggested in his essay 'Patterns of aggression in Western society' that in all Western societies there has been a strong tendency to identify morality with feminine influence. The reaction against morality or 'softness' can be explained in terms of the difficulty for the adolescent of achieving a satisfactory identification with the father after his care and upbringing have been left almost exclusively to the mother. It makes sense that the reaction should have been especially fierce in Italy, where the cult of the mother was so powerful. Anti-feminism was a conspicuous feature of the Fascist mentality. In different forms, it can be found in the writings of Corradini, Papini, Marinetti and Mussolini. Fascist ritual can be read at one level as a complex of virility symbols.

Even if Marinetti was too eccentric a figure to remain prominent for long in Fascist politics, the contribution of Futurism to the ideological appeal of Fascism was extremely important. Many of the Fascist slogans which conveyed a sense of rebellion and novelty were borrowed from the vocabulary of Futurism. No one stated the fundamental political intuition of early Fascist propaganda more clearly than Marinetti: patriotism was to be identified not with traditional reaction, but with 'the destructive action of lovers of freedom'. Such an 'anarchic nationalism' could inspire the action of the Fascist squads during the phase of Fascism's rise to power. However, the heroic mystique of the deed, whether syndicalist or activist, did not offer satisfactory guidance for the reconstruction of the state and the restoration of authority. Mussolini's 1922 article 'Which way is the world going?' shows that he was committed to an interpretation of Fascism which placed it in the context of a secular reaction against democracy and the values of 1789. Fascism might be revolutionary in origin and demagogic in style, but no one after 1922 should have doubted that it was none the less a right-wing ideology. The coherence which Fascist ideology lacked was supplied by the nationalism of Corradini and above all of Rocco. In 1923 the Fascist movement fused with the older Nationalist Association, and the influence of the nationalist doctrinaires could henceforward be officially acknowledged. The nationalists contributed a realism and expertise which the Fascist intellectuals usually lacked. The syndicalists and the Futurists were at one in their suspicion and contempt for bureaucracy; the nationalists appreciated the realities of power and sided with the officials.

In his 1914 introduction to *Vecchio e nuovo nazionalismo* Prezzolini attacked his one-time colleague Corradini without mercy. He attempted to dissociate his own contribution to *Il Regno*, and that of Papini, from that of Corradini and his group. The former was characterized by 'practical and social concerns', the latter by imperialist rhetoric and aestheticism. Prezzolini had come to see that serious analysis of Italy's internal problems and action to solve them had to take precedence over imperialist adventure. However, he admitted that in the years between 1903 and 1914 the nationalists had in part outgrown their original exclusively literary frame of mind, and had made the acquaintance of Italian economic realities. Although Corradini never perhaps understood much about economics, he knew how to flatter businessmen. After 1910, they became his best audience, and his rhetoric was increasingly tailored to suit the requirements of the boardroom rather than those of the café. The celebration of the class of 'producers', i.e. industrialists, in contrast to the old cultivated middle class from which Parliament was recruited, became a dominant theme in Corradini's writings, especially after 1915. As Nolte has observed, Corradini, while not jettisoning the old rhetoric about the superiority of 'ideal' to 'material' forces, none the less accepted 'the mode of thought and terminology' of his Marxist opponents. In 1919 he went as far as to define the nation as 'primarily an economic society', to the scandal of some of his supporters. Before that date he had attempted to turn socialism on its head by his slogan of the 'proletarian nation'. This memorable formula, which he had borrowed from the poet Pascoli, expressed the sense of grievance at the exclusion of the latecomer Italy from the imperial table. The fact on which Corradini seized was the high rate of emigration, which reached an all-time peak in 1913. The conquest of Libya (1911–12) was no serious answer, of course, to the problem of overpopulation; but the mirage of new land in Africa had genuine popular appeal. The battle of the 'young' proletarian nations against the old decadent plutocracies was to become the central motif of Fascist propaganda from the time of the First Abyssinian War (1896) onwards. If Italy was a proletarian nation, paying a tribute to foreign capital, then the remedy was to be found in developing Italian national consciousness. Just as socialism had educated the proletariat to the realities of the class struggle, so nationalism would educate all classes to the realities of the international struggle. An advantage of the analogy with socialism was that it enabled Corradini to stress the need for unity and social discipline. Corradini is deliberately ambiguous about whether war is valuable as a means to creating social discipline, or vice versa. Rocco was more explicit: 'the most important item' on the nationalist agenda was not preparation for war but 'a strengthening of society from within through the creation of national awareness and strong national discipline'.

It was an important feature of nationalist and Fascist ideology that it claimed to 'transcend' socialism. It was at least identifiably post-socialist. Corradini's other important innovation was that he recognized the potential value of the revolutionary syndicalists' attack on democratic socialism. He sensed that their temperament might make them ultimately into allies, and that there was much common ground to be found in the criticism of the 'decadent' humanitarian ruling class. At times, Corradini appears to embrace a doctrine rather like that of Machiavelli in the *Discourses*: the tensions arising from the class struggle, when it is vigorously waged by both sides, generate a drive to expansion. In 1919, like Luigi Einaudi and some other liberal economists, he was willing to argue that class conflict would create a natural equilibrium favourable to economic efficiency providing its conduct was not falsified by extraneous political ideologies. However, his acceptance of syndicalism or the class struggle was never sincere. National power and expansion were linked to the growth of industry; therefore the subordination of the class struggle to the need for national discipline implied also the recognition that the problem of distribution must take second place to that of production. Wages should rise, but only in accordance with productivity.

Corradini's vague phrases about the 'co-ordination' of class interests into 'units of power' leave the contradiction between syndicalism and nationalism unresolved. Rocco put things more plainly. The growth of unions and other associations should be recognized as a fact of modern life. Further, their authority over their members should be legally sanctioned and reinforced. The individual should once more be subjected to a corporate discipline, and his political and economic rights should belong to him not as an 'abstract' atom within the state, but as the living cell of an organic professional body, governed by the principle of hierarchy, not that of equality: 'The isolated individual, the amorphous and inorganic mass of individuals who still dominate our political life are nothing.' However, this recognition of the syndicates' or corporations' power over their members was not to weaken the indivisible authority of the state; recognition signified control and discipline by legal norms and sanctions. The corporations were to be links in the chain which bound the citizen tightly to the state. For old-fashioned conservatism, the corporations or guilds had been idealized not only as an instrument of social discipline but also because they protected individual rights and privileges against the overriding power of the state. The peculiar oppressiveness of Rocco's system lies in its combination of the sanctions of organized social discipline with those of undivided and unlimited sovereignty.

Rocco's vision of history was, like Pareto's, cyclical, but it was framed in different terms. The unending struggle of history was essentially the struggle of state authority against the centrifugal forces of disintegration. 'Now the life of all social bodies is an unceasing struggle between the principle of organization represented by the state and the principle of disintegration, represented by individuals and groups, which tends to disrupt them and thus lead to their decline and fall.' Feudalism, the Reformation, bourgeois individualism, socialism: all these were for Rocco manifestations of the same 'individualistic, anti-social, and anti-state ideology'.

Ultimately, Rocco recognized no imperatives except those of power politics. His state, a Leviathan far more terrible than that of Hobbes, was a collective organism engaged in a remorseless struggle for survival with other states. Natural selection through conflict would ensure that the fittest and best states survived and expanded. Like Corradini, Rocco pointed to the rapid increase of the Italian population as a sign of vitality. The great powers had now entered the imperialist period, and this demanded an unprecedented co-ordination of all spheres of social life: 'the open competition between imperialist powers has become an iron law which no nation can afford to overlook and still survive ... each nation must plan and adapt and organize its whole life, energy and organization to meet this necessity. This basic truth is the sole measure by which to judge all political values.'

The utter subordination of all individual purposes to the state's drive for power over other states could not be more clearly expressed. The state according to Rocco and Fascism does not exist in order to reconcile or protect individual interests and rights, but concedes the satisfaction of the latter only as a means to realizing its own ends. The public interest is identified with external power. The possible conflict between the two is obscured by the questionable assumption that wealth and power are indivisible.

Rocco's nationalism, as befitted an eminent professor of law, was cast in a more consistent and rational mould than that of a Papini or a Corradini. The heroic affirmation of the individual was not Rocco's concern; his only heroes were legislator-conquerors like Napoleon who had restored the undivided sovereignty of the state and buttressed it by a structure of laws and institutions. This was a very different cast of mind from the early Fascist preference for fluidity; Rocco did not believe that chaos was creative.

Undoubtedly, Rocco had a good understanding of the development of contemporary capitalism. The rise of the cartel and the trust were to him symptoms that capitalism was passing into a new organized phase, and that the old liberal ideal of unrestricted competition between free entrepreneurs was obsolete. 'Organized capitalism' was not only a reality but an ideal to be furthered. Seemingly, Rocco, as the chief legislator of the 'corporate state' set up between 1926 and 1934, was able to realize his ideal. Production was to be planned and controlled by the 'organized classes of producers' acting 'under the overall guidance and control of the state'. This formula proved very useful for reconciling industry with dictatorship. However, it could not eliminate the tension between corporate self-interest and arbitrary political intervention. The formal mechanisms of the corporate state were bypassed both by Mussolini's personal government and by the informal agreements among industrial groups. In addition, the discipline of labour relations was one-sided and false, since the employers chose their representatives more or less freely while the workers had little or no say in choosing theirs.

Rocco's whole framework of legal institutions was designed to serve a single political will. In his insistence that the power of the state should be unfettered he failed to perceive the danger that the will of the dictator would by overriding the norms of all particular institutions (party, corporations, etc.) disorganize them. His attempt to maximize both stability and power was ultimately contradictory.

Unlike the other writers discussed, Gentile had the function of justifying a regime already in existence. The metaphysic of 'actualism', as Gentile's philosophy was known, rested on the conception of thought as pure act. Croce had objected when Gentile first formulated his philosophy that this conception annulled the possibility of making distinctions or rational classifications, and reduced the process of thought to a mystical undifferentiated intuition. 'Your pure act, which you call Thought, could equally well be called Life, Feeling, Will, or anything else, since any denomination implies a distinction ... ' Croce's concern that Gentile's metaphysic would make impossible the formulation of criteria of judgment is relevant to the consideration of his political thought. The irrationalist activism of the Fascist movement and Mussolini's scorn for systematic political doctrines were interpreted favourably by Gentile. They exemplified the identity of thought and action which was his fundamental principle: 'The true resolutions of the Duce are always those which he has both formulated and put into effect'; this was for Gentile not a harmless tautology but a subject for praise. The irony of Gentile's position was that while on the one hand his philosophy, because of its extreme abstraction, was quite incapable of serving as the basis for a concrete political orientation, he was committed to the belief that true philosophy must inspire, and indeed be, action. By becoming the philosopher of Fascism he could, at least in appearance, overcome this difficulty.

Gentile saw Italian history as a struggle by those who possessed faith, ideals, or a 'religious sense of life' to overcome the passive resistance of sceptical individualism. It had become a commonplace of Risorgimento historiography that in the Renaissance culture had become divorced from politics, thought from action, and that the intellectuals' loss of civic sense bore much of the blame for Italy's failure to become a united nation. Both his metaphysical reflections and his view of history led Gentile to his insistence that any system of thought, to be either true or historically effective, must be a total *Weltanschauung*, embracing all aspects of man's activity. Men are 'one and indivisible', and a partial or specialized commitment was therefore worthless. 'Nothing can live or be of value in the spirit except what takes hold of the spirit leaving nothing over.' This totalitarian principle sanctioned the transformation of Fascism from a movement with political objectives in the narrower sense of the term into a regime which claimed to co-ordinate all the activities of its citizens.

The denial of diversity is the central characteristic of Gentile's political thought. Gentile derived from the Hegelian tradition the assumption that there is a single collective will, which is also the true, rational or universal will of the individual. The fact that in a modern society citizens can and do belong to different groups, churches or parties with incompatible principles and standards was never admitted by Gentile's intransigent monism. Gentile's revisions of Hegel's thought greatly accentuated its nationalist and statist tendencies. The single national state was the only possible 'spiritual reality', and it absorbed all others; it could neither be transcended nor limited. Gentile discarded Hegel's concept of the spheres of family and civil society as 'purely abstract'; the moral will knew no distinctions, and the good citizen in acknowledging his family obligations would see them only as an instance of his will to identify with the conscience of the whole community. In other words, the political order should embrace within itself all other forms of social integration.

There was a contradiction between Gentile's principles and Mussolini's religious policy. Gentile regarded any limitation on the sovereignty of the state as an illegitimate denial of its ethical nature, which demanded that religion must be 'indissolubly absorbed' by the law and authority of the state. Gentile fought against the Conciliation between Church and state (1929) and was repaid by the fierce hostility of the Catholics.

Gentile had been sharply critical of the nationalist thinkers and his position remained distinct from theirs. Whereas, he said, they regarded the nation as a 'given fact of nature' to which the individual owed obedience, it should instead be viewed as a continuous act of creation within the individual consciousness. This theory, at first sight morc liberal, can also be regarded as more subtly totalitarian. For it is characteristic of totalitarian regimes that they demand not merely obedience but active identification. In Gentile's thought the Fascist Party has a more central place than it has for the nationalists. The party, 'an elite ... with a forward-looking morality', is that part of the nation which has a clear consciousness of national purpose. The party's task was to transmit this national consciousness to the people. The mass membership of the party and its auxiliary organizations were for Gentile the proof that Fascism derived both its authority and power from the people. It is perfectly true that the Fascist regime differed from old-style authoritarianism in so far as it was created with the aid of a mass movement and in so far as it allowed and indeed demanded certain forms of popular participation. But this participation did not signify participation in the making of decisions, merely in their execution or celebration. Even the Fascist Party was in practice reduced to this secondary role. Gentile during the 1930s came to recognize the failure of Fascism to make totalitarianism a reality. It is probably true that the totalitarian ideal of unanimity can never be fully realized; the tensions between obedience and fanatical enthusiasm, coercion and conviction, cannot be resolved except verbally, and the characteristic atmosphere of any totalitarian regime is one of bad faith. In the case of Italian Fascism widespread cynicism, and the survival of old institutions behind the new façade combined to make this atmosphere particularly pervasive. Gentile, on the other hand, was tragically sincere, and denounced with some courage the Fascist reliance on coercion rather than on persuasion. But his disillusionment could not lead him to abandon his conviction that the Fascist Party, and Mussolini in person, were the embodiment of national destiny.

During the 1930s the cultural poverty of Fascism became more and more evident. Official doctrine produced a kind of uneasy symbiosis between a traditionalist cult of order and the family, reinforced by clerical influence, and the activist exaltation of force, vitality and the amoral superman. These incompatible schools of thought were united only by their dislike and fear of free discussion and reasoned argument.

ADRIAN LYTTELTON

NOTE: Footnotes indicated by number are editor's notes: those indicated by an asterisk are in the original texts.

BENITO MUSSOLINI
(1883–1945)

THE DOCTRINE OF FASCISM

(Written in 1932 in collaboration with Giovanni Gentile)

I. *Fundamental Ideas*

1. Like every sound political conception, Fascism is both practice and thought; action in which a doctrine is immanent, and a doctrine which, arising out of a given system of historical forces, remains embedded in them and works there from within. Hence it has a form correlative to the contingencies of place and time, but it has also a content of thought which raises it to a formula of truth in the higher level of the history of thought. In the world one does not act spiritually as a human will dominating other wills without a conception of the transient and particular reality under which it is necessary to act, and of the permanent and universal reality in which the first has its being and its life. In order to know men it is necessary to know man; and in order to know man it is necessary to know reality and laws. There is no concept of the State which is not fundamentally a concept of life: philosophy or intuition, a system of ideas which develops logically or is gathered up into a vision or into a faith, but which is always, at least virtually, an organic conception of the world.

2. Thus Fascism could not be understood in many of its practical manifestations as a party organization, as a system of education, as a discipline, if it were not always looked at in the light of its whole way of conceiving life, a spiritualized way. The world seen through Fascism is not this material world which appears on the surface, in which man is an individual separated from all others and standing by himself, and in which he is governed by a natural law that makes him instinctively live a life of selfish and momentary pleasure. The man of Fascism is an individual who is nation and fatherland, which is a moral law, binding together individuals

and the generations into a tradition and a mission, suppressing the instinct for a life enclosed within the brief round of pleasure in order to restore within duty a higher life free from the limits of time and space: a life in which the individual, through the denial of himself, through the sacrifice of his own private interests, through death itself, realizes that completely spiritual existence in which his value as a man lies.

3. Therefore it is a spiritualized conception, itself the result of the general reaction of modern times against the flabby materialistic positivism of the nineteenth century. Anti-positivistic, but positive: not sceptical, nor agnostic, nor pessimistic, nor passively optimistic, as are, in general, the doctrines (all negative) that put the centre of life outside man, who with his free will can and must create his own world. Fascism desires an active man, one engaged in activity with all his energies: it desires a man virilely conscious of the difficulties that exist in action and ready to face them. It conceives of life as a struggle, considering that it behoves man to conquer for himself that life truly worthy of him, creating first of all in himself the instrument (physical, moral, intellectual) in order to construct it. Thus for the single individual, thus for the nation, thus for humanity. Hence the high value of culture in all its forms (art, religion, science), and the enormous importance of education. Hence also the essential value of work, with which man conquers nature and creates the human world (economic, political, moral, intellectual).

4. This positive conception of life is clearly an ethical conception. It covers the whole of reality, not merely the human activity which controls it. No action can be divorced from moral judgment; there is nothing in the world which can be deprived of the value which belongs to everything in its relation to moral ends. Life, therefore, as conceived by the Fascist, is serious, austere, religious: the whole of it is poised in a world supported by the moral and responsible forces of the spirit. The Fascist disdains the 'comfortable' life.

5. Fascism is a religious conception in which man is seen in his immanent relationship with a superior law and with an objective Will that transcends the particular individual and raises him to conscious membership of a spiritual society. Whoever has seen in the religious politics of the Fascist regime nothing but mere opportunism has not understood that Fascism besides being a system of government is also, and above all, a system of thought.

6. Fascism is an historical conception, in which man is what he is only in so far as he works with the spiritual process in which he finds himself, in the family or social group, in the nation and in the history in which all nations collaborate. From this follows the great value of tradition, in memories, in language, in customs, in the standards of social life. Outside history man is nothing. Consequently Fascism is opposed to all the individualistic abstractions of a materialistic nature like those of the eighteenth century; and it is opposed to all Jacobin utopias and innovations. It does not consider that 'happiness' is possible upon earth, as it appeared to be in the desire of the economic literature of the eighteenth century, and hence it rejects all teleological theories according to which mankind would reach a definitive stabilized condition at a certain period in history. This implies putting oneself outside history and life, which is a continual change and coming to be. Politically, Fascism wishes to be a realistic doctrine; practically, it aspires to solve only the problems which arise historically of themselves and that of themselves find or suggest their own solution. To act among men, as to act in the natural world, it is necessary to enter into the process of reality and to master the already operating forces.

7. Against individualism, the Fascist conception is for the State; and it is for the individual in so far as he coincides with the State, which is the conscience and universal will of man in his historical existence. It is opposed to classical Liberalism, which arose from the necessity of reacting against absolutism, and which brought its historical purpose to an end when the State was transformed into the conscience and

will of the people. Liberalism denied the State in the interests of the individual; Fascism reaffirms the State as the true reality of the individual. And if liberty is to be the attribute of the real man, and not of that abstract puppet envisaged by individualistic Liberalism, Fascism is for liberty. And for the only liberty which can be a real thing, the liberty of the State and of the individual within the State. Therefore, for the Fascist, everything is in the State, and nothing human or spiritual exists, much less has value, outside the State. In this sense Fascism is totalitarian, and the Fascist State, the synthesis and unity of all values, interprets, develops and gives strength to the whole life of the people.

8. Outside the State there can be neither individuals nor groups (political parties, associations, syndicates, classes). Therefore Fascism is opposed to Socialism, which confines the movement of history within the class struggle and ignores the unity of classes established in one economic and moral reality in the State; and analogously it is opposed to class syndicalism. Fascism recognizes the real exigencies for which the socialist and syndicalist movement arose, but while recognizing them wishes to bring them under the control of the State and give them a purpose within the corporative system of interests reconciled within the unity of the State.

9. Individuals form classes according to the similarity of their interests, they form syndicates according to differentiated economic activities within these interests; but they form first, and above all, the State, which is not to be thought of numerically as the sum-total of individuals forming the majority of a nation. And consequently Fascism is opposed to Democracy, which equates the nation to the majority, lowering it to the level of that majority; nevertheless it is the purest form of democracy if the nation is conceived, as it should be, qualitatively and not quantitatively, as the most powerful idea (most powerful because most moral, most coherent, most true) which acts within the nation as the conscience and the will of a few, even of One, which ideally tends to become active within the conscience and the will of all—that is to

say, of all those who rightly constitute a nation *by reason of* nature, history of race, and have set out upon the same line of development and spiritual formation as one conscience and one sole will. Not a race, nor a geographically determined region, but as a community historically perpetuating itself, a multitude unified by a single idea, which is the will to existence and to power: consciousness of itself, personality.

10. This higher personality is truly the nation in so far as it is the State. It is not the nation that generates the State, as according to the old naturalistic concept which served as the basis of the political theories of the national States of the nineteenth century. Rather the nation is created by the State, which gives to the people, conscious of its own moral unity, a will and therefore an effective existence. The right of a nation to independence derives not from a literary and ideal consciousness of its own being, still less from a more or less unconscious and inert acceptance of a *de facto* situation, but from an active consciousness, from a political will in action and ready to demonstrate its own rights: that is to say, from a state already coming into being. The State, in fact, as the universal ethical will, is the creator of right.

11. The nation as the State is an ethical reality which exists and lives in so far as it develops. To arrest its development is to kill it. Therefore the State is not only the authority which governs and gives the form of laws and the value of spiritual life to the wills of individuals, but it is also a power that makes its will felt abroad, making it known and respected, in other words, demonstrating the fact of its universality in all the necessary directions of its development. It is consequently organization and expansion, at least virtually. Thus it can be likened to the human will which knows no limits to its development and realizes itself in testing its own limitlessness.

12. The Fascist State, the highest and most powerful form of personality, is a force, but a spiritual force, which takes over all the forms of the moral and intellectual life of man. It cannot therefore confine itself simply to the functions of

order and supervision as Liberalism desired. It is not simply a mechanism which limits the sphere of the supposed liberties of the individual. It is the form, the inner standard and the discipline of the whole person; it saturates the will as well as the intelligence. Its principle, the central inspiration of the human personality living in the civil community, pierces into the depths and makes its home in the heart of the man of action as well as of the thinker, of the artist as well as of the scientist: it is the soul of the soul.

13. Fascism, in short, is not only the giver of laws and the founder of institutions, but the educator and promoter of spiritual life. It wants to remake, not the forms of human life, but its content, man, character, faith. And to this end it requires discipline and authority that can enter into the spirits of men and there govern unopposed. Its sign, therefore, is the Lictors' rods, the symbol of unity, of strength and justice.

II. *Political and Social Doctrine*

1. When in the now distant March of 1919 I summoned to Milan through the columns of the *Popolo d'Italia* my surviving supporters who had followed me since the constitution of the Fasces of Revolutionary Action, founded in January 1915, there was no specific doctrinal plan in my mind. I had known and lived through only one doctrine, that of the Socialism of 1903–4 up to the winter of 1914, almost ten years. My experience in this had been that of a follower and of a leader, but not that of a theoretician. My doctrine, even in that period, had been a doctrine of action. An unequivocal Socialism, universally accepted, did not exist after 1905, when the Revisionist Movement began in Germany under Bernstein and there was formed in opposition to that, in the see-saw of tendencies, an extreme revolutionary movement, which in Italy never emerged from the condition of mere words, whilst in Russian Socialism it was the prelude to Bolshevism. Reform, Revolution, Centralization—even the echoes of the terminology are now spent; whilst in the great

river of Fascism are to be found the streams which had their source in Sorel, Peguy, in the Lagardelle of the *Mouvement Socialiste* and the groups of Italian Syndicalists, who between 1904 and 1914 brought a note of novelty into Italian Socialism, which by that time had been devitalized and drugged by fornication with Giolitti, in *Pagine Libere* of Olivetti, *La Lupa* of Orano and *Divenire Sociale* of Enrico Leone.

In 1919, at the end of the War, Socialism as a doctrine was already dead: it existed only as hatred, it had still only one possibility, especially in Italy, that of revenge against those who had wished for the War and who should be made to expiate it. The *Popolo d'Italia* was then given the sub-title – 'The Newspaper of Combatants and Producers'. The word 'producers' was already the expression of a tendency. Fascism was not given out to the wet nurse of a doctrine elaborated beforehand round a table: it was born of the need for action; it was not a party, but in its first two years it was a movement against all parties. The name which I gave to the organization defined its characteristics. Nevertheless, whoever rereads, in the now crumpled pages of the time, the account of the constituent assembly of the *Fasci Italiani di Combattimento* will not find a doctrine, but a series of suggestions, of anticipations, of admonitions, which when freed from the inevitable vein of contingency, were destined later, after a few years, to develop into a series of doctrinal attitudes which made of Fascism a self-sufficient political doctrine able to face all others, both past and present. 'If the bourgeoisie', I said at that time, 'thinks to find in us a lightning-conductor, it is mistaken. We must go forward to meet Labour ... We want to accustom the working classes to being under a leader, to convince them also that it is not easy to direct an industry or a commercial undertaking successfully ... We shall fight against technical and spiritual retrogression ... The successors of the present regime still being undecided, we must not be unwilling to fight for it. We must hasten; when the present regime is superseded, we must be the ones to take its place. The right of succession belongs to us because we pushed the country into the War and we led it to victory. The present method of political representation cannot be sufficient for us, we wish for a direct representation of individual interests ... It might be said against this programme that it is a return to the corporations. It doesn't matter! ... I should like, nevertheless, the Assembly to accept the claims of national syndicalism from the point of view of economics ... '

Is it not surprising that from the first day in the Piazza San Sepolcro there should resound the word 'Corporation' which was destined in the course of the revolution to signify one of the legislative and social creations at the base of the regime?

2. The years preceding the March on Rome were years during which the necessity of action did not tolerate inquiries or complete elaborations of doctrine. Battles were being fought in the cities and villages. There were discussions, but —and this is more sacred and important—there were deaths. People knew how to die. The doctrine—beautiful, well-formed, divided into chapters and paragraphs and surrounded by a commentary—might be missing; but there was present something more decisive to supplant it—Faith. Nevertheless, he who recalls the past with the aid of books, articles, votes in Parliament, the major and the minor speeches, he who knows how to investigate and weigh evidence, will find that the foundations of the doctrine were laid while the battle was raging. It was precisely in these years that Fascist thought armed itself, refined itself, moving towards an organization of its own. The problems of the individual and the State; the problems of authority and liberty; political and social problems and those more specifically national; the struggle against liberal, democratic, socialist, Masonic, demagogic doctrines was carried on at the same time as the 'punitive expeditions'. But since the 'system' was lacking, adversaries ingenuously denied that Fascism had any power to make a doctrine of its own, while the doctrine rose up, even though tumultuously, at first under

the aspect of a violent and dogmatic negation, as happens to all ideas that break new ground, then under the positive aspect of a constructive policy which, during the years 1926, 1927, 1928, was realized in the laws and institutions of the regime.

Fascism is today clearly defined not only as a regime but as a doctrine. And I mean by this that Fascism today, self-critical as well as critical of other movements, has an unequivocal point of view of its own, a criterion, and hence an aim, in face of all the material and intellectual problems which oppress the people of the world.

3. Above all, Fascism, in so far as it considers and observes the future and the development of humanity quite apart from the political considerations of the moment, believes neither in the possibility nor in the utility of perpetual peace. It thus repudiates the doctrine of Pacifism—born of a renunciation of the struggle and an act of cowardice in the face of sacrifice. War alone brings up to their highest tension all human energies and puts the stamp of nobility upon the peoples who have the courage to meet it. All other trials are substitutes, which never really put a man in front of himself in the alternative of life and death. A doctrine, therefore, which begins with a prejudice in favour of peace is foreign to Fascism; as are foreign to the spirit of Fascism, even though acceptable by reason of the utility which they might have in given political situations, all internationalistic and socialistic systems which, as history proves, can be blown to the winds when emotional, idealistic and practical movements storm the hearts of peoples. Fascism carries over this anti-pacifist spirit even into the lives of individuals. The proud motto of the *Squadrista*, 'Me ne frego', written on the bandages of a wound is an act of philosophy which is not only stoical, it is the epitome of a doctrine that is not only political: it is education for combat, the acceptance of the risks which it brings; it is a new way of life for Italy. Thus the Fascist accepts and loves life, he knows nothing of suicide and despises it; he looks on life as duty, ascent, conquest: life which must be

noble and full: lived for oneself, but above all for those others near and far away, present and future.

4. The 'demographic' policy of the regime follows from these premises. Even the Fascist does in fact love his neighbour, but this 'neighbour' is not for him a vague and ill-defined concept; love for one's neighbour does not exclude necessary educational severities, and still less differentiations and distances. Fascism rejects universal concord, and, since it lives in the community of civilized peoples, it keeps them vigilantly and suspiciously before its eyes, it follows their states of mind and the changes in their interests and it does not let itself be deceived by temporary and fallacious appearances.

5. Such a conception of life makes Fascism the precise negation of that doctrine which formed the basis of the so-called Scientific or Marxian Socialism: the doctrine of historical Materialism, according to which the history of human civilizations can be explained only as the struggle of interest between the different social groups and as arising out of change in the means and instruments of production. That economic improvements—discoveries of raw materials, new methods of work, scientific inventions—should have an importance of their own, no one denies, but that they should suffice to explain human history to the exclusion of all other factors is absurd: Fascism believes, now and always, in holiness and in heroism, that is in acts in which no economic motive—remote or immediate—plays a part. With this negation of historical materialism, according to which men would be only by-products of history, who appear and disappear on the surface of the waves while in the depths the real directive forces are at work, there is also denied the immutable and irreparable 'class struggle' which is the natural product of this economic conception of history, and above all it is denied that the class struggle can be the primary agent of social changes. Socialism being thus wounded in these two primary tenets of its doctrine, nothing of it is left save the sentimental aspiration—old as humanity—towards a social

order in which the sufferings and the pains of the humblest folk could be alleviated. But here Fascism rejects the concept of an economic 'happincss' which would be realized socialistically and almost automatically at a given moment of economic evolution by assuring to all a maximum prosperity. Fascism denies the possibility of the materialistic conception of 'happiness' and leaves it to the economists of the first half of the eighteenth century; it denies, that is, the equation of prosperity with happiness, which would transform men into animals with one sole preoccupation: that of being well-fed and fat, degraded in consequence to a merely physical existence.

6. After Socialism, Fascism attacks the whole complex of democratic ideologies and rejects them both in their theoretical premises and in their applications of practical manifestations. Fascism denies that the majority, through the mere fact of being a majority, can rule human societies; it denies that this majority can govern by means of a periodical consultation; it affirms the irremediable, fruitful and beneficent inequality of men, who cannot be levelled by such a mechanical and extrinsic fact as universal suffrage. By democratic regimes we mean those in which from time to time the people is given the illusion of being sovereign, while true effective sovereignty lies in other, perhaps irresponsible and secret, forces. Democracy is a regime without a king, but with very many kings, perhaps more exclusive, tyrannical and violent than one king even though a tyrant. This explains why Fascism, although before 1922 for reasons of expediency it made a gesture of republicanism, renounced it before the March on Rome, convinced that the question of the political forms of a State is not pre-eminent today, and that studying past and present monarchies, past and present Republics it becomes clear that monarchy and republic are not to be judged *sub specie aeternitatis*, but represent forms in which the political evolution, the history, the tradition, the psychology of a given country are manifested. Now Fascism overcomes the antithesis between monarchy and republic

which retarded the movements of democracy, burdening the former with every defect and defending the latter as the regime of perfection. Now it has been seen that there are inherently reactionary and absolutistic republics, and monarchies that welcome the most daring political and social innovations.

7. 'Reason, Science', said Renan (who was inspired before Fascism existed) in one of his philosophical Meditations, 'are products of humanity, but to expect reason directly from the people and through the people is a chimera. It is not necessary for the existence of reason that everybody should know it. In any case, if such an initiation should be made, it would not be made by means of base democracy, which apparently must lead to the extinction of every difficult culture, and every higher discipline. The principle that society exists only for the prosperity and the liberty of the individuals who compose it does not seem to conform with the plans of nature, plans in which the species alone is taken into consideration and the individual seems to be sacrificed. It is strongly to be feared lest the last word of democracy thus understood (I hasten to say that it can also be understood in other ways) would be a social state in which a degenerate mass would have no other care than to enjoy the ignoble pleasures of vulgar men.'

Thus far Renan. Fascism rejects in democracy the absurd conventional lie of political equalitarianism clothed in the dress of collective irresponsibility and the myth of happiness and indefinite progress. But if democracy can be understood in other ways, that is, if democracy means not to relegate the people to the periphery of the State, then Fascism could be defined as an 'organized, centralized, authoritarian democracy'.

8. In face of Liberal doctrines, Fascism takes up an attitude of absolute opposition both in the field of politics and in that of economics. It is not necessary to exaggerate—merely for the purpose of present controversies—the importance of Liberalism in the past century, and to make of

that which was one of the numerous doctrines sketched in that century a religion of humanity for all times, present and future. Liberalism flourished for no more than some fifteen years. It was born in 1830, as a reaction against the Holy Alliance that wished to drag Europe back to what it had been before 1789, and it had its year of splendour in 1848 when even Pius IX was a Liberal. Immediately afterwards the decay set in. If 1848 was a year of light and of poetry, 1849 was a year of darkness and of tragedy. The Republic of Rome was destroyed by another Republic, that of France. In the same year Marx launched the gospel of the religion of Socialism with the famous *Communist Manifesto*. In 1851 Napoleon III carried out his unliberal *coup d'état* and ruled over France until 1870, when he was dethroned by a popular revolt, but as a consequence of a military defeat which ranks among the most resounding that history can relate. The victor was Bismarck, who never knew the home of the religion of liberty or who were its prophets. It is symptomatic that a people of high culture like the Germans should have been completely ignorant of the religion of liberty during the whole of the nineteenth century. It was, there, no more than a parenthesis, represented by what has been called the 'ridiculous Parliament of Frankfort' which lasted only a season. Germany has achieved her national unity outside the doctrines of Liberalism, against Liberalism, a doctrine which seems foreign to the German soul, a soul essentially monarchical, whilst Liberalism is the historical and logical beginning of anarchism. The stages of German unity are the three wars of 1864, 1866 and 1870, conducted by 'Liberals' like Moltke and Bismarck. As for Italian unity, Liberalism has had in it a part absolutely inferior to the share of Mazzini and of Garibaldi, who were not Liberals. Without the intervention of the unliberal Napoleon we should not have gained Lombardy, and without the help of the unliberal Bismarck at Sadowa and Sedan, very probably we should not have gained Venice in 1866; and in 1870 we should not have entered Rome. From 1870–1915 there occurs the period in which the very priests of the new creed had to confess the twilight of their religion: defeated as it was by decadence in literature, by activism in practice. Activism: that is to say, Nationalism, Futurism, Fascism. The 'Liberal' century, after having accumulated an infinity of Gordian knots, tried to untie them by the hecatomb of the World War. Never before has any religion imposed such a cruel sacrifice. Were the gods of Liberalism thirsty for blood? Now Liberalism is about to close the doors of its deserted temples because the peoples feel that its agnosticism in economics, its indifferentism in politics and in morals, would lead, as they have led, the States to certain ruin. In this way one can understand why all the political experiences of the contemporary world are anti-Liberal, and it is supremely ridiculous to wish on that account to class them outside of history; as if history were a hunting ground reserved to Liberalism and its professors, as if Liberalism were the definitive and no longer surpassable message of civilization.

9. But the Fascist repudiations of Socialism, Democracy, Liberalism must not make one think that Fascism wishes to make the world return to what it was before 1789, the year which has been indicated as the year of the beginning of the liberal-democratic age. One does not go backwards. The Fascist doctrine has not chosen De Maistre as its prophet. Monarchical absolutism is a thing of the past and so also is every theocracy. So also feudal privileges and division into impenetrable and isolated castes have had their day. The theory of Fascist authority has nothing to do with the police State. A party that governs a nation in a totalitarian way is a new fact in history. References and comparisons are not possible. Fascism takes over from the ruins of Liberal Socialistic democratic doctrines those elements which still have a living value. It preserves those that can be called the established facts of history, it rejects all the rest, that is to say the idea of a doctrine which holds good for all times and all peoples. If it is admitted that the nineteenth century has been the century of Socialism, Liberalism and Democracy, it

does not follow that the twentieth must also be the century of Liberalism, Socialism and Democracy. Political doctrines pass; peoples remain. It is to be expected that this century may be that of authority, a century of the 'Right', a Fascist century. If the nineteenth was the century of the individual (Liberalism means individualism) it may be expected that this one may be the century of 'collectivism' and therefore the century of the State. That a new doctrine should use the still vital elements of other doctrines is perfectly logical. No doctrine is born quite new, shining, never before seen. No doctrine can boast of an absolute 'originality'. It is bound, even if only historically, to other doctrines that have been, and must develop into other doctrines that will be. Thus the scientific socialism of Marx is bound to the Utopian Socialism of the Fouriers, the Owens and the Saint-Simons; thus the Liberalism of the nineteenth century is connected with the whole 'Enlightenment' of the eighteenth century. Thus the doctrines of democracy are bound to the *Encyclopédie*. Every doctrine tends to direct the activity of men towards a determined objective; but the activity of man reacts upon the doctrine, transforms it, adapts it to new necessities or transcends it. The doctrine itself, therefore, must be, not words, but an act of life. Hence, the pragmatic veins in Fascism, its will to power, its will to be, its attitude in the face of the fact of 'violence' and of its own courage.

10. The keystone of Fascist doctrine is the conception of the State, of its essence, of its tasks, of its ends. For Fascism the State is an absolute before which individuals and groups are relative. Individuals and groups are 'thinkable' in so far as they are within the State. The Liberal State does not direct the interplay and the material and spiritual development of the groups, but limits itself to registering the results; the Fascist State has a consciousness of its own, a will of its own, on this account it is called an 'ethical' State. In 1929, at the first quinquennial assembly of the regime, I said: 'For Fascism, the State is not the night-watchman who is concerned only with the personal security of the citizens; nor is

it an organization for purely material ends, such as that of guaranteeing a certain degree of prosperity and a relatively peaceful social order, to achieve which a council of administration would be sufficient, nor is it a creation of mere politics with no contact with the material and complex reality of the lives of individuals and the life of peoples. The State, as conceived by Fascism and as it acts, is a spiritual and moral fact because it makes concrete the political, juridical, economic organization of the nation and such an organization is, in its origin and in its development, a manifestation of the spirit. The State is the guarantor of internal and external security, but it is also the guardian and the transmitter of the spirit of the people as it has been elaborated through the centuries in language, custom, faith. The State is not only present, it is also past, and above all future. It is the State which, transcending the brief limit of individual lives, represents the immanent conscience of the nation. The forms in which States express themselves change, but the necessity of the State remains. It is the State which educates citizens for civic virtue, makes them conscious of their mission, calls them to unity; harmonizes their interests in justice; hands on the achievements of thought in the sciences, the arts, in law, in human solidarity; it carries men from the elementary life of the tribe to the highest human expression of power which is Empire; it entrusts to the ages the names of those who died for its integrity or in obedience to its laws; it puts forward as an example and recommends to the generations that are to come the leaders who increased its territory and the men of genius who gave it glory. When the sense of the State declines and the disintegrating and centrifugal tendencies of individuals and groups prevail, national societies move to their decline.'

11. From 1929 up to the present day these doctrinal positions have been strengthened by the whole economico-political evolution of the world. It is the State alone that grows in size, in power. It is the State alone that can solve the dramatic contradictions of capitalism. What is called

the crisis cannot be overcome except by the State, within the State. Where are the shades of the Jules Simons who, at the dawn of liberalism, proclaimed that 'the State must strive to render itself unnecessary and to prepare for its demise'; of the MacCullochs who, in the second half of the last century, affirmed that the State must abstain from too much governing? And faced with the continual, necessary and inevitable interventions of the State in economic affairs what would the Englishman Bentham now say, according to whom industry should have asked of the State only to be left in peace? Or the German Humboldt, according to whom the 'idle' State must be considered the best? It is true that the second generation of liberal economists was less extremist than the first, and already Smith himself opened, even though cautiously, the door to State intervention in economics. But when one says liberalism, one says the individual; when one says Fascism, one says the State. But the Fascist State is unique; it is an original creation. It is not reactionary, but revolutionary in that it anticipates the solutions of certain universal problems. These problems are no longer seen in the same light: in the sphere of politics they are removed from party rivalries, from the supreme power of parliament, from the irresponsibility of assemblies; in the sphere of economics they are removed from the sphere of the syndicates' activities —activities that were ever widening their scope and increasing their power, both on the workers' side and on the employers'—removed from their struggles and their designs; in the moral sphere they are divorced from ideas of the need for order, discipline and obedience, and lifted into the plane of the moral commandments of the fatherland. Fascism desires the State to be strong, organic and at the same time founded on a wide popular basis. The Fascist State has also claimed for itself the field of economics and, through the corporative, social and educational institutions which it has created, the meaning of the State reaches out to and includes the farthest offshoots; and within the State, framed in their respective organizations, there revolve all the political, economic and spiritual forces of the nation. A State founded on millions of individuals who recognize it, feel it, are ready to serve it, is not the tyrannical State of the medieval lord. It has nothing in common with the absolutist States that existed either before or after 1789. In the Fascist State the individual is not suppressed, but rather multiplied, just as in a regiment a soldier is not weakened but multiplied by the number of his comrades. The Fascist State organizes the nation, but it leaves sufficient scope to individuals; it has limited useless or harmful liberties and has preserved those that are essential. It cannot be the individual who decides in this matter, but only the State.

12. The Fascist State does not remain indifferent to the fact of religion in general and to that particular positive religion which is Italian Catholicism. The State has no theology, but it has an ethic. In the Fascist State religion is looked upon as one of the deepest manifestations of the spirit; it is, therefore, not only respected, but defended and protected. The Fascist State does not create a 'God' of its own, as Robespierre once, at the height of the Convention's foolishness, wished to do; nor does it vainly seek, like Bolshevism, to expel religion from the minds of men; Fascism respects the God of the ascetics, of the saints, of the heroes, and also God as seen and prayed to by the simple and primitive heart of the people.

13. The Fascist State is a will to power and to government. In it the tradition of Rome is an idea that has force. In the doctrine of Fascism Empire is not only a territorial, military or mercantile expression, but spiritual or moral. One can think of an empire, that is to say a nation that directly or indirectly leads other nations, without needing to conquer a single square kilometre of territory. For Fascism the tendency to Empire, that is to say, to the expansion of nations, is a manifestation of vitality; its opposite, staying at home, is a sign of decadence: peoples who rise or re-rise are imperialist, peoples who die are renunciatory. Fascism is the doctrine that is most fitted to represent the aims, the states

of mind, of a people, like the Italian people, rising again after many centuries of abandonment or slavery to foreigners. But Empire calls for discipline, co-ordination of forces, duty and sacrifice; this explains many aspects of the practical working of the regime and the direction of many of the forces of the State and the necessary severity shown to those who would wish to oppose this spontaneous and destined impulse of the Italy of the twentieth century, to oppose it in the name of the superseded ideologies of the nineteenth, repudiated wherever great experiments of political and social transformation have been courageously attempted: especially where, as now, peoples thirst for authority, for leadership, for order. If every age has its own doctrine, it is apparent from a thousand signs that the doctrine of the present age is Fascism. That it is a doctrine of life is shown by the fact that it has resuscitated a faith. That this faith has conquered minds is proved by the fact that Fascism has had its dead and its martyrs.

Fascism henceforward has in the world the universality of all those doctrines which, by fulfilling themselves, have significance in the history of the human spirit.

THE NATURE OF FASCISM

(From *The Preamble to the Statuto of December 20th, 1929*)[1]

The National Fascist Party is a civil militia for the service of the nation. Its objective: to realize the greatness of the Italian people. From its beginnings, which are indistinguishable from the renaissance of the Italian conscience and the will to victory, until now, the party has always thought of itself as in a state of war, at first in order to combat those who were stifling the will of the nation, today and from henceforth to defend and increase the power of the Italian people. Fascism is not merely an Italian organization connected with a programme partly realized and partly still to be realized; it is above all a faith which has had its confessors, and under the impulse of which the new Italians work as soldiers, pledged to achieve victory in the struggle between the nation and its enemies. The Party is an essential part of this new organization, and its function is fundamental and indispensable to the vitality of the regime. In the hour of vigil, its organization was fixed according to the necessities of battle, and the people recognized the Duce by the marks of his will, his strength and his achievements. In the heat of the struggle, action took precedence of law. Every stage was marked by a conquest, and the assemblies were only gatherings of officers and men dominated by the memory of the dead. Without dogmatic formulas or rigid projects, Fascism knows that victory lies in the possibility of its own continuous renewal. Fascism lives today in terms of the future, and regards the new generations as forces destined to achieve the ends appointed by our will. Without order and hierarchy, there can be neither discipline nor effort nor education of the people, which must receive light and guidance from that high place where is to be found the complete vision of rewards, tasks, functions and merits, and where the only guidance is in the general interest.

[1]Officially attributed to Mussolini, the authorship of this Preamble is uncertain.

WHICH WAY IS THE WORLD GOING?

(Article published in the review *Gerarchia*, February 25th, 1922)

I

Three years have now gone by since the soldiers laid down their arms; three turbulent years containing enough incident for three centuries; so much so that the Great War seems extraordinarily remote in space and time to those who fought in it, even more than to those who did not. Sometimes we wonder whether we really did live through the Battle of the Marne or Vittorio Veneto; we have experienced so much and events have followed so thick and fast that we feel overwhelmed by the past, almost as if we were already looking back on the present. When, three years ago, tens of millions of men left the trenches where, day in, day out, they had submitted to the iron discipline and sacred duty of Death, and more or less in chaos streamed back into the lives of their countries, those who were students of society and those who formed the political minority in their governments found themselves wondering what would happen to this immense flood of tortured old veterans now that they were leaving the precarious shelter of their countless trenches: which way would they go? Left or right? Before answering this question, we need to clarify the meaning of those two words. What, in the normal language of the time, was meant by right-wing? And what was the Left? Let us give examples. In politics, the monarchy was, for example, on the Right; on the Left was the Constituent Assembly or the Republic; economically, capitalism was right-wing, socialism, left; spiritually, traditional religion, art and philosophy represented the Right, while the Left contained all the avant-garde: in Catholicism, this meant Christian Democracy (Loisy and Murri); in philosophy, Bergsonism and, artistically, *Futurismo*. Right meant immobility, conservatism, reaction and aristocracy; the Left, dynamism, revolution, democracy and, above all, progress. The best criterion was socialism; those who accepted its doctrines were obviously left-wing; those who rejected them, right-wing; the expression right- or left-wing had meaning in the social-political sphere, above all in relation and with reference to socialism. Moving to the Left meant moving towards a period of history in which socialism would reign triumphant; moving Right meant either remaining static in the present moment of history or else moving towards other forms of civilization very different from those dreamt of by the socialists. Is the world, or more exactly, are the white societies of Europe and America, since the other three continents do not come under the terms of our investigation, moving to the Left, that is to say towards a socialist type of civilization or to the Right, that is to say towards a non-socialist society? In brief: are we or are we not moving towards the 'Socialist Revolution', towards the concrete realization of the Socialists' ideologies, which range from the abolition of private property to the creation of the International, towards the accession of the proletariat to power as the ruling class in their countries? Are we moving towards a lasting peace or must we accept that this is a Utopia?

II

Immediately after the Armistice there was a violent swing to the Left, both in the political and social spheres. Two empires collapsed: the Hohenzollern and the Habsburg, while a third one, the empire of the Romanovs, had already suffered a like fate. Republics sprouted like mushrooms, too many of them, some of which, such as the German Republic, did not even represent a final desperate endeavour of patriots, like the Paris Commune of '71, but merely an expedient to fall in with President Wilson's peace terms. In the years 1919 and 1920, the whole of Central and Eastern Europe was in a ferment of political crisis, as new regimes struggled to establish themselves, a ferment that was aggravated and complicated by the crisis, which we shall describe as socialist, that is, by the attempts to bring about some of the precepts of socialist doctrines. In the countries that had been beaten, the political and social crisis took extremely acute forms—as in Prussia, Bavaria and Hungary—but even the countries on the winning side, such as France and England, were not spared, as they found themselves faced by immense mass movements; and in Italy, the poorest amongst the victorious powers, the crisis assumed alarming proportions, starting with the 'caro-viveri' [high cost of living] movement in 1919 and continuing with the occupation of the factories in 1920.

The general impression of these years was that the world was swinging wildly to the Left; that the Left, in the historical, not in the Italian parliamentary sense, was represented by Russia, who was showing the way for all the peoples of Europe and the world. All the traditional values were turned upside down; the heroism of war was jeered at and desertion praised to the skies; the whole traditional social order was smashed (a Cossack took over command of the Petrograd garrison and the unknown Krilenko was promoted supreme commander of the Soviet army); nor did the economic and technical establishment, the end-product of long selection and painstaking scientific labour, escape the fate of the others: the engineers in the Putiloff works were relegated to the coke-ovens. It seems that after that no further ore was smelted in those works. Even in this sphere, the various European countries offered a whole range of differences based on their degree of civilization and the greater or lesser extent of the social upheaval. In Russia, the Tsar's family was summarily massacred; in Germany, the Hohenzollerns were allowed to go into exile. In Russia, the whole so-called capitalist economic system was brought to a standstill and paralysed—even the slaughter of the 'bourgeois' in Germany, including Bavaria itself, never reached the extremes of the Russians either in political or social action. All the same, in these first two post-war years, these critical developments seemed so horrifying that many of the middle class—especially the politicians—became resigned to the inevitable and, firmly convinced of an impending catastrophe, abandoned any sort of resistance; while the Italian shopkeepers handed over their keys to the *Camere del Lavoro* [trade councils], democratic ideologists and a large part of the middle-class intelligentsia all tended towards the Left, which was very frequently committed, in theory and practice, to injudicious reforms, thus spreading throughout the masses the steadily increasing belief that the old world—the world of the Right—was doomed to extinction. How all these expectations coloured the minds and the actions of the working masses belongs to the history of the recent sorry past.

III

There is no doubt that over the whole of Europe the end of 1920 marked the highest point of this 'left-wing' social crisis. But in the fifteen months since then, the situation has changed. At present, the swing is towards the Right. After the wave of revolution, we have the wave of reaction; the Reds have had their time and the hour has now come for the Whites.

As always, the nation that had deviated most strongly to the Left is the one which, in recent times, is moving most rapidly to the Right: I mean Russia. The sun of the Russian myth has already set. Light is no longer shining from the East, where terrible news of death and famine is coming out of Russia; we are receiving desperate appeals by socialists and anarchists in Petrograd against Lenin's reactionary policies. Professor Ulianov is now a Tsar scrupulously following the internal and external policies of the Romanovs. The former Basle professor did not perhaps imagine that he would end up as a reactionary; but obviously governments have to suit themselves to those they govern and the enormous human army of Russians—patient, resigned, fatalistic and oriental—is incapable of living in freedom; they need a tyrant; now more than ever, they, like every other people in fact, even those in the West, are anxiously looking for something solid in their institutions, ideas and men, havens where they can cast anchor for a while and rest their souls, tired out with much wandering. Without fear of Germanophilia—our only 'philia' is for Italy—it may be asserted that we are chiefly indebted to Germany for this present move to the Right in modern societies. Not only has what may be called the German bourgeoisie offered magnificent resistance to the attacks from the Left (the most recent example of this being the end of the latest railway strike) but the most interesting phenomenon in Germany today is the reluctance of the workers to be tainted by Russian ideas. Bolshevism has failed to infect the German working-class movement. The various uprisings, the 'Putsches' (the word is in itself significant), even the attempt to create a soviet in Munich, in no way invalidate my statement. The truth is that the large masses of the German working-class population have remained untouched by the Russian type of Bolshevism, which is restricted to a few tiny sects that are completely insignificant in the life of Germany. We need only recall that Kautsky, the greatest Marxist theoretician, has shown and proved categorically that socialism and Bolshevism are at opposite poles. It is pointless to discuss whether Bolshevism is a German product imported into Russia for the purposes of war—a sort of ideological poison gas—with the object of putting the famous Russian steam-roller out of action; Bernstein's revelations suggest that this is plausible, but we can say with certainty that having brought about Russia's military downfall and realizing how useless was Bolshevism even for this very purpose, Germany then provided the major barrier to protect the Western world from the deadly infection of Russian Bolshevism; Germany brought the advance of Bolshevism in Europe to a standstill, helped in this by the instinctive contempt that every German feels for every Russian. Following in Germany's footsteps, the nation that escaped most quickly from the obsession of the Russian myth was Italy, thanks to the upsurge of Fascism. We could extend our examination of Europe in the present day to the other countries, but this is unnecessary. The three nations that contain the greatest potential for future development in Europe today are Russia, Germany and Italy and it is the society and ideas of these three countries that are in fact moving markedly towards the Right.

IV

Now that we have established beyond any shadow of doubt that men's minds are moving to the Right, a question arises which we should like to pose in the following terms: are we moving Right in the sense that all the exaggerated extremism of the immediate post-war period is being wiped out or are we going Right in the sense that we are undertaking a much broader and more radical revision of our values? Is it merely the events, the myths and the history of the last two years that are affected or is it a whole century of history, beginning with the convocation of the French Estates-General and ending with the outbreak of the World War in August 1914?

Will the trend to the Right, like the trend to the Left, last a couple of years only or will it last a good deal longer? We answer the second question in the affirmative. If the nineteenth century was the century of Revolution, the twentieth seems the century of Restoration. The two immediate post-war years in which the trend to the Left reached its highest point are the last links in the chain forged in 1789 but briefly cut short by the Holy Alliance in 1815. Why did the Holy Alliance not succeed in completely destroying the movement that Napoleon had aroused amongst the nations of Europe? Because in these nineteenth-century ideologies were contained vital and necessary elements by which the flame that was extinguished on the plains of Waterloo in 1815 was to flare up again in 1848. The left-wing regimes that were set up in the whole of Europe between 1848 and 1900, based on universal suffrage and social legislation, made what contribution they could. The two years from 1919 to 1920 represent the final thread in the skein of democracy as it had been elaborated over the century. We have a whole range of republics; democracy has realized all its basic assumptions; socialism has achieved its minimum programme and has given up its maximum demands. Now we are beginning to bring the century of democracy to trial. Now democratic ideas and categories will be subjected to pitiless and destructive scrutiny. And thus it will become plain that the democratic justice of universal suffrage is the most blatant injustice; that government by all – the Ultima Thule of all democratic hopes – leads in practice to government by nobody; that progress is not necessarily a corollary of the rise of the masses and above all, that there is no proof, in fact, that the century of democracy must lead to the advent of socialism. This probing at the political level is matched by a similar examination on the philosophical level: if matter was worshipped for a whole century, today it will be replaced by the spirit. As a result, all the manifestations peculiar to the spirit of democracy are going to be repudiated; casual attitudes and makeshift solutions, lack of any sense of responsibility, the worship of the majority and of that mysterious divinity called 'the people'. Spiritual creation of every sort – starting with religion – will move into the centre of the stage and nobody will dare to persist in the anti-clericalism that was for so many decades the favourite democratic occupation. When we say that God is returning, we mean that spiritual values are returning. Nobody believes any longer in determinism or in the pseudo-scientific attitude of socialism. The century of democracy expired in 1919–20. It expired with the Great War. The century of democracy reached its apogee between 1914 and 1918 with the terrifying, necessary and inevitable sacrifice of ten million lost lives. Did not universal conscription form part of the intellectual beliefs of democracy? Thus the Great War appears to us at one and the same time as the sacred epic and blundering failure of democracy, its masterpiece and bankruptcy, its supreme heights and its bottomless pit. The immense historical importance of the Great War lies in the fact that this democratic war *par excellence*, which was supposed to achieve its immortal principles for all nations and classes—shades of Wilson's famous fourteen points and the sad, sad, decline of the Prophet!—this democratic war, then, ushers in the century of anti-democracy. The chief epithet of democracy is *all*, a word which completely filled the nineteenth century. The time has come to say: the *few* and the *elite*. Democracy is on its last legs in every country in the world; in some of them, as in Russia, it was murdered, in others it is falling prey to increasingly obvious decadence. It may be that in the nineteenth century, capitalism needed democracy; today, it has no such need. The War was revolutionary in the sense that it liquidated—in rivers of blood—the century of democracy, the century of the majority, of numbers, of quantity.

The process of reconstruction on the Right is already to be seen in concrete form. The orgy of licence has come to an end, the enthusiasm for social and democratic myths is over. Life is flowing back to the individual. A classical revival is taking place. The soulless, drab egalitarianism of democracy, which had taken the colour out of life and crushed all personality, is on its death-bed. New kinds of aristocracy are arising, now that we have proof that the masses cannot be protagonists but only the tools of history. Where this trend to the Right will lead is, at the moment, impossible to say; it will certainly range far, if we may judge by its beginnings and by the sudden collapse of all the post-war cardboard castles of the 'demagogues', while the old strongholds are being battered by the younger generation. This reaction is our revolution. A salutary revolution because it will save Europe from the miserable fate that awaited it had democracy continued its evil ways. Democracy in the factories lasted only the space of some ghostly dream. What has become of the German *Betriebsräte* or the Russian works' councils? Now it is the turn of the other form of democracy, political democracy, to come to an end—and come to an end it must. The present century promises, in a thousand and one ways, that it will be not the continuation but the antithesis of the last. And this antithesis will form the fabric and the glory of life in Europe in the coming decades.

VILFREDO PARETO
(1848–1923)

In his youth Pareto studied engineering, and unlike the other writers in this anthology he was a convinced believer in the extension of the methods of natural science to human phenomena. The model for his concepts of economic and social equilibrium was derived from his early study of mechanics.

Between 1876 and 1893 Pareto engaged actively in business, politics, and journalism. He was a fierce and outspoken critic of protectionism, high military expenditure and corruption. In 1893 he left Italy to take up the chair of political economy at Lausanne, and never returned. He often asserted, perhaps with some exaggeration, that he would have been in danger of arrest or worse if he had stayed in Italy and continued his outspoken attacks on the governments of the day. In this early phase Pareto had been moved by patriotic and radical ideals. His disillusionment explains his later stance of embittered detachment.

Pareto's interest in sociology grew out of his study of economics. He began to lecture on sociology in 1897, the year after he published his first major work, the *Cours d'économie politique*. The basic intuition which Pareto sought to develop in his sociological works is to be found in his distinction between logical and non-logical actions, and the assertion that the latter are the most important in determining the social system.

At the turn of the century Pareto's political views underwent a great change. From 1900 onwards, his hostility to democracy and socialism became more and more apparent. Pareto remained more attached to the 'liberal Utopia' of free trade than he cared to admit; moreover he liked to shock, and now that socialism had become respectable it became the object of his derision, along with other accepted prejudices.

Pareto's major sociological work, the *Trattato di sociologia generale*, was only published in 1916. Although many Fascists had read Pareto and were influenced by him, it is probable that few troubled to wade through the ponderous volumes of the *Trattato*. Pareto intended to add another volume to the *Trattato* which would have examined contemporary events in the light of his theories. This was never written, but instead Pareto wrote a number of short articles on contemporary themes, a number of which were later published in the two volumes *Fatti e teorie* (1920) and *Trasformazioni della democrazia* (1921).

Mussolini treated him with great respect and made him a senator in 1923.

FROM *LES SYSTÈMES SOCIALISTES* (1902)

IV. *Aristocracies; Circulation of Elites; Spoliation*

1. *Aristocracy*. The curve of the distribution of wealth in western societies varies very little from one period to another. What has been called the 'social pyramid' is, in reality, a sort of upturned top. The figure here gives an idea of it. The rich occupy the summit, the poor the base. Only the section A-B-C-G-F is at all known to us, thanks to statistical data. The section A-D-E-F is purely conjectural. We have adopted the form of it given here from Otto Ammon whose suggestion seems probable enough.

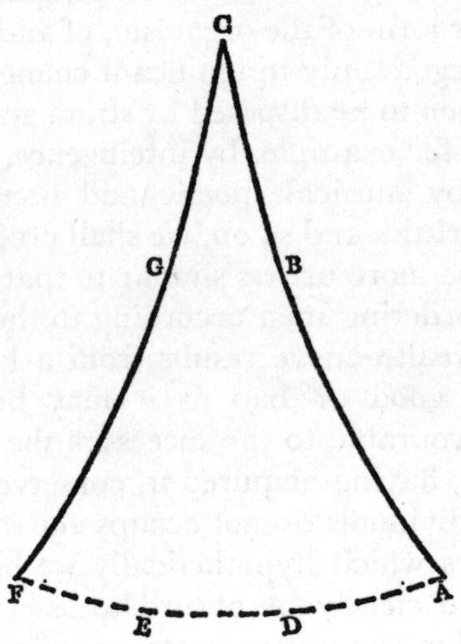

The form of the curve is not due to chance, of that we may be certain. It probably relates to the distribution of the physiological and psychological characteristics of human beings. On the other hand, it can partly be associated with theories of pure economics; that is to say, with human choices (these choices being in strict relationship with physiological and psychological characteristics), and to the obstacles encountered by production.

If we imagine men as disposed in strata according to their wealth, the whole figure represents the exterior form of the social organism. As we have just said, this form hardly changes; on average and over a short period it may in fact be supposed to be well-nigh constant. But the molecules composing the social aggregate are not stationary. Some individuals are growing rich, others are growing poor. Movements of an appreciable extent are therefore taking place within the social organism, which in this respect resembles a living organism. In a living organism the circulation of the blood carries along certain molecules in rapid motion; the processes of assimilation and secretion are incessantly changing the molecules composing the tissues, but the exterior form of the organism, of an adult animal for example, undergoes only insignificant changes.

Supposing men to be disposed by strata according to other characteristics, for example, by intelligence, by aptitude for mathematics, by musical, poetic and literary talents, by moral characteristics and so on, we shall probably get curves whose forms are more or less similar to that which we have just found by ordering men according to the distribution of wealth. This wealth-curve results from a large number of characteristics, good or bad as it may be, which taken together are favourable to the success of the individual who seeks wealth or, having acquired it, conserves it.

The same individuals do not occupy the same positions in the same figures which hypothetically we have just traced. In fact it would clearly be absurd to assert that the individuals occupying the upper strata in a figure representing the distribution of mathematical or poetic genius would be the same as those occupying the upper strata in the figure representing the distribution of wealth. This different distribution in relation to moral qualities (or those regarded as such), and in relation to wealth, has given rise to endless denunciations. Yet it is wholly understandable. The qualities, for example, of a St. Francis of Assisi, are quite different from those of a Krupp. People who buy steel cannon need a Krupp, not a St. Francis.

But if human beings are disposed according to the degree of their influence and political and social power, then it will be found that in most societies, to some extent at least, the same men will occupy the same position in a figure relating to influence and power as in our figure representing the distribution of wealth. The classes called 'superior' are also generally the richest.

These classes constitute an elite, an aristocracy (in the etymological sense of 'aristos' *the best*). So long as the social equilibrium is stable, the majority of the individuals composing these classes appear highly endowed with certain qualities—good or bad as may be—which guarantee power.

A fact of extreme importance for social physiology is that aristocracies do not last. They are all subject to a more or less rapid decline. We do not have to go into the reasons for this here; it is enough to note the existence of this fact, not only in regard to elites perpetuated by heredity, but also—albeit to a lesser degree—in regard to elites which are recruited by co-option.

2. *Circulation of elites.* War is a powerful cause of the extinction of military elites. This has always been realized, and some even have been inclined to see in war the only cause of the disappearance of elites. But this is not the case. Even in the depths of the most profound peace, the movement of the circulation of elites continues; even the elites which suffer no loss through war disappear and often very quickly. It is not only a question of aristocracies being extinguished through the excess of deaths over births, but also of degeneracy in the elements composing them. Hence aristocracies can subsist only by the elimination of these elements and the adhesion of new ones. Here is involved a

process similar to that observed in the living animal, which survives only by eliminating certain elements and assimilating others to replace them. If this circulation is halted, the animal is destroyed: it dies. The same applies to the social elite. If its destruction may be slower, it is none the less sure.

Merely a slowing down of this circulation may have the effect of considerably increasing the number of degenerate elements within the classes still possessing power, and – by contrast – of increasing the number of elements of superior quality within the subject classes. In such case, the social equilibrium becomes unstable; the least shock to it from within or without destroys it. A revolution or a conquest leads to the overturning of everything, bringing to power a new elite and establishing a new equilibrium which will remain stable for a longer or shorter period.

Ammon and Lapouge in their writings go too far when they seek to give us the anthropological characteristics of these elites, dealing with them as eugenic groups and identifying them in particular with the dolichocephalous fair-haired races. At present, this point remains obscure and much more research will be necessary before it will be possible to decide whether the psychic qualities of elites are indicated by external, anthropometric characteristics, and what precisely these characteristics are.

For contemporary European societies, conquest by foreign eugenic groups has been of no significance since the last great barbarian invasions, and it no longer exists as a factor in the European social organism. But there is nothing to indicate that it cannot appear again in the future. If European societies were to model themselves on the ideal dear to the humanitarians, if they should go so far as to inhibit selection, to favour systematically the weak, the vicious, the idle, the ill adapted – the 'small and humble' as they are termed by our philanthropists – at the expense of the strong, the energetic who constitute the elite, then a new conquest by new 'barbarians' would by no means be impossible.

At the present time in our societies, the adhesion of the

new elements indispensable to the subsistence of the elite comes from the lower classes and principally from the rural classes. These are the crucible in which are being formed, in the dark, the future elites. They are the roots of a plant the flower of which is the elite. The flower droops and withers, but it is soon replaced by another if the roots are healthy.

The fact is certain: the reasons for it are still not clearly understood. However, it seems highly probable that the rigorous selection occurring in the lower classes, especially in regard to children, has a significant effect. The rich classes have few children and almost all of them survive; the poorer classes have many children and lose a great number of those who are not particularly robust and well equipped for life. Similarly we find that highly bred plants and animals are very delicate in comparison with ordinary breeds. Why are Angora cats much more delicate animals than alley cats? Because they are surrounded by constant attention; care is taken to save all the kittens in an Angora mother's litter, whereas of the litter of a wretched starved alley cat only the kittens who are in very good health survive. The care taken with wheat over many centuries has made this plant unable to withstand the competition of natural life; wild wheat does not exist.

The high-minded people who would persuade the rich classes in our societies to have many children, the humanitarians who—wishing (for good reasons) to avoid certain modes of selection—give no thought to replacing them by others, are working without realizing it for the enfeeblement of the race, for its degeneracy. If the rich classes in our societies had many children, it is probable they would save almost all of them, even the sickliest and the least gifted. This would increase further the degenerate elements in the upper classes and delay the emergence of the elite coming from the lower classes. If selection no longer exerted its influence on the lower classes, these would cease to produce elites and the quality-level of society would fall considerably.

It is less easy to explain why, amongst the lower classes, it is especially the rural classes which seem to have the privilege of producing choice individuals. There are a good many analogous phenomena in regard to plants and animals which also, for all that they are well known, remain inexplicable. It is essential to use Riga flax seed to produce linen of a certain quality. The corn seed which, cultivated in Tuscany produces the straw called Florence, comes from the Romagna and degenerates rapidly. The most beautiful hyacinth bulbs are grown in Holland and degenerate in other countries.

It may be that the simple fact that the rural classes develop their muscles and let their brains rest has the precise effect of producing among them individuals who can let their muscles rest and work excessively with their brains. At all events, rural life seems eminently suitable for producing the reserves for the devouring, excessively active life of the great centres of civilization.

There are different and somewhat obscure reasons for the decadence of the elites which recruit by co-option or some other similar method. The example which most readily comes to mind in this connection is that of the Catholic clergy. What a profound decadence this elite underwent between the ninth and eighteenth centuries! Heredity plays no part in this phenomenon. The decadence originates from the fact that the elite, in recruiting itself, chose subjects of increasingly mediocre calibre. This is partly due to this elite's gradually losing sight of its ideal, being less and less sustained by faith and the spirit of sacrifice; and partly also to external circumstances: the emergence of other elites and their attracting choice individuals away from the elite in decadence. The proportion of these choice subjects to the rest of the population varies very little, so that one social sector's gain is another's loss. If commerce, industry, administration and so forth offer them a large outlet, they will necessarily be rare in any other elite, for example in the clergy.

This phenomenon of new elites which, through an incessant movement of circulation, rise up from the lower strata of society, mount up to the higher strata, flourish there, and then fall into decadence, are annihilated and disappear—this is one of the motive forces of history, and it is essential to give it its due weight if we are to understand great social movements.

Very often the existence of this objective phenomenon is obscured by our passions and prejudices, and the awareness we have of it differs considerably from the reality.

... The circulatory movement which carries to the summit elites born in the lower strata, and leads to the decline and disappearance of the elites in power, is very often concealed by several factors. As it is in general a fairly slow movement, it is only by studying history over a long period of time—for several centuries, for example—that one can perceive the general direction and the main lines of this movement. The contemporary observer who brings his gaze to bear only on a short period of time perceives only the secondary circumstances. He sees the rivalry of castes, the oppression of tyrants, popular uprisings, liberal protests, aristocracies, theocracies and ochlocracies; but the general phenomenon, of which these are but particular aspects, often wholly escapes him. Amongst the illusions thus produced are some which, because very common, deserve to be singled out for attention.

It is very difficult to avoid the influence of sentiment in dealing with a concrete example; to prevent our discussion from being clouded by this influence, let us deal with the matter in an abstract way. Let A be the elite in power, B the social element seeking to drive it from power and to replace it, and C the rest of the population, comprising the incompetent, those lacking energy, character and intelligence: in short, that section of society which remains when the elites are subtracted. A and B are the leaders, counting on C to provide them with partisans, with instruments. The C on their own would be impotent: an army without commanders. They become important only if guided by the A or B. Very often—in fact almost always—it is the B who put themselves at the head of the C, the A reposing in a false security or despising the C. Moreover, it is the B who are best able to lure the C for the simple reason that, not having power, their inducements are long-dated. It sometimes happens, however, that the A endeavour to get the better of the B, seeking to content the C with apparent concessions without going too far in the direction of real concessions. If the B gradually take the place of the A by slow infiltration, if the movement of social circulation is not interrupted, the C become deprived of the leaders capable of spurring them to revolt, and there ensues a period of prosperity. The A usually strive to resist this infiltration, but their resistance may be ineffective and amount in the end only to an inconsequent resentment. But if the resistance of the A is effective, the B can wrest the position from them only by open conflict, with the help of the C. If they succeed and get into power, a new challenging elite, D, will be formed and will play the same role vis-à-vis the B as the B played vis-à-vis the A, and so on.

Most historians do not perceive this movement. They describe the phenomenon as if it were the struggle of an aristocracy or an oligarchy, always the same, against a people, likewise always the same. But in fact:

(i) What is involved is the struggle between one aristocracy and another;
(ii) The aristocracy in power changes constantly, that of today being replaced, after a certain lapse of time, by its adversary.

When the B attain power, replacing the A elite in full decadence, it is generally observed that a period of great prosperity follows. Certain historians ascribe all the merit of this to the 'people', that is, to the C. Such truth as there is in this observation subsists only in the fact that the lower classes produce new elites. So far as these lower classes themselves are concerned, they are incapable of ruling; ochlocracy has never resulted in anything save disaster.

But more significant than the illusion of those who see things from afar is that of those who are involved in the movement and take an active part in it. Many of the B genuinely believe that they are pursuing, not a personal advantage for themselves and their class, but an advantage for the C, and that they are simply struggling for what they call justice, liberty, humanity. This illusion operates also on the A; many among them betray the interests of their class, believing they are fighting for the realization of these fine principles all to help the unfortunate C, whereas in reality the sole effect of their action is to help the B to attain power only to fasten on the C a yoke which may often be more severe than that of the A. Those who finally understand that this is the outcome sometimes make accusations of hypocrisy against the B or the A—as the case may be—who claimed they were guided solely by the desire of helping the C. But on the whole, this accusation of hypocrisy is ill-founded, for many of the B as well as the A are irreproachable in point of sincerity.

A sign which almost invariably presages the decadence of an aristocracy is the intrusion of humanitarian feelings and of affected sentimentalizing which render the aristocracy incapable of defending its position. Violence, we should note, is not to be confused with force. Often enough one observes cases in which individuals and classes which have lost the force to maintain themselves in power make themselves more and more hated because of their outbursts of random violence. The strong man strikes only when it is absolutely necessary, and then nothing stops him. Trajan was strong, not violent: Caligula was violent, not strong.

When a living creature loses the sentiments which, in given circumstances are necessary to it in order to maintain the struggle for life, this is a certain sign of degeneration, for the absence of these sentiments will, sooner or later, entail the extinction of the species. The living creature which shrinks from giving blow for blow and from shedding its adversary's blood thereby puts itself at the mercy of this adversary. The sheep has always found a wolf to devour it; if it now escapes this peril, it is only because man reserves it for his own prey. Any people which has horror of blood to the point of not knowing how to defend itself will sooner or later become the prey of some bellicose people or other. There is not perhaps on this globe a single foot of ground which has not been conquered by the sword at some time or other, and where the people occupying it have not maintained themselves on it by force. If the Negroes were stronger than the Europeans, Europe would be partitioned by the Negroes and not Africa by the Europeans. The 'right' claimed by people who bestow on themselves the title of 'civilized' to conquer other peoples, whom it pleases them to call 'uncivilized', is altogether ridiculous, or rather, this right is nothing other than force. For as long as the Europeans are stronger than the Chinese, they will impose their will on them; but if the Chinese should become stronger than the Europeans, then the roles would be reversed, and it is highly probable that humanitarian sentiments could never be opposed with any effectiveness to any army.

In the same way, for right or law to have reality in a society, force is necessary. Whether developed spontaneously or whether the work of a minority, law and order cannot be imposed on dissidents save by force. The utility of certain institutions, the sentiments they inspire, prepare the ground for their establishment, but for them to become established fact it is quite obvious that those desiring these institutions must have the power to impose them on those who do not desire them. Anton Menger fancies he proves that our present law needs to be changed because it 'rests almost exclusively on traditional relationships based on force'; but such is the characteristic of all laws that have ever existed, and if the law desired by Menger ever becomes reality, this will only be because he, in his turn, will have at his disposal the force to make it so; if he hasn't, then it will always remain a dream. 'Right' and 'law' originated in the force of isolated individuals; they are now maintained by the force of the community; but it is still force.

In considering successful changes of institutions, persuasion should not, as is so often the case, be contrasted with force. Persuasion is but a means for procuring force. No one has ever persuaded all the members of a society without exception; to ensure success only a section of the individuals in a society need to be persuaded: the section which has the force, either because it is the most numerous or for some quite different reason. It is by force that social institutions are established, and it is by force that they are maintained.

Any elite which is not prepared to join in battle to defend its positions is in full decadence, and all that is left to it is to give way to another elite having the virile qualities it lacks. It is pure day-dreaming to imagine that the humanitarian principles it may have proclaimed will be applied to it: its vanquishers will stun it with the implacable cry, 'Vae Victis'. The knife of the guillotine was being sharpened in the shadows when, at the end of the eighteenth century, the ruling classes in France were engrossed in developing their 'sensibility'. This idle and frivolous society, living like a parasite off the country, discoursed at its elegant supper parties of delivering the world from superstition and of crushing 'l'Infâme', all unsuspecting that it was itself going to be crushed.

Parallel with the phenomenon of the succession of elites, another of great importance is observable among civilized peoples. The production of economic goods goes on increasing, thanks mainly to the growth of personal capital, the average amount of which per head is one of the surest indices of civilization and progress. Material well-being is thus expanding more and more. On the other hand, foreign and civil wars, becoming less and less lucrative, as an industry, are diminishing in number and intensity. In consequence, habits are growing softer and morals becoming purer. Outside the vain agitations of politicians, there is being accomplished what G. de Molinari has called 'the silent revolution' – the slow transformation and improvement of social conditions. This movement is impeded, sometimes halted, by the squanderings of state socialism and by protectionist legislation of all kinds, but it is not the less real for that, and all the statistics of the most civilized peoples bear traces of it.

Having noted the importance in history of the succession of elites, we must not fall into the kind of error which is only too common, and claim that all is explained by this single cause. Social evolution is extremely complex; we can identify in it several main currents, but to seek to reduce them to one is a rash enterprise, at least for the present. For the time being, what is necessary is to study these great classes of phenomena and endeavour to discover their relationships.

3. *Spoliation.* We must again stress the point ... that historians often see these events only through the veil of their passions and prejudices, depicting to us as a battle for liberty what is a straightforward struggle between two competing elites. They believe – and wish us to share the belief – that the elite which in reality is seeking to get hold of power to use it and misuse it in just the same way as the elite it is opposing, is moved only by pure love of its fellow men; or, if we prefer the phraseology of our day, by desire for the well-being of the 'small and humble'. It is only when they seek to join issue with certain adversaries of theirs in historical and political debate that such historians alight on the truth, at least so far as these adversaries are concerned. Thus Taine produces the declamations of the Jacobins and shows us the greedy interests lurking beneath them. Likewise Jan Jensen shows us theological dissensions which are no more than very transparent veils cloaking exclusively worldly interests. His work is a remarkable description of how new elites, when they achieve power, deal with their allies of the day before, the 'small and humble', who discover that they have merely exchanged yokes. The socialists of our own day have clearly perceived that the revolution at the end of the eighteenth century led merely to the bourgeoisie's taking the place of the old elite. They exaggerate a good deal the burden of oppression imposed by the new masters, but they do sincerely

believe that a new elite of politicians will stand by their promises better than those which have come and gone up to the present day. All revolutionaries proclaim, in turn, that previous revolutions have ultimately ended up by deceiving the people; it is their revolution alone which is the *true* revolution. 'All previous historical movements' declared the *Communist Manifesto* of 1848, 'were movements of minorities or in the interest of minorities. The proletarian movement is the self-conscious, independent movement of the immense majority, in the interest of the immense majority.' Unfortunately this *true* revolution, which is to bring men an unmixed happiness, is only a deceptive mirage that never becomes a reality. It is akin to the golden age of the millenarians: for ever awaited, it is for ever lost in the mists of the future, for ever eluding its devotees just when they think they have it.

Socialism is motivated by certain factors, some of which are present in almost all classes of society, while others differ according to the classes.

Among the first we should reckon the sentiments which move men to sympathize with the troubles and misfortunes of others, and to seek a remedy for them. This sentiment is one of the worthiest and most useful to society; indeed, it is the very cement of society.

Today almost everyone pays court to the socialists because they have become powerful. But it is not very long ago that many people were reckoning them to be scarcely better than criminals. Such an attitude could not be more false. So far, the socialists have certainly not been morally inferior to the members of the 'bourgeois' parties, especially of those parties which have used legislation to exact tribute from other citizens and which constitute what one may term 'bourgeois socialism'. If the 'bourgeois' were being animated by the same spirit of abnegation and sacrifice for their class as the socialists are for theirs, socialism would be far from being as menacing as it actually is. The presence in its ranks of the new elite is attested precisely by the moral qualities displayed by its adepts and which have enabled them to emerge victorious from the bitter test of numerous persecutions.

The sentiment of benevolence men have for their fellows, and without which society probably could not exist, is in no way incompatible with the principle of the class struggle. Even the most energetic defence of one's own rights may perfectly well be allied to a respect for the rights of others. Each class, if it wishes to avoid being oppressed, must have the force to defend its interests, but this does not at all imply that it must aim at oppressing other classes. On the contrary, it should be able to learn from experience that one of the best ways of defending these interests is in fact to take account, with justice, equity and even benevolence, of the interests of others.

Unfortunately, this sentiment of benevolence is not always very enlightened. Those who have it at times resemble the good women who crowd round a sick friend, each recommending a remedy. Their desire to be useful to the unfortunate is beyond question; it is only the efficacy of the remedies which is doubtful. However great their devoted concern for him, this cannot supply them with the medical knowledge they lack. When they find themselves in like-minded company, all of them advocating their own special nostrums, they usually end up by choosing a remedy almost at random, because really 'one must do *something*', and the ailing victim is lucky if his malady does not grow worse.

V. *Socialism as a Particular Case of Spoliation*

Societies which admit private property—which is to say almost all and every society known up to the present—offer men two essentially different ways of acquiring wealth. One is by producing it directly or indirectly through the work and services of the capital they possess. The other is by acquiring the wealth thus produced by others. These two methods have at all times been employed, and it would be rash to believe that they will cease to be employed in the foreseeable future. But because the second method is generally under moral reproof, people willingly close their eyes to its employment, holding it to be something sporadic and incidental. In fact it is a general and enduring phenomenon.

Social movements generally follow the line of least resistance. The direct production of economic goods is often a very laborious process, whereas appropriating those goods produced by others is sometimes a very easy matter. It has become considerably more easy ever since the idea took root of accomplishing the spoliation, not by transgressing the law, but by using the law. In order to save, to refrain from consuming all he earns, an individual has to have a certain degree of control over himself. Tilling a field to produce corn is an arduous labour; lurking at the corner for a passer-by to rob is a dangerous venture. On the other hand, going along to the polling station to vote is a very easy business, and if by so doing one can procure food and shelter, then everybody—especially the unfit, the incompetent and the idle—will rush to do it.

From another point of view, it may be said that of the two procedures by which the property of others can be appropriated, i.e. directly by violence or fraud or indirectly by the help of the public powers, the second is much less harmful to social well-being than the first. It is a refinement and improvement on fraud and violence, just as the rearing of domestic animals is a refinement and improvement on hunting wild animals. The socialists who are willing, when collectivizing the means of production, to grant fair compensation for expropriation of property to the existing owners, cannot be accused of seeking to employ either of these two procedures. Other socialists, who would expropriate gradually or immediately without indemnifying the existing possessors, clearly intend to appeal to the second procedure, but they cannot truly be represented, as some legislators have done, as wishing to have recourse to the first. It is solely by means of the law that the socialists and communists seek to alter the distribution of wealth, to give to some what they take away from others. In this sense, their systems do not in any way differ from the various protectionist systems. These latter, properly speaking, represent the socialism of the entrepreneurs and the capitalists.

Classical political economy has only incidentally, and in order to condemn it, been concerned with appropriation occurring with the assistance of the law. Every science necessarily has to limit its field of enquiry. In this respect there is nothing to be said against the method used by political economy. But after separating, by analysis, the various parts of a real phenomenon in order to study them in isolation, there must then be a synthesis, bringing them together again to obtain an idea of reality. Political economy may not study appropriation by aid of the law, but this study must be undertaken by some other science if we wish to understand the concrete phenomenon. So important a part of it cannot be neglected.

The class struggle, to which Marx has specially drawn attention, is a real factor, the tokens of which are to be found on every page of history. But the struggle is not confined only to two classes: the proletariat and the capitalist; it occurs between an infinite number of groups with different interests, and above all between the elites contending for power. The existence of these groups may vary in duration, they may be based on permanent or more or less temporary characteristics. In most savage peoples, and perhaps in all, sex determines two of these groups. The oppression of which the proletariat complains, or had cause to complain of, is as nothing in comparison with that which the women of the Australian aborigines suffer. Characteristics to a greater or lesser degree real—nationality, religion, race, language, etc.—may give rise to these groups. In our own day the struggle of the Czechs and the Germans in Bohemia is more intense than that of the proletariat and the capitalists in England. People who are engaged in the same occupation naturally tend to group together. In many countries, the makers of sugar have banded together to exact tribute from their fellow citizens. This phenomenon is similar to that occurring in former times when armed bands levied tribute from the peasants, and it is only a variant of the same thing. The shipowners combine to get shipping bounties; the retailers act in concert to crush the big shops by taxes; fixed stall-holders cabal to prevent or hamper itinerant street-sellers; business men in one region unite to do down those of another region; 'organized' workers to deprive 'non-organized' workers of jobs; the workers of one country to exclude from the 'national market' the workers of another country; the workers of one town to keep out the workers of another. In Italy the shoemakers in certain towns have attempted, by imposing municipal import duties, to keep out the footware of shoemakers living outside these towns.

Past history and contemporary observation show us men at all times and in all places divided into groups, each of which generally procures economic goods for itself partly by producing them directly and partly by despoiling other groups, who despoil it in their turn. These activities interact in a thousand ways and their direct and indirect effects are extremely varied. One could draw up a sort of balance sheet for each group. For example, some manufacturers produce merchandise of a certain type; through protective duties on the materials they use, they pay tribute which goes to other groups of manufacturers, to farmers, merchants, etc. Other tribute is exacted from them by the circulation of paper-money or by government measures of monetary policy; they pay tribute money to politicians, laying out cash to maintain certain prejudices which they judge favourable to their interests. In compensation they receive tribute from the consumers in the shape of protective duties on foreign products which might compete with theirs, and from the workers through the issuing of paper-money or through measures taken by the government to prevent the workers from freely negotiating the sale of their labour. They levy toll on the taxpayer by getting favourable terms in supplying government departments, etc. With certain industrial groups, it is easy to see to which side the balance tips; with others it is difficult to know whether, on balance, they are gainers or losers by this system—one which, moreover, entails an enormous destruction of wealth for society in general. Cases are by no means rare in which those concerned are deceived into thinking that they end up on the right side in the balance of gains and losses produced by this system of mutual spoliation. For certain groups state socialism may well bring with it cruel disillusion.

There are groups for which the question is simpler, for example, those which produce nothing of importance, pay no tribute, or almost none, but which simply receive tribute. Other groups, the most numerous and important, directly produce goods and very often pay tribute without getting any in return or only to an insignificant degree. Such has often been the fate of the workers; such also is the fate which certain regimes would reserve in time to come for the entrepreneurs and the capitalists.

Generally, for individuals to be able to constitute a group and to win for themselves the possessions of others, certain conditions are necessary.

1. The members of the group must not be too widely dispersed; they must have an easily recognizable common characteristic, such as the same race, the same religion, the same occupation, and so forth. Herein lies one of the most effective reasons why the consumers can scarcely ever organize themselves successfully to resist the producer combines. For example, in our societies, we are all to a greater or lesser extent consumers of cloth and clothing, while there is only a very small number among us engaged in making cloth and clothing. The fact that we all wear clothes cannot serve to determine a group, whereas the fact of making cloth and clothes can perfectly well determine a group.

2. Centuries of civilization have impressed on man's mind the sentiment that he should refrain from seizing the goods of others. This sentiment must not be directly impugned, so an indirect method has to be employed for appropriating these goods, and some reason must be found to justify it.

But there is never any very great difficulty on this point, for the most paltry reasons find acceptance when they serve powerful interests or minister to fixed inclinations. Since most men make convictions of their interests, one is preaching to the converted. A hollow phraseology, empty, high-sounding, emotional formulas, abstract and repetitive phrases, vague and airy expressions with never a firm meaning—this is all that men ask for when they are looking, not for truth, which they wouldn't know what to do with, but only for a justification of actions which are advantageous or simply agreeable to them. There are periods, like the end of the eighteenth century in France and the present epoch, in which the despoiled themselves give reasons for justifying and increasing spoliation by their ethical declamations about 'sensibility', 'solidarity', etc., etc.

... It is a curious circumstance, and one meriting attention, that men are often observed to act with much more energy in appropriating the property of others than in defending their own. As we have noted elsewhere (*Cours*, 1047) if, in a nation of thirty million, it is proposed to levy one franc per annum on each citizen and to distribute the total to thirty individuals, these latter will work night and day for the success of this proposal, while it will be difficult to get the others to bestir themselves sufficiently to oppose the proposal, because, after all, it is only one franc! Another example: it is proposed to establish a 'minimum salary' for the employees of a public administration. The people who in consequence of this measure will receive an increase of salary are perfectly well aware of the advantage this proposal has for them. They and their friends will exert themselves all they can for the success of the candidates who promise to provide them with this manna. As for the people who are going to have to pay for this salary increase, each of them has great difficulties in working out what this is going to cost him in tax, and if he manages to assess it, the amount seems of small significance. In most cases, he doesn't even think about it. He follows discussions about this measure with an inattentive ear, as if it were something which in no way affected him. One of the hardest things to get taxpayers to understand is that ten times one franc makes ten francs. Provided the tax increases occur gradually, they can reach a total amount which would have provoked explosions of wrath had they been levied at one swoop.

Spoliation therefore seldom meets with a really effective resistance from the despoiled. What sometimes stops it is the destruction of wealth consequent upon it, which may entail the ruin of the country. History shows us that more than once spoliation has finished by killing the goose that lays the golden eggs.

The behaviour of these groups, each of which tries to get hold of the goods produced by others, would in all probability survive radical changes in the social organization, like, for example, the abolition of private property. But experience suggests that private property inevitably emerges again after its destruction. However perfect the profoundly thought-out rules for the distribution of goods which have to be consumed, these rules will have to be applied by human beings, and their conduct will reflect their qualities and their defects. If today there are arbiters who always decide against persons belonging to a certain class and in favour of persons belonging to certain other classes, there will very likely be 'distributors' in this society of tomorrow who will share out the loaf in such a way as to give a very little piece to A and a very big piece to B.

FROM *TRASFORMAZIONI DELLA DEMOCRAZIA* (1921)

III. *The Plutocratic Cycle*

1. *Elements composing demagogic plutocracy.* If we consider the economic and social development which has occurred in our society over the last hundred years, and endeavour to distinguish the mean trend from various disturbing secondary factors, we shall recognize the following characteristics:

(i) A very large increase in wealth and savings and in the capital engaged in production.

(ii) An unequal distribution of this wealth. Some people try to make out that this inequality has increased; others contend that it has diminished. Probably the norm of distribution has remained about the same.

(iii) The ever-growing importance of two social classes: rich speculators, and those whom we may generally term 'workers'. This period appears notable for the growth and flourishing vigour of 'plutocracy' if particular consideration is given to the first of these two phenomena. If emphasis is placed on the second, then the period can be seen as marking the growth and flourishing of 'democracy'. Of course, we are here using the terms 'plutocracy' and 'democracy' in the rather vague sense they have as employed in everyday speech.

(iv) A partial alliance between these two elements; this is especially noticeable from the end of the nineteenth century and up to the present day. Although as a general rule speculators and workers do not altogether share common interests, it nevertheless happens that some among both groups find it profitable to travel in the same direction, with the object of getting the upper hand over the state and of exploiting other social classes. At times the plutocrats are able to achieve this kind of alliance by cunningly playing on the sentiments (residues) of the masses, thereby pulling the wool over their eyes. Herein lies the origin of the phenomenon which ordinary people and empirical observers identify by the name of 'demagogic plutocracy'.

(v) While the power of the two forementioned classes increases, there is a decline of the power of two others: (a) the rich propertied class, or simply the well-to-do who are not speculators; and (b) the military class. The power of the latter has now indeed been reduced to very small dimensions. Before the 1914–18 war one would have had to make an exception in the case of Germany, for until then the power of the military was still very considerable there. But this is no longer the case. A clear sign of the strength and prevalence of this phenomenon is the ever-increasing extension of the suffrage from the 'haves' to the 'have-nots'. It must be noted that among the 'haves' there are many who are not speculators, while among the 'have-nots' there are some who share common interests with the speculators, and yet others whose sentiments (residues) the speculators can make use of. Hence it is of advantage to the speculators – an advantage which they have frequently seized – to weaken the power of the 'haves' and increase that of the 'have-nots'.

(vi) Slowly but surely the use of force passes from the upper to the lower classes. This characteristic forms, with the following factor, one of the features of the disintegration of the central power.

(vii) The modern parliamentary system, to all intents and purposes, is the effective instrument of demagogic plutocracy. Through elections and then through political transactions in parliament, considerable scope is given to the activities of individuals who are well endowed with instincts of combination. Indeed it now seems clear that the modern parliamentary system is to a great extent bound up with the fate of plutocracy – prospering with it, declining with it. Transformations of the parliamentary system – which can also be termed transformations of democracy – closely follow the vicissitudes of plutocracy.

What is now occurring in our society is in no way unique. To understand them correctly, the main features of the present situation need to be placed in their proper historical context. We must resist the tendency to give exaggerated and exclusive importance to what is happening under our eyes, disconnecting it from the evidence of past history. Equally we must avoid the opposite error of purporting to see in the present situation a faithful and exact reduplication of the past. Movements recorded by history which have points of similarity with present developments do not tend uniformly in the same direction; they fluctuate now in one direction, now in another. None the less, we can perceive in them a general trend, a basic line of development discernible amid the various fluctuations. These undulations in the general line of movement result from the very nature of human beings who, where government is concerned, are regulated in the main by two agencies: consent and force. The social system oscillates between these two poles.

Consent is achieved by means of subsidiary agencies; 'identity of interest' is one such, and another derives from religious sentiments, customs, prejudices and so forth, corresponding to the residues which in the *Treatise* we have termed residues of aggregate-persistence (Class II). Persuasion is often employed in the operation of these agencies; sometimes genuine sound reasoning is used, but much more often sophistries (derivations) are deployed, corresponding to the residues we have classified under the term of instinct of combinations (Class I).

We have to bear in mind the different roles played in matters of government by two major groups of citizens. One group consists of farmers and owners of landed property; the other consists of merchants, industrialists, public works contractors, financial operators, 'speculators' and the like. The tendency of the first category is almost invariably in the direction of reinforcing the persistence of aggregates, while that of the second fosters the instinct of combinations. The prevalence of one or the other gives rise to markedly different types of society. When the first is dominant, its own inherent qualities may serve to maintain it. The predominance of the second category usually produces plutocratic societies and therefore, since plutocracy is deficient in inherent strength, the end-result is almost inevitably demagogic or military plutocracy ...

The readiness to use force and the preference for obtaining consent are manifestations not only of distinct but also of conflicting attitudes. Exceptional individuals may possibly possess both attitudes in equal measure, but in the majority of men within the governing class one or the other attitude predominates; and we find that the circulation between the various social classes is very closely linked with the oscillations in the social order.

As is the case with living creatures, every type of society contains within itself the seeds of its florescence and its eventual decay; the major oscillations correspond to these periods of rise and fall in societies ...

2. *The end of the plutocratic cycle*. Modern Italy was established by the bourgeoisie against the indifference and at times the opposition of the agrarian masses. The new regime soon turned into a demagogic plutocracy which reached the height of its power at the time of Depretis and a little after. As might be expected, it is now suffering from the consequences of the war, but it is far from being overcome.

Demagogic plutocracy now seems in general to be wholly triumphant. In England it may well be able to hold its own for a long time to come, thanks to the benefits accruing from the hegemony England has created and to which all other countries, America only excepted, now willy-nilly submit. Rome exploited merely the Mediterranean basin: England is exploiting vast areas of the world's surface. It remains to be seen whether effective forces within England will arise against its demagogic plutocracy, or whether military plutocracy in other countries will emerge and challenge England's hegemony. It also remains to be seen what part will be played in the future by those two unknown quantities: Russia and Asia.

Plutocracy is in much greater danger in other European countries; but at all times and in all countries it is rich in expedients for turning to its own advantage circumstances which on the face of it seem to be overwhelmingly unfavourable. To all appearances plutocracy gives way to hostile forces. But it does so with the set purpose of regaining by devious means what it has had to abandon to force, outflanking the obstacle which cannot be overcome by frontal attack – and, in conformity with its general rule, passing on payment of the bill of the conflict to the savers and investors: those meek sheep who lend themselves so readily to fleecing. It has by now devised innumerable expedients: vast public debts which it knows very well cannot in the end be honoured; capital levies; taxes which sap and exhaust the incomes of the ordinary, non-speculating investor; sumptuary laws, proved ineffective time and time again in the past – all these and many other devices of the same sort are employed with the set purpose of gulling the masses.

In Italy, Signor Falcioni's proposed legislation for dealing with the large landed estates and for granting land to the peasants will prove no more harmful to the interests of our plutocrats than were, after a brief period of storm and stress, the agrarian laws of the Gracchi to the interests of the Roman plutocracy. Our plutocrats stand to suffer much more harm from the proposal, if it is implemented, of the 'populists' who are aiming at increasing the numbers of small proprietors, for this group in the agrarian class is the sole adversary plutocracy need fear.

As long as the increment from savings is not too severely curtailed, as long as food-prices and rents are kept low, and provided there are on tap all the other benefits which the plutocracy can make available to its supporters and dependants, there is nothing in the present state of affairs to prevent the plutocrats from continuing to make fat profits, just as the general prosperity of the Roman plutocracy was in no way jeopardised by the corn doles and the annonary laws introduced under the Republic, maintained and then extended under the Empire. This similarity between the conditions prevailing and the measures taken in ancient Rome and the conditions and measures obtaining in our own society derives from the intrinsic nature of things. As it was and is, so will it continue to be in the future. In the decadence of the Roman plutocracy we discern what could very well be, to some degree at least, the image of the decadence which is threatening our own plutocracy.

It is certain that we have now reached a point where there are close parallels with the situation of the Roman plutocracy towards the end of the Republic. By analogy with cycles observed in other periods and in other countries, it is probable—highly probable—that, being close to the peak, we are close also to the downward slope. Realization of this does not of itself amount to much and we would want to know far more about it. Yet something, however small, is better than nothing, and a limited knowledge now does not preclude—on the contrary, it lays the foundation for—a fuller knowledge in the future. The only trustworthy guide we have in attaining this is experimental science.

GIOVANNI PAPINI
(1881–1956)
AND
GIUSEPPE PREZZOLINI
(1882–)

The son of an atheist, Mazzinian, Florentine artisan, Papini was largely self-taught. The sense of being an outsider who had had to make his way against great difficulties no doubt contributed to the resentment which Papini displayed in his ferocious attacks on official academic culture.

His early autobiography, *Un uomo finito* (1912), gives a romantic and often rhetorical account of his intellectual crises. The restless dissatisfaction with which he passed from one philosophy to another made him the representative of a whole generation's search for truth. As an intellectual popularizer he had few equals, but he lacked the stamina and patience needed to become a really original thinker. His pragmatism, which influenced Mussolini, was more mystical than empirical in character, and served to justify his conception of the superman as the creator of his own reality.

He founded his first review, *Leonardo*, in 1903, together with Prezzolini. Although he wrote an article criticizing the imperialist ideal, shortly afterwards he agreed to collaborate with Corradini. The 'Nationalist programme' printed here was read by Papini to audiences in Florence, Siena and Arezzo, and in later years he could claim with some justice that he was 'the first evangelist of nationalism'. His co-operation with Prezzolini continued when the latter founded *La Voce* (1908). The *Voce* welcomed radical contributors such as the socialist historian Salvemini, and opposed the nationalist campaign for the annexation of Libya. However, Papini eventually found the *Voce*'s reformism too sober for his taste and left to found a new review, *Lacerba* (1913). *Lacerba* united

Papini, Ardengo Soffici and the Futurists led by Marinetti. In a 1913 article Papini called for 'a bath of blood', and when war broke out the *Lacerba* group was in the forefront of the interventionist campaign. Papini and the other writers of *Lacerba* saw war as the means to the internal regeneration of Italy, and the destruction of the false values of democracy. They combined nationalism with the subversion of established cultural and moral values.

For Papini, however, *Lacerba* was only another phase. He was rejected for military service on account of his short sight and this fact perhaps helped to isolate him from his friends of the interventionist campaign. In the postwar period he did not share the nationalist enthusiasm of intellectuals like Soffici or Marinetti. He despised D'Annunzio, and in 1919 he wrote that 'the domesticated and imperialist Bolshevism in the service of Mammon' propagated by the *Popolo d'Italia* seemed to him worse even than the crude version preached by the Socialists. At this time he became a convert to Catholicism, and in 1921 he published his most popular book, the *Storia di Cristo*. From then on he became an increasingly orthodox reactionary, deploring industrial civilization and the spread of scepticism. He was one of the intellectual mentors of the literary movement known as *Strapaese* which interpreted Fascism as the defence of traditional rural and popular values. During the 1930s Papini played an important role as an apologist for the regime, identifying the cause of Fascism with that of the Church. In his intellectual development from atheism to Catholicism and from heroic individualism to the defence of tradition and the family, Papini was a precursor.

GIOVANNI PAPINI

A NATIONALIST PROGRAMME

(Extracts from a speech made in February 1904)

We have no desire to found the usual sort of party with its programmes for public or private consumption, its maximum or minimum policies, its list of patron saints, its cliques and sects, a breeding ground for petty vanity. Italy has no shortage of that kind of party and I believe that you would be more ready to welcome someone who promised to get rid of an old party than one who announced a new one.

If you go to the remotest and most obscure village of Italy you will find some old property owner, conservative to the marrow, bemoaning, in tired tones, the disappearance of the principles of earlier days, some garrulous lawyer expounding liberal principles and wanting to get into Parliament under the sacred banner of progress and freedom, a surly pharmacist who is still hoping for Mazzini's Republic, a smart young priest who preaches Christian democracy with a catch in his throat, a left-wing worker who, when he's had a drink or two, can reel off the phrases he's picked up in some 'Clarion Call of the Workers', and some half-brigand of a fellow who has been unsuccessful in his vocation and instead talks animatedly about Ravachol's bombs and Caserio's dagger. And perhaps there'll even be a Utopian pacifist who, from the appropriate shelter of his garret, will expound his grandiose plan for the society of the future where men will all be virtuous, happy and live for ever after, each with a chicken in the pot and the Absolute in his head.

In this traditional land of phrase-mongers we do not want to add any more formulas to those that delight the councils, congresses or committee rooms of the kingdom of Italy. All the ideas and formulas we need have already been drawn up and reiterated. We wish merely to give life, new life, to these formulas and ideas.

We are not putting forward programmes but a passionate attitude of mind to make an end to words and turn programmes into action.

Almost all our political parties are nothing but words, words, words.

The monarchists, for example, seize every opportunity of talking about the king, the country and the army, but they employ the platitudes of '48 and '59 that no longer arouse any feelings in us, they talk in clichés and formulas; they talk coldly, mechanically, rhetorically. Very few of these old liberals have any deep, close or passionate *feeling* for what a king, a country or an army ought to be.

The middle classes talk about the socialist peril and the arrogant claims of the workers; they think about how best to defend themselves, but it remains entirely a matter of words; it is not translated into a real awareness of the danger, a living and conscious will or desire to take action.

The republicans talk to us about the people, about duty, about the individual and other splendid things, but they are merely repeating the fine phrases used by Mazzini or the declamatory periods of Saffi. When it's a question of action, they show a complete misunderstanding of what a great democracy could be and confine themselves to aping a party, the Socialists, whose spirit is as different as possible from theirs.

So our parties remain in the rarified sphere of hot air and a limbo of words. They chatter a great deal but they feel very little; they are very keen on symbols but they show no enthusiasm for things.

Now here lies our difference from the rest and this is our novelty. We want not to prattle but to feel, not to use eloquent phrases but to show real awareness.

The party that possesses or at best has shown up till now that it possesses this awareness is precisely the party which we are most proud to oppose—the Socialists.

But socialism, since it is class-conscious and has no sense of history, is, by its origins and its needs, an international, that is to say an anti-national, party.

Now if we middle-class monarchists want to maintain our position as the ruling class and leading caste, those who own the property and give the orders, we must follow above all a national policy. But if there is one thing nowadays that is not really *felt* it is the nation. I am not saying that we do not still hear resounding phrases about the Old Country or that in boys' books and official speeches the great star of Italy does not still make her blushing appearance in all her tinsel finery, but all the platitudes about the blue sky, the cradle of the arts and the fair land of Italy are of absolutely no use whatsoever if we do not have a strong, constantly alert, national consciousness.

It is the absence of this which shows that Italy has not as yet even started to create a national form of life. I am speaking not of Italy as a geographical expression, which is still bathed by the water of her three seas, nor of the official Italy that has its seat at Montecitorio and goes to sleep in the Ministries, but of Italy as a nation, as a people, as a living organism. No powerful overall direction of all its forces can be discerned in the life of this nation which, however, in the epic and tragic hours of its history reveals such a prodigious wealth of energy in conquest and organization.

Every day and at every moment we feel that Italy is moving onwards not as a result of her own foresight, with a clear vision of her strength and her destiny, but through the inertia of her traditional structures, as a result of external forces and contradictory movements of men, groups and classes. If there are still some Italians who give thought to that tiny organism known as the individual or that greater organism known as class, there is no one or hardly anyone who thinks of that mighty organism known as the nation. Hemmed in between personal selfishness and class selfishness, the mother country no longer represents a living force and is by way of becoming an historical memory. If, in an attempt to restrict selfishness, people try to give the appearance of looking beyond themselves, they move directly from the idea of class not to the idea of nation, which could be an immediate reality, but to that vague, confused and useless word Mankind.

Thus we see that the two largest classes that are or seem to be opposed to each other at the present time possess, amongst other similarities, that of both being anti-national.

The proletariat is what it is because it has a lively class consciousness and this, although it enables it to offer its platonic support to internationalism, none the less prevents it from having any sense of those national needs that, in its view, tend to safeguard its own special interests. On the other hand, the bourgeoisie are anti-national because, as we shall see, they are insufficiently class-conscious. So they are forgetful of their origins which are intimately connected with the recent formation of our nation and have never realized that the only means whereby a governing class can preserve its power is by exercising a function useful to the whole country. But as they are flabby and apathetic and have no thought of how to save themselves, they cannot even see the means by which they might do so, one of which would, in fact, be nationalism, that is to say the pursuit of aims that would concentrate all the energies of every individual and every class on one single aim.

So between the starving proletariat and the inept bourgeoisie, the country cannot yet experience a real rebirth. And so Italian life pursues its course between the demagogic tyranny of one party which loudly proclaims its desire for freedom, and for that very reason wants to take it away from the rest, and the inertia of the bourgeoisie which is incapable of seeing anything beyond its own narrow ephemeral interests and is capable neither of defending itself nor harming its opponents.

It is necessary, it seems to us, to escape from this sad depression and feverish vacuum in which our country is struggling.

We need to restore a deeper meaning to our life, a full meaning to the life of the nation.

This Italy deprived of any unity of vision or any programme of action needs someone to castigate her in order to arouse her from her slumbers and urge her on to action.

And so, in the midst of the arrogance of the proletariat and the lack of awareness of the bourgeoisie, we should like to utter a message, not of peace, which would be unworthy of us, but of renewal. We want, in fact, both arrogance and lack of awareness to come to an end and these wretched classes to rise above themselves and form a Country. We should, in fact, like to be not party men or men of a class but men of a nation and a race.

Thus our work will have to be first of all destructive and negative. Our programme is both uncompromising and resolute. We do not like to tie ourselves to other parties, to form alliances, to use ambiguous formulas to increase our numbers but thereby losing in effectiveness and organization.

We are not fond of those who boast that they are broad-minded. Too often have we seen baseness and indifference and lack of any personal belief hiding under a mask of broad-mindedness for this to satisfy our love of clear and exact statement.

In order to act, you have to be one-sided, to have, indeed, restricted, narrow ideas – but clear and precise ones. Multiple viewpoints and dilettante scepticism may be all right for literature or speculative thinking but not for politics.

And in order to love something deeply you need to hate something else. No perfect Christian can love God without loathing the Devil. So we should not really love our country or greatness or energy unless we have a deep-rooted hatred of everything that is anti-national, petty, base, weak or vulgar. And there are indeed many things that we hate, many things that we should like to drive out and destroy and repress with all our might.

And first and foremost there is what might be called the democratic mentality: by which we mean not the noble forms of democracy that a government inspired by the people may assume, as in Rome under the Republic and the Empire before the Caesars, in the large and small medieval and Renaissance city-states which were republican in the aesthetic and warlike senses of the word, in the great republic of North America, democratic and expansionist; but that confused medley of debased feelings, empty thoughts, defeatist phrases and brutish ideals ranging from comfortable established radicalism to the snivelling anti-militarism of Tolstoy, from bogus positivism with its facile belief in progress and superficial anti-clericalism to the resounding *blagues* of the French Revolution – Justice, Fraternity, Liberty and Equality.

This democratic mentality that now colours every aspect of life and has robbed it of all its earlier values, which pours out of speeches and floods into newspapers, takes root in universities, booms out in committee rooms and Parliament and infiltrates everywhere, whether in the form of pity for the gaol-bird or fear of war, in the disparagement of religion as well as in reliance on meaningless phrases, this mentality we despise and oppose and hate and guard against with every means within our power. Loathing it as we do, we are against the majority. That is to say, not only the democratic mentality but, in a way, the whole mentality of our times. You can feel its hostile and dominating presence in everything at every moment. It has penetrated into the very fabric of our society.

Because it is not only a mentality, that is to say, something intellectual. It is composed not only of ideas and formulas but also of feeling and passion. And even its ideas and formulas serve mostly to justify both our feelings and passions. The thing most to be feared therefore is not only democratic ideology but democratic sentimentality, since the former is merely the rational expression of the latter. Anti-war theories are not produced by reason but reasons are found to excuse the reluctance to accept bloodshed, the fear of conflict and other similar sentimental weaknesses. Theories do not justify economic processes as materialist historians assert, but states of mind. What interests us therefore is to ferret out and bring to light the sentimental substratum of that ignoble attitude which is not so much democratic as mediocratic.

You know its more obvious symptoms and characteristics. The first of them is the one which I have already talked about in *Il Regno*, the irrational respect for human life.

'Every man', I wrote, 'has the right to live and everyone must live: this is the steadfast belief, tacit or overt, of every socialist and bourgeois, individualistic conservative or collectivist revolutionary. It is such a fundamental principle that it lies at the root of all the claims of the proletariat, every anti-war protest or sentimental excess.

'No one ever doubts for a moment that a man has the right to live, that he possesses within himself that sacred and intangible something that is normally considered the mysterious attribute of divinity. Ordinary morality, which has now become so much inflated by squeamish and wordy philanthropy, is nowadays based on that respect and belief.

'Hatred of war, dislike for bloodthirsty repression, the cult of the suffering worker or the victims of misfortune, an obsession with public health, compassion for the gaol-bird, the abolition of capital punishment, pity for those who are murdered or commit suicide, these are all facts, and signs of this one single predominating idea. Human life is sacred, the breath of life in some miserable little man is worth more than an empire and the death of a few thousand soldiers is more important than the power of a nation.

'Fear of death has become the modern man's nightmare: he is pursued like so many feeble women, little nineteenth-century Lady Macbeths, by the ghosts of the dead. Every man has his own little body, his skull full of obscure desires and words he doesn't understand, his ever-grasping hands, his little mechanism of bones, fat and muscles, limited in space, limited in time; and he wants to live out his life at all costs. And in order to succeed in doing this, he wants to respect the lives of others and so that they won't kill him, he takes good care not even to scratch them.

'So the ephemeral, fragile and narrow life of the little man imposes itself upon important class and national interests and sets itself up against them. Fear of taking one tiny life makes the lives of a whole people shorter and meaner.

'The way to a grander life is barred in order to save the life that lasts but a moment.'

Rationally, this feeling is quite inconsistent, but in practice, it is highly dangerous. Modern life, precisely because it is more intense, demands an ever-increasing sacrifice of lives—lives of explorers, scientists, workers, soldiers—and the sentimentalist who sheds tears over every graze and is horrified at every massacre is opposing the important and essential needs of the development of a nation. For a people to be great and powerful, it needs many of its members to understand the value of the supreme sacrifice. The enlargement of life, I said, needs and leads to the enlargement of death. Anybody who is opposed to the former is opposed to the latter.

Faced by the immensity of modern life, in which Italy has to participate if it is not to fall asunder, those fragile and ephemeral lives, narrow and restricted, must and will disappear. Mourning over the dead, wasting one's time in sentimentality, humanitarian moaning, drawing back in the face of all the platitudes on the sacredness of human life, would be to deny the force of the life that is throbbing and growing and glowing all around us. And life is not worth living unless it is full and intense: sacrificing the heroic intensity of such a life in favour of life that is merely ephemeral would deprive the world of its greatest value.

And as we ourselves wish for a richer world, for some great word to be uttered, some great act to be accomplished, some great conquest to light up our narrow horizons, so we reject all our early weakness and tears and meanness of spirit.

When lives have to be sacrificed we are not saddened if we can see arising in our mind's eye the grandiose harvest of a better life that will be born from the dead. And while the democratic mob raise their outcry against war as a barbarous relic of outgrown savagery, we look on it as the greatest possible tonic to restore flagging energy, as a swift and heroic means to attain power and richness.

And a people needs not only proud feelings but another quality which is increasingly despised and misunderstood: obedience. For any enterprise to be brought to a successful conclusion, it needs to be directed by a few people. A people is a flock which always needs competent shepherds; whether it be kings by the grace of God, or demagogues by the grace of the mob, we always need someone to give orders and be in command. The individual will diverts and dissipates its forces without achieving anything. Thus the secret of the great strength of the Jesuits, who were able to dominate so many people with so few means, lies in the principle of absolute obedience when men meekly follow the orders of their chief.

But it is our misfortune that there is nothing which is falling into so lamentable a decline as the principle of authority. A blind feeling of indiscipline, revolt and insubordination is spreading throughout every class. As in the happy days of the *raison raisonnante* of the Encyclopaedists, people think that everybody can decide how best to conduct his life by the use of this intelligence. Never did more serious error take root in man's mind and I am sure that unless this inability to obey is banished from our thoughts, it will be the major factor in the disintegration of our society.

There are a thousand and one signs by which we can recognize this dangerous lack of reverence, from the sneers directed at anything that is superior, the hero or the genius, to the myth of universal equality that everyone believes because he wants to be the equal of those at the top, from the decline of the military virtues, which depend above all on discipline, to the hostility shown towards the Church, which was and is the finest example of organized hierarchy in modern times. This refusal to accept any yoke or any tie or any leader is a sign not of strength but of weakness because it shows that we are incapable of understanding either the necessity for submission or the noble and difficult task of being able to carry out orders. A society is not an organization unless it contains a minority that gives the orders, but this minority cannot exercise its function of ruling unless there is someone to carry them out and any right-thinking man can understand that obedience is as noble and necessary as authority.

Instead, this wind of rebellion and ill-conceived individualism which is blowing through Italy and elsewhere at the moment is disrupting all those things that seem most secure. It has been forgotten that power for all would mean a diminution in the power of everyone, a universal lowering, an illusory levelling, and that in practice real individualism consists not in preaching revolt but in submission. In fact, the ideal towards which all this revolutionary ferment is tending is, fundamentally, anarchy. All those people who keep nagging at their masters are far closer to the anarchists than they imagine. Indeed, it might well be maintained that the anarchical ideal, in which everyone could do as he likes and in which the inner moral law would make leaders and law pointless, is the finest of ideals, not possible but imaginable. But for this very reason it presents one minor defect: it is impractical. An anarchical society cannot be conceived, and equal freedom for all would lead to complete lack of liberty for everyone.

There are thus two fundamental weaknesses in what I have called bourgeois sentimentality: a superstitious belief in life and a superstitious belief in independence. There is too much respect for life and not enough for authority: these are the real and deep-rooted causes, unseen but frightening, of our present disintegration.

As is only to be expected, this sickness of feeling is matched by a sickness of intelligence and on this matter there would be a great deal to say. But I shall consider only that collection of words that go to form democratic ideology and have come into current use with the French Revolution: I am referring to Progress, Equality, Justice and Freedom. At every opportunity, out these words come, day in, day out; the bourgeoisie use them as well as the socialists, but just try to find any one of them capable of explaining to you rationally what they mean by these words that fall so pleasingly on the ears of the mob.

What, for example, is progress? If you ask, you'll receive the answer that it is all those things that show that a society is developing and evolving towards better things. Splendid, we reply, but then what is meant by developed and evolved? Is it perhaps a society that is better than the old one or does it merely mean the next one? In the first case, my dear democrat, it seems to me that the judgment as to which is better is a strictly personal matter, so that, for example, for a theologian our times represent a regression compared with the greatness of the Middle Ages, when the pulpits in Paris or Cologne resounded to the immortal words of St Thomas and Albertus Magnus. And then if you merely mean the succeeding one, you will also have to admit that in some ways later times were not better than earlier ones for that reason alone, because in some forms of activity, such as art, we have not, despite our extra weight of centuries, been able to attain the heights of Greek sculpture or Italian Renaissance painting.

So this idea of progress that people talk about at every opportunity in such grand or sometimes such uncertain terms cannot possibly have any meaning, because if it means time it excludes the idea of betterment and if it means better it is bound to leave out the idea of time. In general, the word progress stands for what the majority finds most to its liking at the present time in any country, but as the majority may change from time to time and pass on to a completely different taste, so all those wonderful myths of continuous, straightforward progress put out by Condorcet and Co. are not historical laws but idle talk for people who cannot see beyond their noses.

The same may be said of all the other much vaunted principles of the immortal Revolution of 1789. To give another example, what does the word 'free' mean? Is it to have the power to do certain things, that is to say, am I freer the more acts I am *able* to accomplish? Free people are those who are the most powerful. Now it is clear that one of the finest and most desirable forms of power is exercising it upon others, that is to say, that in order to be powerful we need to take power away from others, in a word to make others less powerful and thus less free. So the assertion of liberty thus leads to slavery, because there can be no true liberty without slaves. Indeed, if you deprive some men of the freedom to deprive others of theirs, what becomes of the greatest and most obvious advantages of power? And I am not employing sophistry or paradox. Take a look at the party which for the moment seems to enjoy the privilege of talking most loudly about freedom, the Socialist Party. The leaders of that party are bending every effort towards two aims: to prevent the middle classes from using their strength in their own defence, that is, to make them less powerful or less free; and to organize and discipline the proletariat and bring them under the control of the leaders, who then deprive them of their freedom of action. And finally, everybody knows that collectivism would in practice mean an enormous reduction in individual freedom, that is to say, more power for the governing class. So the party of freedom is busily occupied in depriving people of theirs in all directions, both now and for the future.

This is the great and ironic lesson that we can learn from the popular parties, namely that those who want freedom want it only in order to take it away from the rest.

So the socialists ask for freedom and sing its praises so that they can deprive capitalists of the freedom to draw the profits they want from their money, deprive Catholics of the freedom to act according to their faith and deprive the middle classes of the freedom to get rid of them and punish them.

Socialism is nothing but a perpetual conspiracy directed against freedom and if you will allow me the play on words, it wants freedom purely and simply in order to be free to stifle it ...

And it's no wonder if the results of democratic ideas are worthy of their premises.

We have, in fact, witnessed the spectacle of science claiming to be the beginning and end of everything, capable of dispelling every uncertainty and solving every problem, of providing mankind with a sure guide and a firm basis for the universe; but on closer scrutiny it now seems to be nothing but a rough and ready description of facts, useful for practical purposes, but continually needing revision, and in no way competent to give us the last word on the reality of the universe.

And we have also seen pretentious doctrinaires who, under the banner of Positivism, would have tried to reduce all thought to primitive sensation, mankind to his stomach, philosophy to a synthesis of all the sciences and reality to what can be seen. Thus metaphysics was rejected as a form of madness, idealism was considered elegant nonsense and faith an atavistic survival of decrepit old nuns.

And then we see this one-sided science and anti-philosophical philosophy fanning the spirit of revolt against authority in all its vulgar, squalid and superficial anti-clericalism. With four unproven and undemonstrable axioms based on a crude prehistoric materialism which passes itself off as the last word in philosophy and with ten stupid phrases borrowed from Voltaire, who was always spiritually blind, with a few obscene metaphors and a few vulgar phrases, you think you can destroy the profound psychological movement represented by Christianity and the admirable organization known as the Roman Catholic Church. You think you are being eminently sensible in denying God and poking fun at priests and instead you are showing that you have no understanding of either one or the other. If religion may well be the great object of doubt, it ought never to be an object of contempt, because it represents a higher plane of our spiritual life and one of the soundest elements in the organization of our social life. So much so that those persons who would like to bring down Roman Catholicism only succeed in replacing it by new dogmas, less poetic and less profound than the old, and those who laugh at priests are themselves caricatures of the ecclesiastical spirit in their own lack of tolerance.

The same painful feeling of loathing comes over us when we consider the aesthetic products of democracy, the art as well as the architecture of the dominant petty bourgeoisie. Everything grand, outstanding or tragic has been spurned almost with terror as if the souls of our contemporaries did not feel strong enough to accept the mighty ebb and flow of the higher forms of existence. Great feelings and passions, the blast of war and the honouring of great men have all vanished from their anaemic, pallid, colourless, sickly art, produced by mediocrities and praised by nonentities. Recent literature, drama and music have derived what little substance they have from the vulgar triviality of everyday life, from working class sentimentality, from a feeble Romanticism calculated to bring tears to the eyes of any shop-girl and a low realism based on the miserable life of the poor.

Very rarely do you meet a strong voice or a mighty gesture, a man beyond the ordinary, proud tones, a gale of majestic passion, a vast clash of wills.

The man in the street, the manual labourer, the little clerk, the silly woman, betrayed or *femme fatale*, adultery à la nineteenth century and dramas for a public of grocers have taken over in art as well as life. Instead of lifting us beyond the pettiness of life and setting us for an hour or so on a higher plane, into a world that is nobler and more intense, art has brought us down to ordinary life and made it seem even sadder, meaner and more loathsome than it might appear to a superior mind. Instead of creating, it imitates and instead of magnifying, it belittles everything; instead of freeing us from the pettiness of the world, it has shut us up inside it without hope of escape.

All this has been brought about by the democratic mentality which, having achieved predominance during the last century, after the Revolution had finally buried what remained of the noble spirit of the Middle Ages, has now prevailed both in the bourgeoisie which had risen from the plebs and in the plebs which wanted, and indeed have been obliged, to ape the bourgeoisie.

For this reason, of the two classes that hold sway in the world of today neither one of them supports us. We cannot have any liking for the bourgeois as they are, because they show themselves to be weak, without any well defined class consciousness, lacking any nobility of mind, afflicted with the same disease as their enemy, scared by their opponents' specious arguments, and having failed as yet to achieve the proud competence of a caste that intends to govern.

And on the other hand, we are still less able to like the other active force in our public life, namely socialism which underneath all its noisy flagwaving and verbosity hides the vilest, most vulgar and most arrogant animal qualities of man and in the name of freedom wants to create slavery, in the name of idealism thinks merely of filling men's stomachs and in the name of equality is setting up an oligarchical tyranny based on democracy. Socialism is at one and the same time anti-individualistic and anti-nationalistic and since we want the individual to be free to develop and contribute to the resurrection of our country, we are opposed to it in every sense, in every way and on every occasion.

What then will be our attitude towards these two opposing and hostile camps?

A very simple one which contains the whole *raison d'être* of our own party. Arouse the middle classes by means of the aristocracy in order to lead them against socialist or semi-socialist democracy. That is to say, to bring our glorious traditional aristocracy back into the life of the nation, make it the centre for the revival of the industrial aristocracy and, once the whole class has recovered its energy and discipline, lead it into battle against the arrogance, oppression and attacks of the forces that are working to destroy our country, and try to promote and awaken a nobler sense of national life, stronger, bolder and worthier of our annals, both in the political and the spiritual sphere.

I have, in saying this, indicated the main positive points of our programme, namely a revival of the aristocracy, nationalism, expansionism and high culture, and now it only remains for me to say a few words of these principles and dreams of ours, so that you may have a complete understanding of those ideas that *Il Regno* has propounded with all the youthful vigour and forcefulness which spring from its belief that the destiny of our dear country has not yet been fulfilled and that Italy is neither dead nor moribund ...

... Indeed, our traditional aristocracy has largely retired from public life and if there are still a few counts or marquises sitting in Parliament or acting as ambassadors, they are isolated cases and in actual fact, as a political class, the aristocracy is no longer of any account; at the most it fulfils, at court or in the diplomatic world, a function that is in itself almost purely decorative. Now today the aristocracy could be achieving something better than this. Consisting as it does of men free from the restricting cares of life, it ought to represent the summit of human endeavour and as such assume the splendid role of controlling high policy and furthering great art. Since the little men ruling us are powerless to provide us with the grand political conceptions which Italy needs in these terrible times, the old nobility which is not eaten up by idleness and has remained uncorrupted by the world ought to come forward and take up once more the fine traditions of the patrician families of Venice, Genoa, Naples and Florence.

But the major function that could be assumed by the aristocracy at this time is organizing the bourgeoisie. As I have already said and repeated on a number of occasions in *Il Regno* and in the course of this speech, the bourgeoisie has become flabby and disorganized and has not acquired that alert class consciousness and determination to govern which is the only safeguard against the pitfalls, hatred and attacks of its class-enemy.

The bourgeoisie does not yet possess adequate traditions to reach the condition of an aristocracy through its own resources. It holds effective power through its wealth and nominal power since it holds the reins of government, but it is unable either to defend the one or to use the other. But the aristocracy has largely the same interests as the bourgeoisie and if it is inferior to it in numbers and wealth, it is superior in tradition and *esprit de corps*. A closer union of that part of the aristocracy that has remained sound and a more resolute and stronger bourgeoisie could at this moment of time save Italy from its present or impending decline and from future disaster ...

... In this war to the death between the only two parties that can play a decisive role in the future of Italy, between the class which still wants to govern and the class that wants to supplant it in order to govern in its turn, the old aristocracy and the new bourgeoisie will be able to fight elbow to elbow and with success against all the united forces of the lower forms of democracy.

But it would be neither useful nor proper should the aristocratic bourgeoisie triumph unless its triumph is of advantage to the country.

The theory of the aristocratic classes which I have outlined contains the principle that when a governing class no longer exercises a function useful to the whole country it will decay, decline and fall apart. Thus, in order for the Italian bourgeoisie not only to continue but to consolidate its power, it is essential that its work be above all orientated towards nationalism.

We have thus now reached the second article of our programme, that is to say, nationalism.

I shall not say a great deal on this matter, since too much rhetoric has been expended on the subject of our dear country and today we need actions rather than words. Our nationalism must not be produced, like that of some Frenchmen, by someone sitting at his writing-desk in dressing-gown and slippers but must be a nationalism of facts, a practical nationalism, willing to act.

So our party will have to call up and reinvigorate all the forces of nationalism which are at the moment held down by the hostility of the democrats; it will have to help to promote the development of our national wealth, the exploitation of all the energy and wealth of our soil, from the power surging through our waterfalls to the gold that is being mined in Eritrea, because wealth gives security, strength and enterprise and stimulates the powers of resistance of those who hold it. In addition, it will keep alive in our minds the memory of those splendid national traditions of a country that three times, in three different ways, was the leading light of the world, with its territorial conquests by the Romans, its conquest of souls by the Church and its conquest of the senses and intellect by the Renaissance. And on every possible occasion we shall sing the praises of the great heroes of our country, the forces that are still alive in our memories, the terrible toll of dead still fresh in our minds who uplift our spirit and strengthen our endeavour. And we shall not shrink should the robust organism of our nation be required to show its mettle in conflict with other peoples because life is really lived only when opposing others and the strength of nations has till now been forged in the mighty blaze and blood of war.

The necessary complement of any nationalism is expansionism. No modern nation can remain within its own confines. Expansion, either in the form of colonies or men or capital or goods, has now become the *sine qua non* of the life of the greatest nations of the world. At the moment, Italy can offer only considerable expansionism in manpower and a lesser one in goods; she almost completely lacks colonies to exploit and populate or capital to export. Our attempts at colonization have been fraught with uncertainty and dogged by misfortune. We could by now have possessed almost the whole of East Africa, and a fair part of North Africa. In fact,

England had suggested to us that we should together occupy Egypt and the Sudan; we could have taken Tunisia and Obok before the French and we should have been able to take possession of Tripolitania and Cyrenaica. Instead we have at this moment only the strongly—but mistakenly—criticized colony of Eritrea, so deeply resented by the democrats and which we were tempted to give up—a notable example of our weakness and ignorance of colonial affairs; only now are we beginning to exploit its agricultural and mineral resources.

But colonies should be more necessary to us than to anyone else: first of all because our large emigration means that we need places of our own where Italians would be under the authority of metropolitan Italy and not have to undergo difficulties and restrictions as foreigners or give up their own language and nationality. The South American colonies do not have the importance that they might have for us were they administered and controlled by us Italians and unfortunately most of the people who make up these colonies remain Italian in name only.

In addition, as Italy is a poor country agriculturally and needs to import a great deal of agricultural produce and many raw materials, and to export many manufactured articles, she needs colonies that would supply her wants on advantageous terms and in their turn provide guaranteed outlets for her national products. Indeed, what would England be without her colonies but a miserable little island with a population subsisting on potatoes?

Now in order to export goods, the outlets must either be our own or under our influence; our interests must be defended by our own administrators; we cannot envisage the possibility of any customs barriers restricting our exports as might be the case in a country not governed by us. So in order to sell a great deal we need a large number of markets of our own and markets are not won by words but by shrewdness and force of arms. In modern society the army has now become an instrument of economic policy and those who indulge in idle talk about unproductive costs have failed to understand this vital function of force of arms in our industrial civilization. We are not one of those who look on an army as a mere ornament useful for reviews and parades or for the physical welfare of the nation: we want it to be one of the great national bodies, and as bodies which are inactive are useless and as the function of the organization known as the army is war, we, unlike many others, are not scared when the whiff of gunpowder and the rumble of guns announce that the fate of nations is being changed. For that reason we are proposing a form of expansionism which is, of course, not purely warlike, but above all economic, that is to say, productive of wealth, but we do not want, because of stupid anti-militarist prejudice, to fail to avail ourselves of the army and navy which have cost us such sacrifices and so much money in order to help and further this expansionist policy.

Even in this matter, the military and colonial policies of the democrats are miserably ludicrous. They say that the colonies we have are not paying dividends while at the same time they do not want us to try and find others that are more productive; they make a great fuss about the army being unproductive and yet they want it to do nothing, that is to say, want it to be really unproductive. It is as if I have a gun in my house and someone tells me that it serves no useful purpose and at the same time stops me from going out on a shoot or off to war so that it might really be used for something.

In fact the policy of democracy consists, as far as the bourgeoisie is concerned, in preventing the army from acting in order then to say that it does nothing and so cast it off as being useless. Thus the bourgeoisie must reply to these accusations not only by defending itself but also by positive action to make the country rich and powerful by internal discipline and external expansion.

Then, in this world of revived energy, once the traditional aristocracy has taught the new masters the virtues of authority, and the new bourgeoisie, having shaken off its sloth, has acquired wealth and abundance which it is able and willing to defend and increase with all the force at its disposal, we shall see great art and great literature flourish, as we so ardently desire, as the supreme culmination of Italian art. Then heroic deeds and superhuman passions, nature in all its light and all its mystery, proud thoughts that wreathe the world with iron bonds, will once more reappear in the music and drama, the poetry and the metaphysics of the rising generation. Meanwhile, we are on the watch for the first gleams of light and in our hearts we feel the first joyful steps of hope as we secretly meditate on the unforgettable words that we hope to broadcast to mankind.

And when the whole life of our country has achieved the wholeness and greatness that we imagine in our dreams and are striving for so earnestly, it will be pleasing to recall the fervour with which we uttered our first prophecies.

GIUSEPPE PREZZOLINI

AN ARISTOCRACY OF BRIGANDS[1]

Since attempts are already being made to find precursors for *Il Regno* and since Enrico Corradini's longstanding attitude of protest against the decadence of the Italian theatre, novel and politics can be seen to be on the same lines as that of the young monarchists, I should like today to undertake that old but very amusing intellectual operation known as the search for our theoretical ancestors. I should like briefly to show the *Italian nature of our thought* and proffer a friendly hand to some writers who, in little-read works, have already expressed part of what we are proclaiming. It would indeed be strange and, let us add, ridiculous if our nationalism were a borrowed one, based on a foreign tradition and on ideas not stemming from our own race; and though it is highly laudable, both where ideas and things are concerned, to make conquests, and though adding to our spoils a doctrine that is life-enhancing (even if it is not Italian in origin) is as good as conquering some splendid province, nevertheless we must prefer ideas that have sprung from Italian minds and are nourished on observations based on things Latin. We have no need to hire our ideas from the French or the English; we do not need either Barrès or Chamberlain or Kipling except as examples and admonishment; we can address ourselves to Gaetano Mosca and Vilfredo Pareto whose works have provided us with scientific and philosophical justification for our own practical efforts. At different times and in various works, those two thinkers, so markedly dissimilar in spirit, have provided us with a philosophy of history that we could call, on the basis of its

[1] A review of works by Gaetano Mosca and Vilfredo Pareto.

central idea, an *aristocratic* theory. Whereas socialism, springing as it does from theories produced by minds foreign to us by race and nation, by Jews and Germans, appears hard, abstruse and tedious to Italian minds and, in order to be adapted to our needs, requires pulling about, tearing up, expanding and changing in every part in order to turn it into something sentimental, plebeian, hooliganesque and violent, the beautiful simplicity and clarity of the aristocratic theory, its absence of mathematical content and its easy universality show it to be one of the finest products of the Latin genius.

At first appearance, this theory seems paradoxical and shocks all our dearest beliefs; both the study of history and the experience of life today have led us to believe that there is either rule by one man or rule by all men; that there are monarchies and democracies, that the Tsar rules in Russia and that the people rule in America. Nothing is further from the truth; government by one man as well as government by all men are both abstractions devoid of any reality; they are merely simple formulas put out to deceive people and to occupy a respectable place in treatises and manuals. Constitutional history shows us on the other hand that at all places and at all times, from small embryonic societies to the largest, richest and most cultivated, from the Papuans to the Yankees, there are always two classes of people, harmonizing or contrasting, one that dominates and the other that is dominated.

The first, the least numerous, assumes all political functions, has the monopoly of power and enjoys the advantages that appertain thereto; the second, more numerous, is governed and controlled by the first, more or less legally, more or less violently, and provides it with its material means of subsistence while being offered in return a well-organized state. The first class is pre-eminent by reason of the individual qualities of its members, their wealth, strength, culture and intelligence; pre-eminent also because it has the advantage of being organized and capable of united action when faced by the scattered movements of the other class. The power of this governing class or, in Mosca's excellent expression, this *political class* (because it has the function of controlling the state) tends in general to run in families, by heredity; but this is never completely achieved either in strictly closed aristocracies or in the more open English type of aristocracy. The political class is continually being renewed and if it does not renew itself adequately, it will fall and be replaced by another one. Neither of them, the one that falls nor the one that moves up only to fall in its turn, justifies its power merely by *de facto* possession, but strives to give it a moral and legal basis by making it appear to be the necessary consequence of doctrines and beliefs acknowledged and accepted by the society which they both successively govern. This purpose is achieved by *political formulas* which, however, being founded more or less on fact, are not vulgar frauds especially invented to trick the masses into obedience but satisfy true, generally accepted feelings, a need of man's social nature.

An example of such formulas can be provided by the two that Spencer so skilfully placed side by side, the divine right of kings and the absolute rights of political assemblies, the first of these underlying the principle of the *ancien régime*, the second that of modern democracy. We all know how little they correspond to reality; but no one fails to recognize their moral value. And just as political formulas meet intellectual and sentimental needs, so the ruling classes meet a practical and social one; it is unbelievable that they would have continued for centuries and been reproduced always in similar forms, whatever the latitude or race, unless they corresponded to an overriding social need: the need for unity of government and state.

This is Mosca's theory, in summarizing which I have often used his own words. Pareto has put forward an extremely similar one in which the *political class* is called the elite, the phenomenon of political formulas is more closely analysed and described, and greater importance, with a more ironical and subtle observation of detail, is given to the struggle between the ruling class and the one that wishes to replace it in power. Except for short intervals, peoples have always been governed by an aristocracy, using this term in the etymological sense of the strongest, most energetic and capable, both for good as for evil. But as a result of a physiological law of the greatest importance, aristocracies do not last, and so the history of mankind is the history of successive aristocracies. This is what actually occurs, although it often appears to us in other forms. The new aristocracy that wishes to oust the old and also to be the sole possessor of its power and its honours does not express this intention openly but puts itself forward as the leader of all those who are oppressed, and maintains that it is not pursuing its own gain but the good of the majority; it moves up to the attack not on behalf of the rights of a restricted class but of those of almost every citizen. Obviously, once it has succeeded, it will subjugate its allies once more or at best make them a few formal concessions.

The best and most vivid example of this theory as well as the most instructive can be seen in the present state of affairs. We have a ruling class, the bourgeoisie, which has rendered great services in the past and is still doing so; which, far from having completed its historic role, has still a long way to go; and which has not lost all its energy but can still exercise a profound moral influence on the minds and the economy of the nation; which has tradition, wealth and the state on its side. Opposing it there stands an armed minority, full both of words and unbridled desires, composed of outcasts and malcontents, lawyers with no clients, unsavoury individuals, who have nothing to lose, and careerists spurred on by vanity, need and hidden anger.

These are the leaders, the *meneurs*, the aristocrats of socialism. They have succeeded in working a most powerful miracle; these men who complain every day, in cartoons and little snippets, light-weight articles and ponderous books, with a lavish use of statistics and dirty pictures, of the lamentable state of the Italian economy and represent the middle classes as being idle, over-fed parasites, have succeeded in extracting from the less prosperous and more naive section of Italian society a standard of living that their peevish desires had not succeeded in procuring for themselves in the struggle for existence. In a word, these group secretaries, socialist deputies, strike organizers, socialist lecturers, authors of inferior works of vulgarization, shameless pamphleteers and liverish cartoonists have become the exploiters of the Italian proletariat and have extorted money from it to support newspapers and journalists, reviews and editors, to live well and pay for their own extravagances and those of their mistresses, and for their wives' fancies, to travel first-class, to give full rein to their vanity and their personality, to play the bourgeois at the expense of the workers, the manual labourers and the peasants.

What the Italian proletariat has gained in recent years in better economic conditions through strikes and social legislation has finished up in the pockets of the demagogues.

We all know what a treasure trove is offered by lectures and little tracts and subscriptions, when your petty vanity can enjoy the pleasures of sacrificing yourself for your comrades, seeing your name in print in the paper and finally giving yourself the feeling of being a real rebel! Our altruistic and lachrymose humanitarians have been using the proletariat as a most fertile breeding ground to cultivate this sort of vanity and sentimentality, where by planting words you can reap money; Marxist formulas have stilled the hunger of more than one disreputable doctor and Lassalle's 'Iron Law' has provided many a jobless schoolmaster with economic support. They even invented persecution and for a long time (the market is now in retreat) martyrdom was a share paying handsome dividends. Really, there never had been such a strange transformation of theories and feelings into good hard cash.

And perhaps this partly explains our demagogues' wrath against the Catholic clergy, whom they criticize for faults they themselves possess; or perhaps they are entirely sincere, in which case the anti-clerical campaign of *Avanti* and *Asino*, consisting of gross obscenity and a rehash of stupid rationalistic platitudes, should be regarded merely as a striking example of professional rivalry and commercial competition. So it should thus not be difficult to find many things in common between lectures and sermons in that a collection is taken after they are over; and to compare subscriptions with offerings, with the difference, for example, that the latter comes after the Sacrament and the former after a drink. So poor old Italy, at a time when she is short of men and perhaps at a turning-point of history, finds herself set upon, as if at a street corner, by this mob of hungry adventurers who set themselves up as political and moral guides and as a ruling aristocracy and who have adopted as their ultimate aim the seizure of public power, neither more nor less than a democratic Italian Tammany Hall. Perhaps a future aristocracy, as Pareto claims, but certainly an aristocracy of brigands.

But a more curious phenomenon than that of bourgeois socialism has been the parallel case—perhaps even more ridiculous and despicable—of the socialist bourgeois. We have seen large numbers of people whose social position, upbringing and material and spiritual interests should have led them to share the cause of the ruling class and defend themselves against the insolent attacks of the demagogues, desert instead, by word or deed, to the opposite camp and provide them with practical or moral support; and even when they did not actually go so far as that, they always either showed condescending sympathy or unconsciously aped their speech and action, or provided them with involuntary support by showing indifference. And finally, there have been deliberate imitation and Machiavellian concessions, partly from those who wished to bring down the socialists by copying their opponents' systems and partly from others who deluded themselves that by making some concessions they could preserve the rest. Such pusillanimity together with more serious blunders have, in the space of a few years, brought the middle classes to a state of moral decadence. Now, when they look back they cannot discover either any signs of energetic defence or examples of fighting spirit. The bourgeoisie has become humanitarian, liberalistic and Tolstoyan, is playing the democrat with the people everywhere and reaching out a brotherly hand to all its opponents. V. Pareto's two volumes, *Systèmes Socialistes*, are full of examples of this decadence, skilfully chosen from newspapers and books and carefully commented on with all the sharpness of his French style of approach. There could be no better lesson than that provided by the lashing tongue of the Lausanne economist; and it is here that we find ourselves in complete agreement with him, that is, we share the scorn he pours on that section of the ruling class that shows its timidity, lack of courage, sickly mysticism and general paralysis of willpower by abandoning its vital sources of energy to its enemies, and that is committing suicide without even the benefit of scepticism or stoicism, a suicide inspired by fear.

But we find ourselves in disagreement with him when he considers that a new aristocracy will shortly appear, consisting, he maintains, of the most cultivated and highly skilled section of the workers; any such aristocracy that might arise (since it is absolutely futile to think of government by all) would merely be a copy of today's bourgeoisie, apart from changing a few platitudes and replacing a few superstitions by others.

On the contrary, the present bourgeoisie, however low it has sunk and however discouraged it may be, still has the energy and will to exercise its powers and continue to leave its forceful mark on the face of the world and the mind and body of mankind. A programme which does not talk about renunciation or retreat, which rejects cowardice, which aims at vast and grand achievements, in a word, a programme of men and not cripples, can provide body and substance to the vigour and wealth which Italy has shown herself to possess.

The modern revival of Italian poetry may be the favourable omen for our future action. When we find Gaetano Mosca speaking many years ago of the necessary work of renewal that 'must never be directed towards changing political formulas and those central governmental mechanisms which, whether altered or simulated, can never lead to a transformation of the whole social organization' but '*must rather aim at achieving a real and true renewal of the whole political class*', in these few words he was already adumbrating the goal to which *Il Regno* is striving, with far greater hopes of success.

CAN THE BOURGEOISIE REVIVE?

(An exchange of letters between Vilfredo Pareto and Giuseppe Prezzolini)

I have been reproached for my belief that the bourgeoisie of today is in decline and on its way to being replaced by another elite springing from the working classes; it seems to me on the contrary that every day new facts appear which confirm my argument.

I am discussing this matter purely objectively, as I might undertake research to discover which is the most aggressive amongst the many species of ants; I feel neither liking nor dislike for either side.

Perhaps the reason for our disagreement lies in the fact that we are struck by different things. It was only after living abroad that I properly understood – or, if you prefer, thought I understood – the meaning of this evolution. In Italy the bourgeoisie is not as decadent as it is in France and in other countries and so it is natural that someone who is principally concerned with Italy should hold a different view from that held by someone who has observed more mature developments.

But even in Italy there could well be certain facts in support of my thesis. Does it not seem to you that there is a big gap between the energy and activity of the socialists and that of the bourgeoisie? A tiny number of socialists, by their vigour and determination, succeeded in overthrowing the parliamentary majority by their obstructive methods. A little courage was needed to bring this masterful minority to heel, just as the English overcame the obstructive tactics of the Irish in Parliament. Not one person showed that courage: neither the Ministers, nor the Speaker nor the Members of Parliament.

Let us make another comparison. Let us see how the

socialists behaved over the Tsar's visit and what the bourgeoisie is doing about the visit of President Loubet.

I am not discussing good manners; in this respect, the middle classes are superior to the socialists; nor does this contradict my thesis; at the time of the French Revolution the nobles showed themselves consistently better mannered and better bred than those who were guillotining them. But the excellent Italian middle classes might well, without falling short on good manners, somewhat temper the spineless adulation that has now gripped and possessed them towards the man who represents those who wish to overcome and destroy them; the head of the government that has now amnestied and allowed to go free and unpunished the men who burnt down factories, looted banks and assaulted harmless citizens in Armentières.

We must not concern ourselves with what is taking place in someone else's house. Look who is preaching this! Is Russia not someone else's house for the socialists? And when they heaped insults on the Tsar, were they not concerned with what was happening in Russia? Then why should it not have been right and proper for the middle classes to be concerned at what is happening in France? The socialists dislike the Tsar because he represents an absolutist regime; so why should the middle classes like Loubet, who represents the radical-socialist regime which is preparing social revolution? Yet the clamour of the socialists was enough to prevent the Tsar from coming to Italy and now to make their opponents kow-tow to Loubet.

Tell me which is the side that is showing energy and courage; tell me which of the two confronting armies seems likely to win when one of them is excessively pugnacious and the other so cowardly and yielding that far from opposing its enemy, it gives it support? Even a poor miserable rabbit bites when you kill it; yet those people give a friendly welcome to the ones who are trying to shatter and destroy them.

I could go on quoting other examples at length. In any

case, I am talking in generalities and it is obvious that there are exceptions; and where these have been overlooked, you must remind me of them, as you and your friends move boldly into battle. But will you find followers? If so, I shall say that my conclusion does not apply to Italy. If not, it will have been confirmed for Italy, too. Scientifically, only facts count; nothing else exists.

Yours etc., VILFREDO PARETO
Céligny, December 31st, 1903

You must allow me to dispense with the usual compliments and thanks. Your letter represents for my friends from *Il Regno* and myself the not unimportant satisfaction of having been noted by someone of high intellectual distinction and analysed by a subtle logician and clear-sighted observer of present-day affairs such as yourself. But it also represents for my friends the welcome pleasure—rare enough to be and to remain so—of finding a thinker similar to themselves, and for me the no less welcome pleasure of spelling out more exactly the criticisms of your *Theory of Aristocracies*. It seems to me that these criticisms arise not from the observation of different facts but rather from our differing approach. Your desire is to be the objective scientist, without prejudice or sympathies, balanced, disinterested and without emotion, observing, experimenting and noting with the cool precision of an instrument of physical science and the clarity of a polished mirror. I am not sure to what extent such a thing is possible and whether an analysis of the human consciousness and the history of the sciences which are, in our case, primarily moral sciences, allow us to assert the possibility of such an attitude. In any case, such an attitude is certainly not mine. Anyone can remain indifferent towards a theorem of mechanics and one can even play with a metaphysical problem. But in political and social studies it is impossible to free oneself from personal aims. Of necessity, the scientist goes hand in hand with the lawyer, the observer owns capital or is a proletarian and so is transformed into a partisan. Of course, we can climb up on to the seats of the circus and calmly look down on the struggle; but if we have committed ourselves to the bookmaker, we feel a certain desire to come down into the arena and take sides with one of the combatants. A hefty punch leading to a decision in favour of our actions causes us pleasure; whilst a blow which not only knocks down the wrestler but also our hopes of winning our bet is as unpleasant as if it had knocked us out ourselves. In a word, you see in the theory of aristocracies a scientific theory; I see it instead as a scientific justification of my present political needs.

Having looked at attitudes, let us also examine the facts. That there exist proofs of bourgeois decadence, no one denies; and if the one you quote so appositely is extremely typical, there are many others no less so that we have commented on in our sections on *Fatti del Mondo* and *Discorsi degli altri*. But it is this decadence that is the real justification for *Il Regno*, which would be irrelevant in England or America where the bourgeoisie has not yet become so spineless as to provide weapons for those who are set on despoiling it. We are certainly, as you say, an exception; we are a minority of heretics courageous enough to despise the sacred cows of the religion of humanitarianism, to laugh at the maudlin sentiments of the pacifiers and to strive to give back to the bourgeoisie the feeling of strength which it has lost.

But we do not merely acknowledge proofs of decadence; we go further and maintain that there are proofs of resurgence to counteract them; just as we also maintain that the theoretical reasons which lead you to prophesy the imminent end of the bourgeoisie can be opposed by other reasons which show that this end is a long way off.

I shall speak of these theoretical reasons in some other place; it would require too much space and time to do so here. But I wish briefly to refer to the symptoms and recall the individualistic attitudes that have recently appeared:

the formation of property-owners' associations to combat the insolence of the socialists and governmental indifference; the introduction of the lock-out into Italy, following its sometimes justifiably savage use by English and American factory owners; as well as various examples of firm and resolute resistance to strikes that would have been inconceivable a few years ago.

The bourgeoisie does not lack power; it would have tradition and the state and the Church to support it; it includes the intellectual and economic wealth of the country.

Socialism relies for its very life on the strength provided by the middle classes, because this does not reside so much in the organized masses which have swallowed, more or less stupidly, the socialist doctrine as in the organizers, who are bourgeois, starting with the more subtle politicians such as Turati and ending with the more practical activists such as Ferri. The victory of socialism would merely be the victory of a bourgeois minority.

What the Italian bourgeoisie has hitherto lacked has been an example and a strong voice. The accepted belief amongst the middle classes themselves at the present time, their internal enemy, is the certain conviction that they are doomed, that sooner or later they will have to hand over everything to the enemy; and this conviction has all too often reduced them to cowardly apathy and led them to make mistaken concessions.

You well know that the prime reason for defeat is being convinced that you are going to be defeated; whereas the prime reason for victory is confidence that you will win.

Up till now, we have lacked an example and a spokesman: that is to say, *a man*. We believe strongly in the power of individuals to influence the history of nations. Chamberlain is the living proof of this. Give the Italian bourgeoisie a Chamberlain adapted to its needs and capable of arousing its class consciousness and the self-interest that will defend itself, attack, subjugate or destroy, the self-interest that is found in all living organisms, the self-interest that is even to be found in the rabbit you spoke of; then you will see that Tsars will be able to come to Italy and obstructionism will be overcome.

And since you still show such great respect for facts as to make them the supreme criterion and the Supreme Court of Appeal for scientific laws and forecasts, I want to remind you of one fact amongst the signs of the revival to which I referred above, namely *Il Regno*.

Does it not seem to you a significant fact that a review such as ours, following such a definite and clear-cut path unswervingly and without cowardice, has been enabled to emerge in Italy?

I should like, Sir, to tell you at greater length where I dissent from your views but it is enough for me to have indicated why I do so. You are an observer or at least you wish to maintain that role; and if at times your arm shoots forward to applaud and you are moved to irony at some despicable sight, you quickly pull yourself together and regain your calm. I on the other hand am a militant, here at least, and as such I cannot countenance the condemnation of my party and myself.

Yours very truly, GIUSEPPE PREZZOLINI
January 1904

ENRICO CORRADINI
(1865–1931)

In youth, Corradini tried his hand as a playwright and a novelist without much success. He was a typical member of that class of struggling literary men with great and unsatisfied ambitions who took refuge in a somewhat facile cultural pessimism. The complaint which he put into the mouth of one of his characters – 'The time does not allow for magnanimous feelings' – sums up their state of mind.

In his two mediocre nationalist novels, *La patria lontana* (1910) and *La guerra lontana* (1911), Corradini dealt with the themes of emigration and war. Emigration and war, he said, were 'protagonist and antagonist'; the former made Italians slaves, the latter would liberate them. Both novels insist on the responsibility of the bourgeoisie for their own defeats, and on the need for nationalism to go to the people. The figure of Lorenzo Orio in *La guerra lontana*, which is set in the days of the First Abyssinian war, is modelled on Alfredo Oriani, the writer and historian, whose *La rivolta ideale* (1911) was very popular in Fascist and Nationalist circles.

Corradini played the central part in the foundation of the Nationalist Association in 1910, and in the propaganda for the conquest of Libya. During the 1915–18 war he devoted himself especially to urging closer collaboration between the government and the industrialists, calling for a regime of 'total responsibility' in which economic and military planning would be closely co-ordinated. With Alfredo Rocco and Luigi Federzoni he remained one of the leaders of the Nationalist Association until its fusion with Fascism in 1923.

ARTICLE FROM *IL REGNO*

(1903, I, I, pp. 1–2)

In founding this review, my friends and I have only one aim: to be one amongst all the voices raised in protest and contempt at the degradation of the nation at this hour.

The Italian people, that great majority which constitutes the real people of Italy, are already showing that they have shaken off their torpor. Ever since the African war, in the fields and cities, the workshops and stores, the prolific and patient Italian people have been working harder every day. So the foundations of prosperity have been laid and on these foundations there will arise the memorials and works of our greatness. In founding this review, we take as our starting point this first, certain fact as we turn towards the certainty of our future. The passage from the obscure labours of humble citizens to the triumph of the nation represents the upsurge of a people. We wish to be one voice amongst those which, if merely by their earnest desires, hasten the upsurge of our fatherland.

A voice, therefore, raised against the present degradation. And first and foremost against the foul degradation of socialism, that gigantic chaos of new forces in the world that has ended with a few men of Saturn who have turned it into their own Saturnalia, using their own dregs. Any kind of generous thought was replaced by the basest of angry instincts of cupidity and destruction. All the other classes were outlawed in favour of one class alone and the manual labourers' wages became the be-all and end-all of human society. Every value came under furious attack from the masses. And before those massive hordes, there came the onslaught of the frenzied men of Saturn, malevolent and faint-hearted, little men who, thanks to the baseness of the age, represent a deadly peril like to that of shrill-voiced

Byzantine eunuchs. And this looting expedition took place in the name of justice, and the noblest words were uttered by lips reeking of falsehood and slander. Morality was dragged into the market-place to support these lies and slanders and turned into a whore as an inspiration for bestial degradation, an assassin hired to kill. The majestic dream of happiness under Saturn which had been handed down over the ages by successive generations of mankind seems to have been revived merely to satisfy that most despicable of all things, the ambition of contemptible men; and they used it as a trick to deceive the masses and, in the name of civil liberty and decency, they erected a tyranny of the streets, that of jungle chieftains, while crying out against condottieri, kings and judges, priests and idols, opposing any other law and order superior to that of the jungle and the street, from the royal court to religion and from the militia to the court of law. Now, the stomachs of us all are turned by such a state of affairs, whatever our political affiliations, even, indeed above all, those of us who believe in socialism when it is not ignoble; but there are few who are as yet daring enough to speak out loud and clear. We who speak for ourselves wish to be one of these few voices, and speak out loudly because our loathing knows no fear.

It is likewise a voice that condemns those who do everything possible to be defeated, a voice that condemns the rule and government of the Italian bourgeoisie. I am not referring to the timorousness that lends strength to the boldness of the aggressors, nor to the even more speedy retreat from their pursuit; I am referring to something which contorts our lips into a bitter laugh full of disgust and anger: the fact that they are willing accomplices of their own destruction. Does the class struggle need to have a free hand within the country and, externally, to break down those great harmonious ethnic and historical entities which are called nations? And every day the Italian bourgeoisie persist in their increasing fondness for the doctrines of freedom and internationalism. They are the sink into which sentimental socialism drains.

Their truths become the lies which socialism discards when it genuinely turns to action. Like some old sewage barge they go to every sewer outlet discharging its lethal effluent and load it until they founder. They have been deeply infected by the contagion of the sociologies, the philosophies, the policies, the atheistic, secular, cosmopolitan mysticism which are the well-manured soil in which the weeds of socialism have grown and prosper. Every sign of decrepitude, sentimentalism, doctrinairism, outmoded respect for transient human life, outmoded pity for the weak and humble, utility and mediocrity seen as the criteria for wisdom, neglect of the higher potentialities of mankind, the ridiculing of heroism, every foul sign of the loathsome decrepitude of degenerate people can be found in the contemplative life of our ruling and governing class, the Italian bourgeoisie.

And their practical life corresponds to their contemplative life. In every organism and body which rules, governs, controls, inspires and represents the Italian people, which produces and conducts their civic acts, base democracy has set up its congregations, its schools, its businesses, its cliques, its clans, its intrigues, its schemes whereby the greater is driven out by the less. If I wanted and was able to quote from amongst countless examples, I should say that the greater was driven out by the less in our concept of royalty, which fluctuates between the two poles of Hamlet's equivocal soliloquy; in the concept that we have begun to acquire of the use of force, inspired by the widespread terror of wars and the general confidence in the peace of nations and the Hague court; it has been driven out of teaching, literature, art, the theatre, philosophy, science, history, wherever the materialistic democracy of tiny little men could drive out an *idea* and replace it by *matter*—replace it by the less, by those deficient in spirit and intelligence and ambition, by worthless ability, lifeless senility, incompetent honesty or dishonesty whose only competence lies in evil-doing. Just as in Rome the statues of the emperors, the heroes and the gods were cast down by infantile wild barbarians, so the higher values of mankind and the nation have been cast down by our townbred citizens, even worse barbarians, now moribund. And should someone try to make the gesture of erecting a statue again, if he were a politician they would cut off his arm and his hand; if he were a poet, at best he might have the good fortune to go on show at village fairs, where the yokels gather round with open mouths. But there are few who think that the poet is pointing to the only life that is worth living.

And thus the Italian middle classes who rule and govern the Italian people, are not the same as the people, who have shaken themselves out of their torpor. The only fact that remains is that, over this land which was called the land of the dead and is now the land of those who have risen from the grave to a life of industry and work, there had been cast the suffocating net of the deeds of the dying, which has now been torn by the fury of the passing festival of Saturn.

In founding this review, we oppose both of these, for though hostile to each other, they are joined in their common liking for all that is basely material in life. Our voice will be raised to help re-erect the statues of the higher human and national values so that they may be seen by those who are resurrecting to a new life.

EXTRACT FROM *LA GUERRA LONTANA*

'Who's accusing the people? It's not the fault of the people!' cried a very loud and angry voice.

The whole room exploded, but on turning round everyone exclaimed:

'Lorenzo Orio!' And no one knew what to say. But Lorenzo Orio, standing in the doorway, was not going to be interrupted.

'No! It's not the fault of the Italian people. They're not to blame. They're not to blame. Who can blame them?'

A wave of protest broke over the head of the man still standing in the doorway. Someone shouted:

'Who can blame them? Anyone who feels sorry for our country!'

'Then by all that's sacred, keep quiet the whole lot of you!'

His anger was such that the mob was quelled, like an animal trapped in a net. And Lorenzo Orio himself stood silent as he looked at them, eyes blazing. He had come to Rome from his little country house in Romagna where his warm heart had for many years been embittered by the many things he had seen. He was of the breed of patriarchs, priests and kings, and he had lived by himself; his only wife and family were his anger, and his studies were his sole domestic comfort. Through his study of history he had achieved the ability to prognosticate human affairs and, by observing the baseness and blindness of his contemporaries and looking into the future, he had, in his solitude, composed tome after tome in which his wrath had broken through like the curses of Hebrew prophets hurled against the gates of the cities of their enemies. He loved his country and, because his vision encompassed the vast expanse of the horizons of history, he loved her greatness.

Now in this night of defeat, he remembered how, from the start, Italy had behaved in Africa. And that was why he had burst out so angrily. With head thrown back and fixing the whole assembly in the eye, he continued amidst a deathly silence.

'Do you expect the people to have the sense of purpose for long-term enterprises and far-away wars? The people who are nothing but the base material of history? Heavens above! But when the first ships and the first soldiers left for Africa, where were the leaders of the people? Where was the sense of long-term purpose? Where was the wise counsel and the will to succeed? How many people realized that Italy was not going to Africa but returning there? That she was launching out once more on her history? That she was laying the foundations of a new civilization, her civilization? We could see that the Parliament and government understood nothing of this immense enterprise! The government did its best to diminish its importance by representing it as reprisals against a few brigands. The democrats saw it as a waste of public funds and raised their usual moans. And so Italy's triumphant entry into world history was turned into something mean and underhand. A moment of glory became a moment of shame! Oh you middle-class Italians! You bad Italians! Heavens above!'

Now he was striding to and fro amongst the assembled company like a bull in the midst of a flock of sheep. His scowling eyebrows bristled as he tugged furiously at his long sparse beard which fell in two separate points from his chin. But he found no comfort for his great anguish. He began to speak again, not for the few, but for the multitude, following his own train of thought.

'You bad Italians! I've heard you howling against foreigners, against those who dragged our flag in the mire in Turin! But frankly, all your howls on that wretched night gave me a dreadful urge to laugh, forgive me, gentlemen! How much better it would be if the voice of conscience could be heard in the country! At this very moment, so that it could be more stern and firm! And now let me raise my voice, and question you, so that your souls may suffer deeper remorse for the past and that you may change for the future. What have you done up till now? What have you done? The people felt hatred, but what love did you feel? The people were made to hate something; but what did you make them love? The people were being preached a new doctrine, a doctrine opposed to our country and to you; but what did you do for the country or for yourselves? Yes, you are everything, here and in the towns where you live! You are Members of Parliament, local councillors, teachers, writers, journalists, lawyers! You've everything in your favour, the vote, commerce, the law, privilege, everything! You are or ought to be the salt of the earth! You are the middle classes, the burgesses! But you've done nothing! Each one of you has lived only for himself and not one of you for all the others! Each one of you has pandered only to his own selfishness! Not one of you has been able or tried or dared to look one inch in front of his face! Yet now you stand there howling because our flag has been dragged in the mire! You utter loud moans over the defeat of the country! Oh, what is your country, you middle classes! And what is the defeat of your country, you bourgeois! And what is your flag, you bad Italians! But when did you ever realize it, until now? When? Answer me!'

EXTRACT FROM *LA PATRIA LONTANA*

'Italy is being forced into a cowardly foreign policy and it's you who are largely to blame!'

A tall thin young man with a long thin face leapt up and sprang towards the socialist Giacomo Rummo. He snapped back:

'It's the fault of the bourgeoisie.' But the other was not listening; he went on: 'You ought to realize that the class struggle is something internal, and externally it's the struggle between nations. But you socialists have never wanted to think about this and you've reduced everything to the class struggle! Through your class selfishness you've destroyed the whole nation! Now you want to turn out the Minister because he won't make war on Austria! That's like you—when you've always been so strongly against rearmament! God save us!'

The voice of the tall thin young man, a journalist from San Paolo, was high-pitched, with a suspicion of a lisp. Without batting an eyelid, Rummo replied:

'It's the fault of the bourgeoisie. As socialists our only duty is to pursue the class struggle. Nothing else! It was the bourgeoisie's job, since they're ruling the nation, to pursue a nationalistic policy by opposing us and even crushing us. So we strongly opposed rearmament? But we should have rearmed. They didn't have the courage. They only had half the courage, when forced by necessity and fear, to spend just the right amount of millions of lire to make the socialists protest but not enough to provide the nation with proper defences. That is, they had only enough courage to succeed in making the so-called unproductive expenses not only unproductive but really expensive. It's not our fault. But we shall certainly be capable of providing Italy with a ruling class with more guts, more energy and more intelligence.'

Approvingly, Buondelmonti voiced his admiration for the socialist:

'I'm with you in blaming the bourgeoisie.'

The socialist stared at Buondelmonti for a second and then said curtly:

'A good job too!'

And he turned and faced the journalist who was giving the latest news of the unsettled state of affairs between the European powers, including Italy and Austria, which in the last few days had been endangering the existing peace.

But after the meal, Buondelmonti again went up to his enemy, whom he had also met in Brazil, because he inspired sympathy and because he wanted to try and tame him. He caught sight of him standing smoking on his own, went up to him and, taking up the thread of the conversation again, he said:

'I've no doubt at all that you socialists would be able to give Italy a more intelligent and more courageous ruling class!'

THE PRINCIPLES OF NATIONALISM

(Report to the First Nationalist Congress in Florence on December 3rd, 1910)

... There is one basic and central general factor from which all the particular factors conditioning Italian life derive, as the whole tree stems from its stump. It is necessary for us to find this stump, which is the seat of evil, and suggest a cure in accordance with our nationalist way of thinking and feeling. So let us attack the heart of our argument without further ado.

We are an emigrant nation, that is to say (and you must not think it otiose to explain the meaning of this very ordinary word at this point), in order to obtain work and our daily bread, we are obliged to leave the country of our fathers and disperse all over the world ...

We must start by recognizing the fact that there are proletarian nations as well as proletarian classes; that is to say, there are nations whose living conditions are subject, to their great disadvantage, to the way of life of other nations, just as classes are. Once this is realized, nationalism must, above all, insist firmly on this truth: Italy is, materially and morally, a proletarian nation. What is more, she is proletarian at a period before her recovery. That is to say, before she is organized, at a period when she is still groping and weak. And being subjected to other nations, she is weak not in the strength of her people but in her strength as a nation. Exactly like the proletariat before socialism came to its aid.

The workers' muscles were as strong as they are today, but to what extent did the workers desire to improve their lot? They were blind to their position. So what happened when socialism started talking to the proletariat? They roused themselves, they had the first glimmerings of their situation, they glimpsed the possibility of changing it, and for the first time conceived the idea of changing it. And socialism carried them along with it, urged them to fight and, through that fight, forged their unity, their awareness, their strength, their very weapons, their new rights, their will to win, their pride in abusing their victory; it freed them and enabled them to dictate their class law to the other classes, to the nation and to other nations.

Well, my friends, nationalism must do something similar for the Italian nation. It must become, to use a rather strained comparison, our national socialism. This is to say that just as socialism taught the proletariat the value of the class struggle, we must teach Italy the value of the international struggle.

But international struggle means war.

Well, let it be war! And let nationalism arouse in Italy the will to win a war.

It is unnecessary to labour the point that our war is not a sudden call to arms and that winning our war is not a simple-minded poetic or prophetic statement but a moral imperative. In a word, we propose a 'means of national redemption' which we sum up, extremely concisely, in the expression 'the need for war'. War is the last act, but asserting the necessity of war means acknowledging the need to make ready for war and to prepare ourselves for war, that is to say, it involves both technical and moral methods. It is a means of national discipline. A means of creating an overwhelming and inevitable reason for the need for national discipline. A means of creating an irresistible need to return to a sense of duty. The nationalists are most anxious that our schools as well as our railways should do their duty. A means of restoring belief in the virtues and their application which the bourgeoisie and their public opinion and their common sense and the governing classes and the politicians and parliamentary rule have outlawed from Italian national life. And a means, finally, of reviving a pact of family solidarity between all classes of the Italian nation. A means of proving the need and usefulness of such a pact. For years and years the socialists, our masters and opponents, have been preaching to the workers that it was in their interest to show solidarity with the workers of Cochin-China or Paraguay and to dissociate themselves completely from their employers and the Italian nation. We must drum it into the workers' heads that it is in their best interests to maintain solidarity with their employers and, above all, with their own country and to hell with solidarity with their comrades in Paraguay or Cochin-China.

To sum up, since Italy achieved freedom and unity, Italy has lost two wars and has not solved the problem of the Mezzogiorno.[1] In her policy of alliances, she has succeeded in being the enemy of her allies and the friend of her allies' enemies and enjoys no credit with either. She has not even had the faintest idea that she could direct her emigration to further national ends, and her institutions are now worn out and her parties all exhausted.

The sum and substance is that our foreign policy and our home policy are both achieving poor results. What are the causes of this? There is need for a general reappraisal. Nationalism proposes to undertake this reappraisal. There is need for a change of system in order to find a better one, both human and material. Nationalism wants to find such a system. Herein lies its justification.

[1] Impoverished and underdeveloped Southern Italy.

THE PROLETARIAN NATIONS AND NATIONALISM (1911)

... Nationalism asserts above all the need for Italy to acquire awareness of herself as a nation, an awareness which is a form of *esprit de corps* as well, a sense of solidarity among citizens, just as class consciousness is a sense of solidarity amongst workers, which I have already praised.

Do we have to prove that national awareness is lacking in Italy?

It is not necessary.

We need to start both changing the colours in the picture and saying more comforting things, because we must have trust in the future of our country.

So we must seek rather to discover the causes for Italy's not possessing any developed national awareness and start straightaway by recognizing that she does not possess one because she cannot.

And here are the reasons why she cannot:

First of all, gentlemen, until quite recently Italy had in fact never been a nation.

Secondly, Italy has never even had and still does not have a national language, except in literature.

Thirdly, she was created after little fighting and little revolution.

Fourthly, Italy was created as the result of the efforts of too many people, often in conflict amongst themselves: an official aristocratic and middle-class monarchy, popular Garibaldianism, cosmopolitan Mazzinianism; and these conflicts persisted and still persist.

Fifthly, Italy was created as a result of diplomatic intrigues and by foreign arms.

Sixthly, Italy too quickly declined into the class struggle and the initial formation of her self-awareness was inhibited.

Seventh and lastly, Italy—and this could not be otherwise because of the slightness of the revolution that created her—Italy fell into the hands of the politicians whom I have already described more closely above, the men left over from her time of bondage, the dregs of traditions, methods and people already decadent and decaying under a regime of tiny, timorous and inept governments.

Recognizing this, nationalism asserts its role as the educator of the national consciousness. It asserts itself (let's say something else comforting!) as a sign of progress for Italy, unhoped-for progress towards the formation of a national awareness.

Nationalism has started to develop this awareness as something active.

The patriotism of the old patriot, the perfect good old Italian bourgeois whom we were talking about earlier on, was a false patriotism, not only because it was, in fact, false but because it was inert. It was a dead patriotism.

But now nationalism is a living patriotism.

Now national awareness is being conceived as a religious awareness, a producer of good works.

It is being conceived both as the result of activity and as productive of activity.

It is being conceived as providing inspiration for the whole life of the citizen.

Gentlemen, the Italian people lacks discipline. Do we have to prove this? It is not necessary. Let us not concern ourselves with the individual. However, the individual is found in the public services and in public administration. But it is not necessary to prove how much the Italian citizen working in the public services and public administration is lacking in discipline. Or how much he lacks a sense of duty.

Now national awareness, as nationalism understands it, can and must be a school for discipline and duty. The pious person, knowing that for each of his acts he must answer to God, strives for his every act to be good and in accordance with God's will. Thus religious awareness inspires the whole life of man and is, as I have said, productive of good works. Similarly, national awareness, which tells the citizen that for certain of his acts he must answer to the nation so that the latter may then fulfil its task, can and must arouse in him a sense of duty and thus the practice of discipline.

NATIONALISM AND DEMOCRACY

(Political Speech, 1913)

And another thing: not only is the class struggle not the opposite of nationalism, we even acknowledge that whatever its action, it has done the nation more good than harm. We acknowledge this because we believe that our convictions are true and we are happy to recognize their remarkable unity. For the basic belief of our essentially dynamic doctrine is struggle, international struggle, and we are pleased to be able to acknowledge that struggle, even struggle at home, has produced quite similar effects; that all in all and despite everything, it has proved useful to the nation because it has made two classes more energetic. So instead of condemning the class struggle, by reason of our nationalistic principles we absolve it. And so two activities that seem opposed to each other, internal and external conflict, become united in the unity of nationalistic thinking.

But then how can we assert that nationalism and socialism are opposed?

Let us take a look at this.

At the Rome Congress I accused our integralist and dissident friend Luigi Valli of being a mystic because of a statement he had made. He very quickly returned the compliment by accusing me of being a mystic because of my statement that nationalism was aiming to put an end to the class struggle and to establish peace at home ... Valli taxed me with mysticism on the grounds that I wanted to abolish the class struggle whereas the class struggle was eternal. And he was indeed right but I was not wrong. Because I had meant something quite different by peace at home, as I shall explain by means of a noteworthy example: the French Revolution. This led one class to clash with the other; but the former instantly identified itself with the nation, and, as a result of its principles and of the slaughter it caused, it released a dynamic force of patriotism such as the world had never seen before, and gave France a moral ascendancy that is still exercised over two continents. And that is what I meant by a *nationalistic* internal peace; not so much peace between the middle classes and the proletariat as the other sort of peace which socialism has disrupted, peace between the proletariat and the nation.

Now we can see the antithesis. And the antithesis between nationalism and socialism is not a single antithesis but a double one. Because what socialism has done and is continuing to do is, by identifying the nation and the middle classes with the state, to urge on the proletariat against the nation and at the same time to attack the nation from outside by uniting the proletariat internationally. In this way the nation is besieged from two sides. And for that reason nationalism, the alert guardian of Italy's development as a nation, is doubly, not singly, antipathetic to socialism, on account of both the class struggle and the international nature of the class struggle.

Having posed these simple premises, it is time to proceed to a review of democracy.

It is obvious to everyone that democracy has become deeply socialistic. Nowadays, democracy is a contamination of democracy by socialism. And I use the term contamination in its double meaning, the Latin one of mixture and the ordinary one of a poisoned mixture. In a democratic-socialistic mixture of this kind, the violent elements of socialism such as class struggle, the final achievement of power by the proletariat, the vicious identification of the nation with the middle classes, are no longer apparent, but in their stead there appears a mild representative of both of them: a system aimed at raising the proletariat by submitting the nation to a course of continuous and progressive parasitical infection. The socialist class struggle is replaced by democratic parasitical infection. At the same time, externally, the socialist international, founded on the solid community of the interests of the proletariat, has been succeeded by the democratic international, fluid, sentimental and rhetorical in nature, an age-old humanitarian and pacifist secretion of decadent peoples, now secreted by the glands of the cultivated cosmopolitan classes of Europe.

It is both curious and instructive to observe the state of equilibrium in which democracy and socialism stand in regard to each other and to everything else. This is because, with its parasitical reformism, socialism aims at emptying the nation and national bodies of all content in order to swell the proletariat and bring it to power, and at the same time democracy, which, when all is said and done, is the political form of the middle classes, intelligent democracy, has understood that the more the parasitical infection of socialism attacks the nation, the more socialism will be distracted from directly dispossessing democracy, that is to say, its representative, the middle-class businessman. And so a reformist democracy grew up around socialist reformism, a vague sort of democracy in which there is much talk of bettering the proletariat, a term which could hardly be vaguer. When socialism keeps on talking of the ultimate triumph of the proletariat, democracy lets it go ahead, to serve its own ends; and when, in turn, democracy talks merely of bettering the proletariat, socialism, similarly to serve its own ends, pretends to be satisfied; and so socialism and democracy agree on the equivocal and thus hypocritical and lying expression: betterment of the proletariat, an expression which in the hands of other wily customers working in more devious ways serves as the formula to justify the abominable electoral coalition of the 'bloc'.[1]

And this is what constitutes the immense lie of present-day democracy. It is so constituted as to be of advantage to the few and harmful to all, harmful to the proletariat itself and to the nation.

[1] The 'bloc' stood for the alliance between Socialists, Radicals and Republicans.

THE CULT OF THE WARRIOR MORALITY

(Speech made at Savona, December 15th, 1913)

The essence of Italian nationalism, ladies and gentlemen, consists in fighting the three aspects of pacifism.

Let me explain in order to remove any possible misunderstandings straightaway.

The 'three aspects of pacifism' means the collaboration of three sorts of pacifism to the same end.

But first, one word. If, immediately after one Italian war and two European wars, I still continue my fight against pacifism, you will think: What is he up to? Is he still not satisfied? Isn't that really going rather far at this moment of time? You must listen to me to the end and then you can judge.

To come to the three aspects of pacifism, the first of them is an old one and is still feeding on nectar in the heavenly regions. This is the idealistic pacifism of the cultivated and cosmopolitan middle classes of contemporary Europe. For these middle-class gentlemen the ideal of peace is the logical consequence of two other logical ideals: first, that everything is capable of being settled by the use of reason; secondly, that the union of peoples can be brought about. Once this has been achieved, war will be a thing of the past. Pious humanitarianism encourages this idealistic pacifism. It is also supported by the principle that human life is sacred. It is superfluous to point out that at the bottom of the theoretical and ethical principle there lies a residue of atavistic cowardice. That is to say that by means of pacifism, the cultivated middle classes are idealizing, theorizing, ethicizing – excuse these horrible verbs – and aestheticizing their own state of mind, which consists in turning their backs on reality and wallowing in decadence.

Now let us come to the second sort of pacifism.

This one feeds on something more substantial: it is class pacifism or, better expressed, the pacifism of the class struggle. It is socialist pacifism. That means international pacifism, which socialism needs in order to have a freer hand to conduct the national class struggle. Socialism wants national strife and wishes to disunite the nation; but since any political action needs ideas, ideals, moral and aesthetic theories, socialism takes over those of its real opponent, the bourgeoisie. So it, too, longs for peace and sentimentalizes over the unification of all peoples; but it doesn't say that it is doing all this in order to make war at home and bring dissension into the family. Socialist pacifism is to middle-class pacifism as a rogue is to an idiot.

And then finally we have the third sort of pacifism, one that was relatively unknown amongst us before the last few days of September of last year. It is plutocratic pacifism, which first the Libyan War and then the Balkan War brought out of the shadows into the limelight. It is the pacifism used by businessmen, traders, bankers, contractors, all those who have concessions from governments. It is pacifism founded on the principle that 'business is sacred and the be-all and end-all of everything', just as middle-class pacifism is based on the principle that 'the life of the individual is sacred and the be-all and end-all of everything', and socialist pacifism on the principle that 'the class struggle is sacred and the be-all and end-all of everything'. For plutocratic pacifism the be-all and end-all of everything was the stability of the status quo of the Ottoman Empire, a very rich field for commerce. A war by any European nation against Turkey was bad business for plutocratic pacifism.

When we urged war against Turkey over Tripolitania, business emerged from the secret hideout where it was at work and rushed to oppose it. And when the Balkan War was about to break out, the governments of the plutocratic states, that is the states which have the welfare of a large amount of their subjects' business to look after, were seen making every possible effort to avoid it. And once it had broken out, to cut it short as quickly as possible. Poincaré, the minister of the most plutocratic country in the world, will go down in history as having agitated for intervention and conferences—without any support. Plutocratic Europe came to an end when it saw war sweep Turkey away and put the four Balkan allies in her place. Then Europe decided that excellent business could also be done with these heirs and successors; so it let the war go ahead and Turkey was as unceremoniously left to her fate as she had at first been unceremoniously protected.

So money allowed the Cross to eat up the Crescent Moon.

Now these three sorts of pacifism, the pacifism of business that doesn't want to be disturbed, the pacifism of the class struggle that wants to be the sole operative force in the world and the idealistic pacifism of the middle classes that wants to settle the affairs of the whole of mankind by peaceful means, are all in collaboration with each other, as I said at the beginning, and this is quite natural. It matters little whether this takes place as a result of a treaty of alliance or not; it is in fact a tripartite alliance. So in our war we were attacked by the pacifism of the international bankers and bitten by all the vipers of cosmopolitan humanitarianism while at home we were plagued by the yelping of obstructive socialists and other mischievous and foolish people, and finally, in the name of civilization, progress and other sacred cows, we were solemnly and loudly cursed by a quarrelsome and servile Swiss congress of idealistic pacifists.

This idealistic middle-class pacifism and realistic socialist pacifism overlap and corroborate each other. Plutocratic pacifism, more realistic still, lacking its own formulas, makes use of both of them. All three together have combined to form part of the public consciousness. They bear witness to three facts and three situations: the decadence of the upper classes in Europe, the greed of the capitalists and the greed of the proletariat; these states and situations add up to a state of mind that is all-pervasive, extending to every class and every institution. It is the pacifist state of mind of our times, compounded of the soft-heartedness of idealist pacifism, the lies of socialist pacifism and the practices of plutocratic pacifism. Our rulers come from the enfeebled upper classes, are exposed, if not subordinated, to the demagogic activities of the socialists in Parliament or amongst the rabble, and have contacts with the plutocracy. Above all, they are rulers of democracies. The pacifist state of mind has even infiltrated the army. The war in Libya offers proof of this ... Nationalism must react against this state of affairs. It must react as a moral force and with a revolutionary dynamism, so that the revolution may build a new Italy, beginning with the conquest of Tripoli, and against the regime of the Italy of the past which came to an end with that conquest. The new Italy urged the old into war, and if the new had not existed and if there had not been any new Italians, not even the 'historic destiny' of the Right Honourable Member Giolitti would have sufficed to send our ships and regiments into action, but once the war had broken out, the old Italy which still held the reins of power in government, diplomacy and the armed forces, overcame the new ... The essential duty of nationalism is to create a warlike state of mind to oppose the pacifistic state of mind.

And when we talk like this, ladies and gentlemen, we do not mean that we are singing the praises of war like some medieval soldier of fortune. We mean that we recognize that war, like peace, is both a necessary and salutary fact of life.

NATIONALISM AND THE SYNDICATES

(Speech made at the Nationalist Convention, Rome
March 16th, 1919)

During the war, nationalism, while aiming, as was its duty, at redeeming the nation and pursuing colonial expansion, was elaborating its social and economic policy. It reached the following conclusions:

First and foremost, since it is by definition national in politics, nationalism cannot be anything other than national in economics also, since the latter is the basis of the former. Being essentially an agent of the state rather than of the government, since it has emerged as a development of the middle-class consciousness, nationalism intends to rise above all class interests by co-ordinating and concentrating them so as to transform them into units of power, wherein lies the specific function of the state.

For this reason nationalism has re-emphasized that the nation is primarily an economic society. The aim of this society is to produce. This aim constitutes its highest and most basic morality, both at the national and international level, if we use the word 'produce' in its fullest meaning, both as producing wealth and as producing civilization. For this reason, nationalism, which at first, during its early years, was faced by the ignorance and reluctance of the whole of Italy, advocated power politics and expansion abroad; and when it turned to home affairs supported that policy by proclaiming the *doctrine of the producers*, insisting first and foremost on the *need for large-scale production*, with the particular meaning in this case of economic production – commercial, agricultural and industrial development. The latter – economic production – was seen for what it really is, the raw material of the other sort of production in its fullest sense, the production of civilization, whereby a nation acquires strength and the right to expand in the world.

But just as the fact that there is more than one producing nation in the world gives rise to competition and sometimes to war, the fact that, in this complex and extremely composite society that makes up the nation, there are more classes than one gives rise to conflict between them and sometimes to revolutions. Production is necessarily competitive and imperialistic as between nation and nation, since it needs raw materials for its livelihood and markets in order to be converted into wealth; and once that is done, it becomes competitive and imperialistic once again in the form of its distribution within its national frontiers. Hence the continuous movements of nations and classes. The movement of nations is contained, inasmuch as it is contained, by a hegemony of powers, without which the world would be Bolshevist; class movements need to be contained by the laws of preservation of that higher body, the nation, which evidence themselves in the power of unity and stability represented by the state.

Where party action is concerned, nationalism supports the state. In the cruel struggle being waged at the moment between capital and labour, nationalism is by definition a unifying force. As such, it begins by asserting the overriding factor of production inasmuch as the latter represents the yield of the firm or of the hereditary estate called the nation or fatherland. Hence the private interests of every producer of capital or labour are subordinate to the laws of production. The struggle between the two can only take place within the framework of these laws. Now, strange as it may seem, such a framework at the present period of history can, as a result of the existence of socialism, be achieved only by the formation of organizations with the liveliest awareness of their private interests, that is to say, *by the formation of syndicates*. These latter supersede the old political parties which are not concerned with economic interests but with political ends that have all too often turned into ideologies and degenerated into individual or group obsessions, remote from any sense of reality of time or place. The same old

Socialist Party, which started from economics, is now crushing rather than promoting the economic interests of the proletariat beneath the heavy mass of its ideology or obsession – the desire to transform the so-called social order. And this is why the political parties hide their complete lack of realism behind the ambitions of their leaders and the fanaticism of their members and use these ambitions and this fanaticism to provide the content of their struggle and to guide it; whereas when the syndicates struggle with each other, they expose their extremely sensitive economic nerves, if I may express myself thus, not so much through the blows they give as those they receive. Where the nerve hurts, there you will discover the economic law that has been offended against. So when the syndicates fight amongst themselves, they compel each other to respect the general laws of production. They eliminate each other's arbitrariness and greed. And so, beneath their restless struggle in pursuit of their private interests, they discover the solid rock of the basic unity of the laws governing production, which neither capital nor labour can afford to neglect unless they want to destroy each other and themselves. Through these laws they achieve that unity of private interests that is usually known as the general interest. This is the *collaborationism* that nationalism advocates. A collaborationism that, in the first instance, is conflict and based on conflict but which can develop into an equilibrium of forces between the various parties, based on the organization of technical agencies – a committee, council, commission or Parliament, call it what you will, composed of directly elected representatives of all the syndicates, whether of industry or labour. Then you will have real collaboration, organic, unifying and complete. Now since, as the specific syndicalist institution for discussion and deliberation, this body may be incorporated side by side with other national institutions, what changes will it produce, how will it stand towards the state and how and to what extent will it modify the latter? When this extremely novel form of Parliament composed of economic producers comes into existence, what will become of the old form of Parliament composed of politicians? We cannot nor must we reply to such questions here. Certainly, the appearance of the first of these, the technical product of organic collectivities, subject to their own laws of selection, must immediately place on trial the second form of Parliament, produced by individualistic private initiative. The parliamentary principle will not need to stand any further trial: the present time is all in favour of organizations, and so individualistic parliamentarism is outdated; and anything outdated has received its *coup de grâce*. We hold the view that the nationalists must go into Parliament, but for reasons of convenience, and they should remain constantly aware of the new goals to be reached. Liberalism is specifically the doctrine of the old cultivated middle classes; it may well be an ideal discipline for a private elite but it has shown itself to be the medium for every sort of disorder in public life. Liberalism must give way to a new national democracy, that is to say, a democracy opposed to the existing one, in fact a democracy offering a firm structure, order and authority based on hierarchies that have been formed from within itself. And it is likewise certain that when class syndicates have reached the stage of collaboration, they must show solidarity by making common cause even in respect of foreign affairs, that is to say, in respect of acquiring markets and raw materials, both of which are matters of world competition. We have now already reached the sphere of the state. The whole thing depends on seeing how the part, that part belonging to the economic producers, will fit into the totality of national politics, raising the standard of productivity even of the producers of the spirit, of high culture, so as to form, as far as is possible in view of the inevitable corruption of mankind, the most genuine producers' state.

Nationalism advocates *strengthening and organizing the middle and industrial classes*, otherwise it is that section which will suffer in the collaborationist struggle and the destructive socialist element will gain the upper hand, dragging with it the other section, the working classes. And nationalism also advocates large-scale production because Italy cannot be a poor nation in a rich civilization and war has clearly shown the prime importance both of the eternal military virtues and of modern productive power. And it also advocates high wages to match large-scale production. There are two principles which are used to support high salaries, one of them socialist, the other nationalist. The first of these supports them as a sort of divine right of the proletariat, leaving aside any question of productivity; the second supports their steady increase in accordance with the gradual increase of the national product. This last principle breaks through the obstacles of overriding selfishness, encourages productivity and is the principle of those who, like ourselves, start from a social view of the nation and of a fair and equitable society. And we likewise think that since the conception of a wealthy people in a powerful nation is one imposed by the nature of modern civilization, we must make a virtue of necessity and stop interpreting the whole of Roman history in accordance with the monastic tradition of the Middle Ages, with its admiration of Cincinnatus who ploughed his fields on the right bank of the Tiber, and realize that the increase of wealth can be accompanied by a religious view of human life and a developing civil awareness. The inborn qualities of the Italian people are such as to lead us to hope that when they reach this happy state they may succeed in becoming a type of people in whom enjoyment of wealth will reduce the malevolence of civil strife and make them loyal and sturdy champions of the fatherland in the fulfilment of its historic task.

ARDENGO SOFFICI
(1879–1964)

The painter Soffici spent much of his youth in Paris, where he became a devotee of Cézanne and later of the Cubists. His picaresque novel, *Lemmonio Boreo* (1912), was designed as a satire on contemporary Italy. The hero, who, like Soffici, has returned from abroad, decides to become a kind of modern knight-errant; he redresses injustice and punishes fraud and hypocrisy with the aid of two assistants from the people, Zaccagna and Spillo, who symbolize force and cunning. The episode reproduced here is a literary anticipation of *squadrismo*. What is notable is the way in which Soffici makes fun of the petty-bourgeois and conventional appearance and oratory of the Socialist deputy, and contrasts it with the feelings of the unspoilt people.

After the First World War, Soffici never wavered in his support for Fascism. Like Papini, he became increasingly conservative. His ideological position resembled that of Maurras and the Action Française; in his writings on art he recommended a middle way between traditionalism and modernism.

EXTRACT FROM *LEMMONIO BOREO*

There he is! There he is!

Puffing and swaying the tram came into the square wreathed in a cloud of dirty white smoke and stopped in front of the station, where it was surrounded by a clamouring throng.

Lemmonio and the others could see from where they were standing a waving mass of heads in front of the lighted windows of the three coaches, from one of which the deputy was about to emerge; they could hear the yells and applause dominating all the other sounds as the crowd started to stream back towards the centre of the town.

A moment later the crowd parted, thrusting them to one side as it suddenly moved back to let the speaker pass by under their noses.

Although Lemmonio had not seen him for a number of years he recognized him at once. He looked a little older but still much the same, with his rather curly reddish beard and his jerky step like that of a marionette. He was dressed as always in his suit of shiny black cloth, with his bright red neckerchief hanging out of the turn-down collar of his coat and his soft grey hat cocked, in popular fashion, slightly over one ear. He was smiling left and right as he strutted along, shaking hands all round as he walked, now and again throwing a word to a pale, emaciated, grubby little shrimp of a man, who had a large pair of spectacles precariously perched on his long nose and a bag under his arm, and who was walking by his side and making strenuous efforts to keep up. Lemmonio had been told by Spillo that this was the famous Pompilio Pelagatti, the Secretary of the Trades' Council. Behind them came the rest of the red-tied mob who had been there either that morning or a short while ago, puffed up with conceit and more insolent than ever now that they were in force and close to their leader.

'What a nasty-looking bunch!' exclaimed Zaccagna loudly.

Two or three of them turned and threw him an ugly look, but without saying anything. They all went across the square towards the café. The populace followed.

It was now after nine o'clock and time to prepare for action. Without wasting time, Lemmonio gathered around him Veleno and his friends, who had been scattered by the crowd, and made the final arrangements. Only a few words were needed to decide on the signal and method of attack. The signal was to be three whistles in quick succession when Lemmonio decided the time was ripe; the separate attacks, as had already been agreed, were to move from the periphery of the audience towards the centre, where they were to join up and group together under the statue of Garibaldi ...

Meanwhile the platform was ready and it was already slightly past the time announced on the red broadsheet which had been distributed that day and was now being reread by a lot of people in the light of the torches fastened to the cart-rails. The only person missing was the speaker but, as the red-tied fraternity were bustling around screening the platform, it was clear that he would not be long. In fact, a moment later, confused shouts were heard from the direction of the café; and with a surge of bodies, a kind of wake opened up across the square and the Right Honourable Ghiozzi appeared beside the podium. A burst of applause rose from the 'red ties' and was taken up by the crowd.

The deputy bowed two or three times in each direction, then glanced briefly at a few sheets of paper that Pelagatti extracted one by one from his brief-case; and finally, helped or rather hoisted by the hands of numerous comrades, he climbed on to the cart. As soon as he was up, he stood there, perching knock-kneed and pot-bellied, assumed a solemn demeanour, stared straight ahead with his pig-like eyes as if to call for silence and, when he saw that everyone was quiet and that the audience was all agog, he spoke:

'Fellow citizens and comrades! I am proud and happy that, in willing response to the kind invitation of the gentlemen of the press of your charming and cultured town, I can have the opportunity, on behalf of my party and myself, of answering the extremely important question: Who are we and what do we want?

'I have already been privileged on earlier occasions to speak to you and everything that I said then and all the things that later on were done to come to the help of the most urgent needs of you hardworking country folk might perhaps be considered as making it unnecessary for me to tell you once again today who we are; but I am anxious to give you a fuller and more complete answer.

'Fellow citizens! Socialism, of which I am merely the most modest servant and pioneer – socialism is the light which, even if it does not descend from heaven as a dove or a pigeon, is destined to undermine and cast down the foundations of any form of tyranny or exploitation, to loosen the shackles in which for centuries a minority has held the vast mass of humble downtrodden producers in bondage, which will sweep away social shams and give new life and hope to the proletariat of the whole world as the sun rises on a glorious future!'

Another burst of applause rose from the 'comrades' surrounding the cart, as well as from other parts of the square. But the orator, accustomed to greater triumphs than this, showed no sign of emotion. He gave a slight nod to acknowledge the applause, stroked his beard which seemed even redder by the light of the torches and shifted his weight on to one leg while waiting for the clapping to die down. Then he began again and, gradually warming to his task, he went on for several minutes, issuing judgments and spelling out definitions in his florid style, now and again interspersing them with a few quips that brought laughter and applause from his sympathetic audience.

Lemmonio remained calm and collected as he listened to the speaker's empty, tortuous, demagogic phrases; while after every interruption the latter proceeded to pour out his relentless flow of empty rhetoric.

'Who are we? We are the real friends of the people, the pioneers of a new era; and it is not without deep significance that this evening I am speaking to you from this place, set as it is between the emblem of nineteen centuries of bondage and obscurantism (pointing to the church) and (pointing to the statue of Garibaldi) the symbol of fratricidal strife, a relic of the greedy and warlike feudalism of the Middle Ages.

'Fellow citizens and comrades! We who are thrusting ourselves like a gigantic wedge between these two images of past ignorance and oppression, we represent the apostles of a new gospel of brotherhood on earth whereby mankind, united and with one resolve, will at last be enabled to fight the good fight for the future.

'That is what we are: and our war-cry is: justice and light, progress and prosperity!'

These words produced even louder and more enthusiastic applause, not only from the deputy's friends and the usual groups of supporters scattered round the square but from a large part of the now spellbound crowd; so that the orator, beginning to realize the great success which was in store for him, was no longer content to wait for silence to return but started strutting up and down, smiling and nodding to those spectators nearest to him, with one hand in his pocket and the other feeling his beard, which was covered in spittle.

But Lemmonio, although far less calm, managed to remain stiller than ever as he watched him closely. He looked at his puffy red cheeks, his podgy nose, his furtive little eyes, the narrow, furrowed forehead, so typical of his mediocrity, which was dominated by a quiff of tousled red hair, the whole vulgarity of his face, and, thinking back on what Spillo had said about him, he was amazed that such a stupid moron could appear with impunity, as he almost invariably did, before different audiences, whom he always regaled with the identical rubbish, and not only escape danger but even draw applause instead of a shower of ripe tomatoes. So it was true that crowds really were so stupid!

'Shall we whistle?' Zaccagna asked, noticing the disgust written on his face.

Lemmonio shook his head.

'Not yet.'

Meanwhile, silence had been more or less restored after a great deal of shushing. The speaker proceeded:

'But I have not come here merely to tell the people of this town, who already know what we are—as do our opponents,' he added sarcastically. 'But I want to explain to you as well what we socialists want.

'Fellow citizens and comrades! The world was a sink of iniquity, injustice and privilege, perpetuated by the combined efforts of the aristocracy and the clergy, when a man appeared, an apostle of scientific doctrine, and with a stroke of genius stripped away the veil that hid the truth. I mean Charles Darwin. This man of science, in the thicket of the web of lies that held mankind in a vice-like grip, destroyed at one fell swoop all the centuries-old fables invented to harm mankind; and by proclaiming that man, instead of having been created from clay like the pots made in Montelupo, was descended from apes, he ushered in a new era that was the forerunner of all the later triumphs of science and thought. From that day forth, the fundamental inequality asserted by the theologians of the Inquisition and the philosophers in the pay of the middle classes was obliterated, any sort of aristocracy was exposed as a fraud, and from the mass of ruins of these errors there arose the shining principle of equality; and emerging from the discoveries of the American naturalist, it began to make its way from that day onwards, thus leading on to the Positivist philosophy that is the very basis of our party.'

The Right Honourable Member continued for a while in this vein, explaining in minute detail how this discovery had given birth to a complete political system of 'noble humanitarianism' in which 'there was no longer room for the fraudulent mysticism which, by the false promise of an after-life, had provided the justification for the immoral distinction between rich and poor, exploiters and exploited', where 'the laws governing the capitalist system had superseded the artificial laws of allegedly spiritual hierarchies' and 'positive individual and social welfare had replaced abstract aspirations that were purely for the benefit of despotic and bloodthirsty minorities'.

'Our opponents will talk to you of history and civilization and kindness. Socialism retorts that its history is not compounded of the blood and tears of the proletariat; its kindness is made up of brotherhood and peace, and its civilization is one that by scientific progress will lead the multitudes to conquer the fruits of the earth and achieve happiness.'

Once again he was interrupted as more and more people joined in the applause and shouts of approval. The crowd, without understanding a syllable, were letting themselves be carried away by the sound of the words and feeding on their own excitement; they were heaving and swaying all over the square as if everyone wanted to press even more closely round the speaker. The latter now nodded his head again several times and wiped the sweat from his face; but instead of waiting to continue his speech, he bent down towards Pelagatti who was leaning against the tie-bar of the cart and had a few words with him while all around his followers gave full rein to their enthusiasm.

'Shall we whistle?' Zaccagna asked again; he had been desperately fidgeting for some time and could no longer contain himself.

'No,' Lemmonio replied again, sharply, in a slightly hoarse voice. 'Wait.' And he started listening to Ghiozzi again as he once more began to speak:

'Yes, this is what socialism wants and it wants something else besides,' he was saying. 'Once knowledge has freed man's thought and science has freed man's arms—now that machinery can take their place—freed them from their long slavery; once these two have made man free and lord of himself and of the world, our crowning task will be the final struggle against the last spectres of age-old oppression.'

And thick and fast there followed a storm, an avalanche, a whole gale of platitudes borrowed from the basest sort of ideology, phrases from electoral posters, an incontinent flood of words from some incompetent cheapjack politician full of resounding nonsense, illiterate solecisms and blind stupidity.

In his bewilderment, Lemmonio Boreo had finally reached the stage of not being able to follow the thread of that relentless flood of twaddle; all he could hear was the noise it made, interrupted now and again by the usual expressions of popular enthusiasm. He was pondering. True enough, he had never had any love or esteem, nor was he feeling now any love or esteem, for those humanitarian phrase-mongers who go from place to place with their quack medicines and panaceas concealed under their cloaks like the mountebanks of old, deceiving the simple-minded with golden words, appealing to their gullibility, their natural baseness, their cowardice and their stupidity; but during his own lifetime he had never chanced upon anyone like this or anyone for whom he felt such a violent dislike. It was true that in coming to listen to him, he knew what he was letting himself in for, but the reality was far more disgusting than anything he had in fact foreseen. And it was not so much the ideas of the party to which Ghiozzi belonged that disgusted him. He knew them and even if they were not exactly his own, he could yet recognize their good side and their effectiveness in practice, as had already been demonstrated by the considerable improvements achieved even amongst our own people. In fact, in that empty claptrap, it was not so much the socialist that offended him as the betrayal of the ideas that the speaker was trying to spread; and in particular, he disliked the person himself. Socialism was not his ideal, certainly; but neither were the anti-socialist doctrines, the 'bourgeois' doctrines; far from it. So what interested him were the men preaching these doctrines. Thus he was prepared to find Bestemmino's and Veleno's anarchy equally as absurd as Ghiozzi's socialism; for him the difference lay in the fact that Bestemmino and Veleno shod donkeys and made spades and ploughshares while the deputy led exactly the same life as his alleged opponents and was as lying and deceitful as they were, not only towards his own like but also towards the poor who were in no position to judge him. If he had been a convinced Utopian, an innocent honestly deceived, an ignoramus of the popular sort, he would even have forgiven him all this tiresome rigmarole. In a speech, basically the words count for much less than we think. According to the man who utters them, they appear to follow an internal rhythm that underlines and enriches their sense, and become tinged with an inner life which contains almost all their meaning. A journalist's phrase can still be fiery, and a mistake that betrays someone's lack of education can increase the psychological value of his speech. The words don't count. All the same, the rhythm and colour of those that were issuing from the gap between Ghiozzi's moustache and his beard, glistening with spittle, were too dreadful. Lemmonio could hear in them the man's whole self-conceit and dishonesty and careerism and incurable obtuseness.

No, his recent reading had indeed not lied. 'There he stands,' he thought, 'one of the modern heroes of my race! A liar, with his "gentlemen of the local press"; a flatterer, a rogue, a windbag, a vulgar ignoramus. And he is one of the representatives of my nation! And perhaps not the worst!' He gave a hysterical laugh. Zaccagna looked at him questioningly; but he continued to look towards the speaker as if he had not noticed it.

Meanwhile the latter, as was to be expected, had very gently come down from his ideal summits to the more profitable field of electoral possibilities; and after having explained to those good folk what socialism wanted in general, he was now suggesting what he, Ghiozzi, was asking for on his own behalf. A lot of votes at the next election. But he wasn't saying this in so many words. Instead he was saying:

'But socialism cannot put its whole marvellous programme into action if the great masses of the people do not close their ranks tightly under the shadow of the Red Flag. Only with the moral and material help of the whole proletariat can our sacred cause triumph and seize power, and this seizure of power can only be realized by gaining control in Parliament through the legitimate representatives of the working masses.'

'Here comes "so turn up as one man at the polling booths",' muttered Lemmonio to himself and was on the point of issuing his order when the orator suddenly veered back to his demagogic balderdash, only returning to the real purpose of his speech now and again, almost as if he wanted to get there rather by surprise, without anyone noticing.

But now Lemmonio was tired and only waiting for a particularly idiotic or dishonest phrase to give Zaccagna his head; the latter was becoming more and more restive beside him and kept on looking questioningly at him every time he heard the roar of applause.

And at last the moment came. Ghiozzi had come down somewhat from the clouds and was now directly apostrophizing his listeners on the subject of peace based on internationalism and depicting it in the most wonderful colours.

'Comrades! Tillers of the soil! The whole proletariat has an interest in putting an end to this long-standing state of affairs. When all frontiers have been destroyed as emblems of bourgeois capitalist savagery, all the nations of the world will be able to clasp each other in a brotherly embrace. But you workers in the fields have a special interest since you will be the first and most numerous victims of this monster of militarism when you are driven to the slaughter in order to save their lordships' fatherland! Fatherland,' he added with a pitying sneer, 'that's another word that ought to be erased from the book of mankind once mankind has been redeemed by socialism. That infamous word has caused rivers of blood to flow all over the world. A Latin author, a forerunner of our times, wrote thousands of years ago, *ubi bene ibi patria*; which freely translated means "your country is where you can best eat and drink". And from now on that is to be the definition of that lying relic of medieval times.

'Yes, victims of every oppression, outcasts, ah, this word fatherland! Our fatherland is where our welfare is to be found and if peoples from foreign lands come to us and descend upon our exhausted soil, oppressed by misgovernment and capitalism, with the full weight of their industrial power, we shall welcome them as brothers and liberators ... '

'Oh God! That's enough!' Lemmonio burst out, ramming his hat down on his head.

And hurriedly turning to Zaccagna: 'Get going! Whistle! Hard!'

For more than half an hour, Zaccagna had been waiting to receive just that order, astounded and bursting with impatience and barely able to prevent himself from swearing because Lemmonio was taking so long to give it. So no sooner did he hear his master's words than he put the index and middle fingers of each hand together, as shepherds do when they see their flock spreading over planted fields, inserted them into his mouth, pressed them on to his palate against his tongue and summoning every breath of air in his lungs, blew three immensely long shrill whistles; then, buttoning up his jacket and huddling even closer to Lemmonio, he stood waiting beside him to see what would happen.

For a moment nothing happened. As if some strange prodigy had unexpectedly appeared in the heavens, no one moved or breathed. Even the speaker, as if he were taken aback, left his sentence unfinished and stood dumbstruck with his mouth agape and his hand poised for a gesture. But as soon as the red-tied fraternity had had time to recover from their surprise and understand what was happening, a burst of applause, calls for silence and invective greeted the unknown whistler.

Shouts of 'Shhh! Shhh! Shut up!' could be heard above the hubbub. 'Down with the exploiters! Down with the scabs! Down with the priests! Down with the spies!'

But the signal had already been given and other whistles and shouts were replying from the back of the square, from the direction of the café, the church, the station, from all around and, amidst wild confusion, swirling masses of men moved forward all together, jostling the crowds of people as they forced their way violently towards the statue of Garibaldi.

'Down with the charlatans! Death to the politicians! Up with anarchy! Boo! Boo!'

In a very few minutes, the square and the whole town were in uproar and confusion.

GABRIELE D'ANNUNZIO
(1863–1938)

D'Annunzio early on announced that he did not wish to be 'a *mere* poet'. He set out to be a patriotic bard in the Risorgimento tradition. However, he remained at heart an aesthete, 'a dilettante of sensations', as Croce described him. One of the most powerful sensations he experienced was in the command of crowds; in a characteristic image he once described the 'hidden beauty' present in the spirit of a crowd, which could only be evoked by an 'inspired artificer'. As a master of rhetorical persuasion D'Annunzio had no equals, not even Mussolini, but he lacked the patience and sense of reality needed for a practical politician.

D'Annunzio's political ideas were not really important. What mattered were his images, his language, the myth which he constructed around his own person. He had a keen sense of the changing mood of the public, and knew how to give expression to its secret desires. Without doubt he was the most eloquent of all those who preached the heroic revolt against mediocrity and the shameful betrayal of the passions and sacrifices of the Risorgimento. Corradini's inaugural article in *Il Regno* shows his influence clearly enough. However, as nationalism acquired a distinctive doctrine, it also emancipated itself to some degree from its D'Annunzian origins.

In 1915 D'Annunzio was living in France. He returned to take the leading part in 'the radiant days of May', when the interventionists won control of the *piazza*. Both then and in his 1919 campaigns for Dalmatia and Fiume, he incited his audience to hatred of 'the internal enemy'. D'Annunzio's effrontery in using Christian language and imagery would be astonishing if it were not seen against the background of a culture in which the confusion between the values of Christianity and nationalism was so far advanced. His May 1915 speech in memory of the Thousand ends with a parody of the Beatitudes ('Blessed are the youths who hunger and thirst for glory, for they will be satisfied', etc.), and in the *Letter to the Dalmatians* printed here the theme of purification through sacrifice is central. To an extraordinary degree, in fact, D'Annunzio's use of religious language and ritual succeeded in winning him the kind of veneration accorded to a religious leader. But the ethic of D'Annunzio was 'Nietzschean' and 'Darwinian', not Christian. The dictates of the 'heroic will' are the highest law, and conflict is the essence of civilization.

In his last phase, after the fall of his extraordinary state of Fiume, D'Annunzio tried to become the apostle of civil concord and the reconciliation of parties. In this role, he caused a good deal of trouble to Mussolini. There was a certain magnanimity about D'Annunzio's National Socialism; even if it was still a pose, it was not a mere disguise for class interests or the pursuit of power. His *ralliement* to Fascism was reluctant and half-hearted.

LETTER TO THE DALMATIANS
JANUARY 15TH, 1919

Tell them over there, when you have recrossed the sea. If, seeing your suffering, the Cause had needed to be consecrated again, you could not have hoped for a nobler reconsecration than this. The day before yesterday in the old Dalmatian oratory of Saint George there surged up a passion and a will straighter than the spear of the Christian hero thrusting at the deformed beast. The beast cannot prevail and shall not prevail. The promise made in September—beyond the power of any disagreement or deception or mistake—I now repeat to soothe your anguish.

And through me and with me this promise is repeated by all those who fought for a pledge that the vanquished can no longer take away from the victor ...

I and my comrades have fought for that express pledge, that accepted pledge, lying between us and the enemy, lying between us and the Austrian, lying between us and that rabble of Southern Slavs whose mask of new found liberty and a bastard name do little to hide their vile old snout as they continue to strive against us for that which we reconquered with our weapons alone and with our sole passion and which we intend to hold for all eternity.

I say, for those who fought on the Piave, that every drop of their most precious blood was carried by the waters throughout the whole expanse of our sea as far as distant Otranto. I say that for us the delta of the Piave stood for the sand and seaweed of the whole Latin strand in the east; and when a noble hero such as Andrea Basile took a handful of it as a sacrament before offering his life, he felt that he was communing with the whole of that further shore as far as the innermost recesses of the labyrinth of Cattaro.

Of what value are the secrets of laborious treaties—expedients bred from weakened faith and untimely fear—compared to an upright heroic will?

He amongst us who advanced on Trieste through double fire, that man took possession of Trieste. He who defied the hell of Pola took over that port for Italy. He who performed the miracle at Premuda seized the whole archipelago. He who first flew over the Bay of Teodo, felt that he was arousing, between Risano and Perasto, the roar of the lion who is awaiting us. He who violated the Carnaro on the night of Buccari, wished to make good the gaps in the London Pact.[1] From beginning to end, I was always of that race.

And so I say and bear witness that each one of us bore within himself the spirit of victory. He made war to win the whole war. He thrust his goals further and further forward. Every death meant certainty. To offer yourself completely, you must never doubt. He who offered himself completely never doubted. The doubters were those who sat still, or rushed for shelter, which was nothing other than decline and denial. Even in the gloom of Caporetto, the faithful did not lose their way. They said: 'Even this is a victory for us, the twelfth!' And it was true. Eleven times had Italy conquered the enemy, and the twelfth time she conquered herself.

And the thirteenth time was the victory of the sun, wherein she was regenerated as a heroine, with her regenerated bread, and was worthy of the praise of her first Interpreter. And the fourteenth victory was the sovereign and exemplary victory, the victory of victories: the Roman wedge, that cleft the strong force of the enemy into two quivering trunks; and so came the collapse of a formidable lie: the destruction of an empire rooted in the most obdurate ignominy; the dissolution of a monstrous structure.

Now all still under arms, victorious Italy should have said to her rivals: 'Here is my sacrifice. Will you weigh it in the balance? But love does not bear weighing. Here is my

[1] The 1915 Treaty between Italy and the Allied powers on the basis of which Italy entered the war.

victory. Will you measure it? But it transcends your measuring as it transcends the old pact. Whether this still holds or does not hold, I care not. It has been absorbed by my rights. And here are my rights, for which I have fought alone, for which I alone have suffered, for which alone I have three times renewed my strength and my courage.'

This is what, in her victory, Italy should have said loud and clear, with composure and discipline and massive will, brief and firm in her assertion: 'My confines in the east are marked by the Bebian Alps and the Dinaric Alps, which continue the Julian Alps. That whole strip of land which was constantly Italian in origin and essence, belongs to me. Earlier persecutions by successful bullies and recent distortions by beaten usurpers carry no weight.'

Instead we witness a piteous sight. We seem almost overcome by our triumphant victory. Some wish to frighten us with the dangers of victory, we who have affronted and overcome every danger. And so we do nothing but prattle on 'with a tongue that seems an outstretched hand'. We are begging for a smile from the arbitrator; we celebrate all the thirty-two teeth of that inscrutable smile. We place the Roman She-Wolf, reissued in solid gold, in the hands of a guest on bargain terms. But if once again universal authority rests in the pocket of a philosopher, why did we neglect to regild in glory the equestrian statue of Marcus Aurelius with dollar gold?'[1]

The affable guardian of the Forum—who is of Venetian stock—offers the visitor the myrtle and the laurel sprung from the dust of greatness. But was that branch of myrtle, which can purify man of the sin of having killed his brothers in civil strife, in the innermost chamber when a most evil citizen came in, more pernicious today than that 'blubber-lipped old executioner'[2] who tried to strangle the bewildered fatherland with a Prussian noose?

Is the Fatherland still bewildered?

[1] References to the visit of President Wilson to Italy.

[2] The reference is to Giolitti.

We had two foes, both equally ignoble, both equally to be feared: an internal and an external foe.

We have conquered the external foe, we have pursued him with our bayonets at his back, we have humiliated and defeated him. And now we see him revive and spit his hatred in our face and abuse and deride us and declare that he is irreconcilable, and once again contend for what is ours by right. And there are those who would persuade us that we should be afraid and that it is necessary to sacrifice our deeply suffering flesh, our most gentle soul, to a rabble of savage louts who had a guarantor in our house, a pettifogging rascal who had grown rich by trading in adulterated wine and defrauding unsuspecting customers.

It seemed that our resounding victory should sweep away the internal enemy or at least render him speechless and break his power. Instead he is more vicious than ever and more hateful: he has the semblance of an honest little man, he claims to support new immortal principles, he confides his new Acts of the Apostles to foreign newspapers and speaks a language that in its structure, novelty and depth vies with that of the late Ernesto Teodoro Moneta.

And so the Italy of San Michele and the Vodice, the Italy of the Grappa and the Piave, the Italy of Premuda and Pola, heroic and patient Italy, the Italy of the indomitable little infantryman, the one who the day before yesterday prayed in your oratory without kneeling down, the Italy who is stronger and more clearsighted than her leaders, greater than her fortunes, nobler than her glories, has, despite a few helpless struggles to raise her head, lived on in bitter and impotent humility for half a century.

But around us, life was never more greedy, the conflict of desires never more savage, the drama of clashing races never more violent. And so, we see our dear Allies biting each other hard in the ear as they embrace, in the manner of Sicilian rivals. Even when they talk of fraternity and fresh sacrifices, we feel that the words are uttered through clenched teeth and are referring to the forbearance of others.

They are hungry. *Improba ventris rabies*. That is it.

After being saturated with victims and waxing fat, the earth seems to have passed on its hunger to the peoples. And if the earth is satiated, men seem insatiable. And if man is not a wolf to other men, a nation is a lioness to other nations.

An ascetic of war, bearing my name, said at the beginning, 'In heralding the most widespread massacre, I believe that war is preparing mystic spheres for the apparition of great ideals. Where the charnel house dissolves, sublimity will be born in ferment. Where the weight of mortality sinks down, the soul's freedom will be uplifted. The greater the offering, the greater will be the wonder and the miracle.'

Was he alluding to that 'better and happier mankind' for which that old surgeon of France was longing, that Celt whose bristle ill disguises his well exercised predatory jaw, whilst he makes plans to pierce our living flesh with steel and then to carve out for himself his own lavish portion?[1]

Even today, after so much grievous suffering, energy and pride of race are triumphant and insatiable in their voracity. Force that has given of its blood is the most to be feared. Fourteen stitches will not suffice to stitch together the torn flesh.[2]

Are we to shake our heads and endlessly moan over the 'sublime insanity of fate?'

Civilization is nothing but the glory of incessant struggle. When man is no longer a wolf for other men, a nation will and must always be a lioness to other nations.

And we want to crouch down in solitary sheep-like submission! The people bent on *revanche*, intoxicated by victory, spread all their plumes to the wind once more and once more prepare to sound their clarion call; they hasten their steps to overtake the swiftest and the most resolute; and we draw hurriedly aside to let them speed through.

The well-fed people with their five meals a day have

[1] Clemenceau.

[2] Wilson's Fourteen Points.

hardly finished their bloody task before they open their jaws again to gobble up all that they can; and we frugally tighten our belts another hole or two.

The people of the star-spangled banner do not disguise the fact that they have brought their business to the best and most successful conclusion, in the cause of eternal ideals; and we are already allowing strangers to muddy the sources of our new wealth.

Those who preach moderation, prudence, self-denial and mortification, are they not rubbing their sweaty palms together?

In what dark museum vaults have we hidden the six thousand cannon captured from the Austrian? In what remote pigstyes, to the detriment of the country folk, are we fattening up our last five hundred thousand prisoners of every race?

In what inaccessible cemeteries have we abandoned our dead, the finest dead in the world? In what unlit ward are we allowing our disabled to wilt, the disabled who allowed themselves to be cut down only that they might give more fruit?

Why, amongst so many blackguards and windbags infesting our streets and market-places, do we not see the silent makers of the Word?

And what will be the peace finally imposed upon us poor Christians?

Pax Gallica?

Pax Britannica?

Pax stelligera?

Miserere nostri ...

Well then, no! Enough is enough! If it were right to repeat the old cry of a defenceless poet, the much abused 'Ah, non per questo ... ' (Oh, not for this ... '),[1] it would resound over an infinitely richer gush of blood and infinitely more cruel than that which spurted at Calatafimi and Milazzo.

[1] A reference to a poem by Carducci.

Victorious Italy, the most victorious among the nations—victorious over herself and over the foe—will have, in her Alps and on her sea, the only peace that is sitting for ever, the *Pax Romana*.

We have fought for a greater Italy. We want a greater Italy. I say that we have prepared the mystic sphere for the apparition of our ideal of her. We are waiting for her at last to appear in the form in which she was heralded.

The 'makers' of the Word knew and know what was and is the Word of Italy: the most luminous in the mother tongue and the proudest, such as outshines the splendour of the earthly spring: a superb affirmation of life, of the whole of life, written on a sublime summit of the history of mankind: the Renaissance.

But today it cannot ring out true and whole except through the iron mouth of the will.

Between that which must be preserved of the past and that which must be won in the future, does the tireless Workwoman prepare to rise up from her travail and to repeat the loud proclamation that will resound throughout the whole Mediterranean basin?

What was spoken and asked during the years of foul ignominy is today being said and asked again in the onrush of victory.

We wish that a feeling of greatness be set up in our nation. Is it not the inevitability of our greatness which today inspires such aversion?

Let us assert it and exalt it. Italy is great and wishes to become greater.

At times, even during the years of ignominy, our heart sprang up when we felt within us what a fund of creative power lay inexhaustible within our land, what nucleus of latent energies was there condensed in order perpetually to restore life as it was consumed.

And today we exult in our hearts if we consider the immense effort put forth by Italy by the sole virtue of her deep hereditary instinct and despite the blind ineptitude of those who guide the fortunes of a country where statecraft came to full bloom with such vigour – an art of government founded not on false scholastic methods and puerile illusions but on living reality, on facts, on experience, on the shrewd study of men and institutions and their analogies and relationships; it was a time when our men of state seemed without peer both in the republics and when, out of the destruction of the free communes, there arose the new principalities, and the magnificent vision of Machiavelli burned bright against foreign bondage.

I say again that the womb of this Mother of Corn and of Heroes, of this female Warrior of the Solstice 'twixt sea and Alp is still the most fruitful amongst all mothers.

Moral ascendency seems to be her destiny. The saddest mistakes can oppress but never destroy her genius.

I repeat amidst the roar of struggle what I had said amidst the silence of the spirit.

'She is the lucid artificer of a confusion of races. In her alone will the diverse molten matter of new life be pressed into grand and perfect shapes. In her alone will ideal forms once again become living; and to men in their frantic struggle as they develop in all directions, trying out every force in every peril, forging ever more complex tools to bring all the spirits of nature together within the spirit of mankind, she will offer once again these forms as examples against which they may judge themselves and as marks which they must make their constant aim in the violence of war as in the jubilation of victory.'

For this divine motherland have we fought. For her we wish to fight again. And he who regretted not having given up his life for her can be glad today that he is able to throw into the battle for the nation what had been left to him.

I and my comrades would not wish to remain Italians in an Italy enervated by the fomentations of our Dr Wilson from across the Atlantic and amputated by the surgery of our Dr Clemenceau from across the Alps.

The cry that was addressed to the people of Rome on a

day of tumult is still valid today, even more valid today: 'Not rags nor bones, not dribs nor drabs, nor fraud nor barter. Enough is enough! Overturn the benches! Smash the false scales!' If need be, we shall face this new conspiracy in the manner of the daring heroes of old, a bomb in each hand and our blades between our teeth.

It is not possible that, one hundred and twenty years later, the Treaty of the Clock should repeat, in another form, the infamy we suffered at Campoformido.[1] Even after one hundred and twenty years, let us bless that sweet island that rose to a man when she heard the news and killed her pusillanimous major because he showed himself ready to accept the abuse. May her vine tendrils garland her in perpetuity, may her peaches and almonds adorn her at the beginning of every spring with a robe lovelier than the robe of her sea and may her Venetian grace never fade *in secula seculorum*.

I know, my friends, how your heart thrills at that recollection, and I know that every one of your brothers in every town of Dalmatia is equal to the pride of that Istrian memory.

Just as, with the secret or overt support of an allied nation, the hybrid band of Slavs tried to cheat us of the booty won by our navy in Pola, will their attempt to cheat us along the coast and in the archipelagos be similarly supported? Ships are ships and lands are lands. A spirited people does not desert its land in the way a crew of mercenaries abandons its ship. You would rather die, in the Italian way, in the Roman way. And people that call themselves Latin wish to help you to your death in order to leave room for Croatian filth in the loggia of the Venetian magistrature and the baptistry of Andrea Alessi, in order to deposit the copious vomit of the Austrian vulture in the hall of Diocletian's Palace. And there are people like this on the other side of the Alps as well as on this.

The weight of grief is such as to stifle anger. And this grief

[1] The treaty by which Napoleon allowed Austria to annex the Veneto.

we must also bless. The day before yesterday, looking round to seek on the newly uncovered façade of the Basilica of St Mark the horses that are no longer there, this grief did not wish to remember who had taken them away, some one hundred and twenty years ago. Nor when the news of the customary insolence reaches it from over the sea does it imagine that the demon of the slaughter of Verona may now be brooding in the lions of your sea gates.

Let us exorcize it. Let us conjure this fraternal misfortune.

But as for me, having offered my all, and if all was not taken from me I regret it, today I am ready to sacrifice all love, all friendship and all advantage to your cause which has been my cause ever since the time when, as a youth, I was dazzled for the first time by the visage of Traù, a kinswoman like the beloved amongst my sisters, who was left in the pure house of my mother.

In this I am your equal, just as the day before yesterday, standing between the altar and the door, I felt myself the equal of the silent young infantryman.

I shall be with you to the end. And you know what I mean by this promise.

Would that all Italians were with you, openly resolute and of one mind. Would that I might impress on every Italian heart this wound that burns me and cannot be dressed except by justice. Would that I might dispel with my breath the spectres of beggary and adulation and arouse an intrepid, victorious people behind their leaders and their legates, a people still desirous and capable of further victory.

Does he who denies you, repudiates you and betrays you know that you are living creatures, peoples and towns, men and stones? If men bleed, stones give up the ghost.

Now a few days ago, in noble Almissa, a younger sister of Spalato, the enemy, our defeated enemy, the foul Croat, pulled himself up by the bosses of the Venetian wall, like a rabid ape, and hacked at the winged lion with a vile chisel. Now a few days ago, in Cattaro, a loyal guest was seized by trickery and violence, placed in a boat, taken to Castelnuovo and there disembarked in a lovely spot and shot in the back 'as an Italian', in sight of the castle by the sea and the land fortresses under the sign of the lion.

So he who denies you is handing you over to the gaoler and executioner. He is condemning you to bondage and to death. He thrusts you into a horror from which there is no escape. He will make you slaves of Slavs.[1] He wishes to crown your long martyrdom with a shameful death. He is killing you and your hope. He is killing in you 'that which no mortal man nor immortal god ever killed'. It is an unpardonable crime. No myrtle can wash it clean, not even the illustrious myrtle in the Forum. When the upright and valiant fratricide was about to enter the room of arbitration, I am certain that the myrtle branch withered like the fig-tree of Judas.

The guardian of the Forum and the august Palatine, Giacomo Boni, on the sad occasion when the bell-tower of St Mark's collapsed, loaded the fragments of the Roman bricks and Venetian rubble on to a boat; and from the lagoon went out into our captive sea and cast his glorious cargo into the sea, where it sank to join the Doge's rings.

Trusty Dalmatians, should the injustice come to pass—and may God avert its imminent shadow—you will load your boats with the glorious fragments of stone and you will embark with them; and you too will go out into the sea of your despairing love; and you will let yourselves sink together with your relics, and in the depths you will find our dead, no longer slaves in chains but free men amongst free men.

And I shall follow my calling and shall be with you: and perhaps not I alone.

And it will be said that the victory of Italy was writ upon the waters.

[1] *Schiavo* means both 'slave' and 'Slav' (translator's note).

AGOSTINO LANZILLO
(1886–1952)

Lanzillo was born in Calabria and studied economics at Rome. Like other southern intellectuals, he was a passionate free trader and criticized orthodox socialism for conniving with the forces of protectionism. As a journalist he took part in the revolutionary syndicalist movement. In 1914 he joined Mussolini and became one of the staff of the *Popolo d'Italia*.

Lanzillo was a disciple of Sorel and also of Pareto; his writings illustrate the way in which Sorelian syndicalism and Paretian elitism could be given a specifically Fascist interpretation. Lanzillo was one of the few active Fascists whose ideological position showed a certain consistency over the years.

EXTRACTS FROM
THE DEFEAT OF SOCIALISM

(Revised second edition, Rome, 1918)

Preface to the first edition

This book, written amidst the vicissitudes of war, after I had been wounded, reflects the way in which, day by day, I became increasingly struck by the mighty events of these momentous years: it has both a subjective and an objective value. While trying to depict the author's moral and psychological crisis, it attempts to sum up and express the more general and far greater crisis in the national and socialist consciousness of today, after the whole traditional structure of thought has been upset by the war. If the present war was unforeseen by all classes and all parties, if the military leaders and rulers of nations themselves were uncertain of the possibility of a European war, if the world conscience recoiled in horror at the mcre thought of this possibility, this war appeared to the socialists not only as improbable, for the same reasons as it appeared improbable to other writers and the traditional parties, but as unfeasible because they were convinced that the strength of socialism itself would make any outbreak of war impossible. It seemed in fact that the capitalist classes themselves, as a result of the complex network of interests which tended to unite them, would be able to prevent war; and in addition it was thought that the international proletariat, faced by the imminent threat of an unlimited war, would make a revolutionary move and receive the necessary impetus for such an immense undertaking from the exceptionally serious situation of the times. When war did break out, however, it was seen how mistaken the socialists' forecasts were: there was no revolutionary opposition and hostilities started with determination and the full support of the whole nation.

This was the moment of crisis: a whole line of thought and action was erased; the historical and ideological structure of socialism, which had dominated the whole of the nineteenth and the first decade and a half of the twentieth centuries, tumbled down in ruins and things took a course in marked contrast to that of socialism.

The phenomenon was too broad and striking not to have complex and deep-seated causes. They were intimately connected with those which gave rise to the war and ... they were mingled in one single causal system, a simultaneous and unambiguous reversal in the life and development of our century.

Thus we can well understand how this reversal of historical factors and their reappraisal must have affected the hearts and minds of the socialists. Many of them, who today support the war, had imbibed a religious faith in socialism with their mothers' milk and lived and drew their being from this single grandiose belief. At one fell swoop, they saw the war open up an abyss beneath their feet; socialism had come to an end and, worse still, the reasons for its existence, which seemed inherent in life itself, had disappeared. Their beliefs were replaced by anxious doubt; something which seemed incontrovertible truth had been torn to shreds by brutal facts whose power could not be denied.

In its general conception, socialism was founded on the differences between the classes and the *political evaluation* of these differences: and war has abolished classes and given the nation back its firm sense of unity. Socialism based its arguments on the diametrical opposition of interests within individual countries, and war showed the possibility of reconciling these interests in the will to defend by force of arms a common heritage and common ideals. It could not even be imagined that this would be a passing, short-lived phenomenon, because war is a long drawn-out, bitter and intense struggle, requiring exceptional nervous endurance, whose agony exhausts both those who fight and those who merely watch, the non-combatants and the neutrals. It proliferates, causing upheaval in other nations, advanced civilizations with the most highly developed workers' movements.

Such hard-fought conflict between people and nations, and the appearance of new nations in the lists, cannot be explained except by the internal agreement of these peoples, by the general support of all classes and *therefore also of the working classes*. If the proletariat had accepted war in a brief moment of intoxication, the years of struggle and suffering would have caused any enthusiasm to flag unless it had been based on a permanent attitude of mind or on a resigned acceptance of the inevitable ...

From Chapter VI (The War)

... Anyone who has read these few pages carefully will recall the brief examination which we made of the fundamental aberration committed by capitalism in Europe towards the middle of the nineteenth century. Capitalist society had quickly abandoned the scientific approach on which it had been based and its whole organization had been fundamentally transformed. Its economic, legal and political structures had changed. Its *laissez-faire* economic principles had been refuted by its practice and this led to the collapse of the whole spirit of conquest and free enterprise, which had provided capitalism with its brief but extremely intense moment of inspiration, representing, as it were, the spirit of the new regime. From that time onwards, the bourgeoisie started on its inevitable decline. I say decline but I am using the word more exactly in the sense of full stop. Capitalist society entered a period which recalls Dante's picture of Hell: *che non può trovar posa in su le piume, ma con dar volta suo dolore scherma.*

Its conservative qualities were weakened and its creative urge broken.

Pacifism is one of the most eloquent and characteristic symptoms of this second stage of our society. Pacifism is the result of a tendency to find an equilibrium, the need to preserve, to call a halt, to tidy up. It is the effort to provide society with the greatest possible stability and permanence. Capitalist society opposed competition in order to pursue durability. A search for durability and security is the predominant psychological force in the second stage of the bourgeois regime. Pacifism is the most authentic manifestation of society's lack of revolutionary spirit. But pacifism must not be merely understood as the sentimental Utopian attitude that preaches the need for peace as it might preach happiness or goodness, with a similar likelihood of success, but as something more comprehensive, a general reluctance of modern nationalities to settle the major conflicts of interests between peoples by recourse to tragic means. It is a related phenomenon and identical with the one which occurs within states themselves: this pacifism between states corresponds exactly to the pacifism within the state which we have already examined at length. The protectionist capitalist society reacts *pacifistically*, that is to say by an uneasy search for an equilibrium, both to the pressure of the class struggle as well as to the pressure of historical, economic and social conflicts between nations.

European history is the proof of this tendency, because after 1870 the century offers us nothing but states of equilibrium between the nations, pursued and maintained at the cost of sacrifices and compromises.

And as the relations between states became more complicated and interlinked, so the arguments in favour of peace and against war became stronger.

The history of international relations in Europe in the second half of the nineteenth century reveals a series of compromises between historical trends in order to maintain, by any means, a state of balance.

Thus a chain is formed: first of all, immediately after 1848, society deviates from its course, accepts protectionism and allows considerations based purely on monetary gain and speculation to take precedence over production. This predominance weakens the spirit of the bourgeoisie and their creative virtues. From this there arises a profound psychological disturbance, in the sense that society becomes progressively more pacifistic. Finally, pacifism brings the need to compromise on controversial issues by providing temporary solutions that leave the status quo intact, by disturbing the normal and more or less methodical development of business as little as possible.

This evolution of pacifistic factors in society was a universal phenomenon; only in Germany did it fail to take place. There, side by side with pacifistic tendencies, which did exist but whose development had been totally inhibited by the political constitution and power of the state, there was the ferment of a warlike attitude and a trend towards domination under the influence of Bismarck and the Prussian tradition.

The trend towards pacifism predominated in every other European country. We need only think of the limited importance achieved by the nationalistic parties in France, England and Italy. Everywhere they were minority factions whose action did not even scratch the surface of their countries' politics. So we must remember that the nationalist movement is an extremely recent one. It began about 1900 in France and about 1908 in Italy. In brief, it is a symptom of the opening up of a new historical horizon. It is not purely by chance that the nationalist and syndicalist movements make their appearance at the same time.

With this double reaction the world crisis begins. The revival of national ideologies and the profound changes in the attitude of the workers' movement brought about by syndicalism represent trends towards reform of the greatest significance, but both of them are phenomena which appear and take shape at the dawn of the twentieth century. The optimistic, pacifistic and reformist democratic processes were too far advanced and too widespread to be halted by these extreme tendencies, whether they aimed at creating a new bourgeoisie through asserting imperialistic ideas or attempted to give new heart to the struggle of the proletariat.

The decadence of society had gone too deep and had become too complex and organic to be stopped by ordinary means and by minority movements.

But it was also true that European society could not fall apart so simply, because in the deep recesses of the lives of nations there smoulder mysterious forces which at the appointed moment are fated to burst to the surface and to assume tragic forms, purifying and transforming society.

Contemporary society was heading for disorder, moral anarchy and paralysis.

War is a reaction against decomposition.* War is the major proof that society cannot decay and collapse because it contains something vague, indefinable and even mysterious which is like some new growth that sprouts from an old trunk and reasserts the everlasting quality of life.

When it seemed that modern society was about to crystallize into fixed forms, when the forces of rationalism and intellectualism, in their various forms of laws, state protectionism, balance and reason, were about to prevail and enclose the historical cycle of capitalism within strict and rigid lines, like a bolt from the blue there burst this unexpected war between nations which overthrew everything. It erupted to cause upheaval, confusion and destruction. Ideas, systems, prejudices and institutions instantly collapsed. The economy was transformed, everything that seemed stable was annihilated, and what seemed to have vanished re-emerged.

It was revolution.

This revolution is the outcome of and epilogue to a

* Some people might object that this opinion is difficult to prove and, to say the least, premature. That, in fact, society is proceeding in the same general direction as before the war and that we can observe moral, political and ideological aberrations similar to, if not worse than, the earlier ones.

Our reply is that war has forced society to accept a system of military and civil discipline hitherto unprecedented which, although it has not yet ended, is causing a marked transformation of our whole view of life as well as basic political and internal changes in the various states ...

century of events because it has enforced the solution of certain historical, ethical, social and psychological problems which have existed for a century and longer.

As in the finale of a Beethoven symphony, this war has taken up all the themes that had appeared on the historical scene in the past period of history and that had remained unresolved. It is the crisis of crises, the conclusion of every event that has been left pending; it exposes as lies what we had considered true for more than twenty years and as truths things that had seemed improbable.

This war has the closest, I would even say visible, links, political, ideological and historical, with the great revolution. Each one of us knows intuitively that at this moment, the epilogue to that great tragedy is being played out on its vast battlefields. None of us dares think or say what will happen tomorrow but we are all convinced that a profound, radical and unpredictable transformation is in store for us. Each one of us feels that millions upon millions of men cannot be dying without this savage hecatomb giving birth to a prodigious renewal.

It is a universal war, that is to say, one which not only involves every nation, every race, every regime and every force but draws on the deepest, most diverse and essential activities of the spirit. A war which has broken out like some devastating storm but which makes the humblest soldier and the most indifferent and sceptical of men feel that it cannot be merely destructive but that it must be constructive, not death but life. There is no smallest part of our world, no activity of our spirit, that has not been overturned, no belief left unshaken, no faith that has not been strengthened or destroyed.

Everything is being transformed in a bloody and legendary regeneration.

From Chapter VIII (*Syndicalism*)

As the main cause of the defeat of socialism lies in its having allowed itself to be won over to the optimistic ideas of democracy, we can see that the truth of syndicalism lies precisely in its longstanding opposition to democratic optimism and socialist materialism, and in its tireless advocacy of the importance of developing a proletarian consciousness which despises the sickly and corrupt democratic mentality of the bourgeoisie.

Today after these long years of war and suffering, we can appreciate the truth of the syndicalists' ideas on violence and the anti-demagogic attitude which the new school preached with such dogged perseverance.

The anti-parliamentary struggle of the groups of syndicalists in Italy and France is the most glorious manifestation of syndicalist activity and will perhaps give birth to further major developments in the immediate post-war future.

No part of the syndicalists' political and historical criticism was better grounded than their refusal to recognize any legitimacy, usefulness or even reality in the strictly electoral attitude of the bourgeoisie and the socialists, as a party. And this rigorous, absolute and uncompromising refusal by the syndicalists was justified, after the war, by the facts, whose consequences we shall see in the immediate post-war period.

The contribution that syndicalism will be called upon to make in the near future will probably be of capital importance.

The downfall of democratic ideology will have grave historical repercussions on the future adaptation of peoples to new conditions. It seems to us that there will be two general consequences:

(a) The need for a new ideology to satisfy the new society as it issues, red hot, from the war.

(b) A deep-rooted contradiction, difficult to resolve, between the fact that a form of society which is democratic in spirit seems likely to continue to exist, and the downfall of that democratic ideology which had arisen and developed in accordance with the formation and historical development of democratic regimes in the course of the eighteenth and nineteenth centuries.

There are two questions requiring discussion:

The crisis in democratic ideology is, as a result of the war, really widespread and all-embracing. If the war has upset the whole scale of values, all the calculations of the socialist pedagogues and all the hopes of the humanitarians, it is certain that this process of subversion has taken place almost entirely at the expense of democratic ideas. This is because the life of the various peoples was so deeply imbued with democratic ideas that the whole material machinery of existence was concretely linked with its premises. We also saw that such a conception had peace as its supreme ideal, the idea of ensuring that society should tend to be peaceful. Nor was this premise entirely erroneous; both because any mercantile society, since and inasmuch as it is mercantile, must logically tend to be and needs to be peaceful, and because the nineteenth century was historically a century which showed a marked diminution in warlike activity. It is also certain that a mercantile civilization finds war deeply disturbing and an almost insuperable obstacle to its existence.

This is why war would be an almost inexplicable phenomenon were one to consider its only cause to lie in the necessity of the various mercantile countries to compete with each other, or in any other purely economic motives.

From the beginning, democratic thinkers made the mistake of interpreting society rationalistically, and of imagining that henceforth nothing irrational could take place. They denied the possibility of war as the most irrational phenomenon in history, and consequently considered that it must disappear in a period dominated more than any previous one by reason.

Instead, society is in perpetual movement and is thus dominated above all by irrationalism, even when it does not seem so. For a variety of hidden and obscure reasons that we have partly considered, the nineteenth century was able to overcome the grandiose irrationality of socialism but could not stand up against the impetus of the historic forces that were to lead to the present war. The failure of socialism is closely linked in so many ways with the war primarily because both are irrational phenomena.

Unfortunately, democratic thinking had gone sour, had lost its critical faculties and, above all, was deaf and dumb to any serious concern with the future of society.

An almost mindless optimism reigned amongst democratic countries and governments regarding the outlook for the future.

When war broke out, the peoples of all nations (except, of course, those of the central imperial powers) were caught completely unprepared. The first emotion in face of the terrible event was one of surprise. The French Republic was totally unready; had Italy been obliged to go to war at once she would have been entirely lacking in resources; even England did not expect war. The lack of preparation was not only military and strategic, but, in addition and above all, psychological: at the beginning, the English, French and Italian peoples considered war as the incredible nightmare of a sleepless night. The fact that military unpreparedness coincided with a democratic regime is obvious and grave in the extreme.

What will happen tomorrow in the highly difficult and regrettable situation that is already looming on the horizon?

I have stated the reasons why I consider it unlikely that the present war will be decisive enough to permit a long period of peace and why on the contrary I consider that the years to come will continue to be marked by serious conflicts against Germanism which will once more spring forth in all its fury.* Faced by this visible impending danger, modern

* It is hardly necessary to observe that in speaking of 'future clashes', 'another war' and 'impossibility of a long peace', I do not mean that new wars will occur a few months or a few years from now. I mean that the international scene will be in unstable equilibrium, in a state of dynamic tension. Neither side will acknowledge that it has been so soundly defeated and conquered as to give up for ever all idea of battle. War will reappear: whether it reappears after two or after twenty years is of no importance. The lives of nations extend over centuries and the historian and politician have the duty to speak in terms of events occurring over the space of centuries.

society, while the war is still raging, is visibly being transformed and is adopting the psychological attitudes appropriate to the demands of the times.

Thus we shall in all probability witness *the formation of a new ideology suited to the historical situation and the particular needs of a new civilization.*

FILIPPO TOMMASO MARINETTI
(1876–1944)

Marinetti was born in Alexandria, the son of a rich Italian merchant. For all his nationalism, he was a highly cosmopolitan figure; he published his first poems in French, and the Futurist manifesto appeared for the first time in *Le Figaro*. Marinetti's energy, optimism and charm, allied to wealth, made him a great impresario; he spent his fortune on the movement he created.

Futurism was in the first place an artistic movement, but Marinetti's fantasy was all-embracing and like others of his generation he was fascinated by war and violence. A political element was therefore present in Futurism from the beginning. He was active in Irredentist demonstrations against Austria, and went to Tripoli in 1912 to report on the Libyan war. The First Balkan War gave him the occasion for his Futurist composition, *Zang Tumb Tumb*. In 1913 the Futurists published their first political programme, and in 1918 Marinetti founded a short-lived Futurist party, which was absorbed by the *Fasci di combattimento* of Mussolini. After standing as a Fascist candidate in the 1919 elections, however, Marinetti left the *fasci* in protest against their willingness to compromise with the Church and the monarchy. But in 1923 he made his peace with Mussolini and from then on he remained a faithful supporter of the regime. His Futurist principles did not prevent him from becoming a member of the new Academy created by Mussolini in 1929. In spite of his age, Marinetti volunteered for active service in the Second World War. In 1943 he adhered with enthusiasm to the Salò Republic.

THE FUTURIST MANIFESTO

We have been up all night, my friends and I, beneath mosque lamps whose brass cupolas are bright as our souls, because like them they were illuminated by the internal glow of electric hearts. And trampling underfoot our native sloth on opulent Persian carpets, we have been discussing right up to the limits of logic and scrawling the paper with demented writing.

Our hearts were filled with an immense pride at feeling ourselves standing quite alone, like lighthouses or like the sentinels in an outpost, facing the army of enemy stars encamped in their celestial bivouacs. Alone with the engineers in the infernal stokeholes of great ships, alone with the black spirits which rage in the belly of rogue locomotives, alone with the drunkards beating their wings against the walls.

Then we were suddenly distracted by the rumbling of huge double-decker trams that went leaping by, streaked with light like the villages celebrating their festivals, which the Po in flood suddenly knocks down and uproots, and, in the rapids and eddies of a deluge, drags down to the sea.

Then the silence increased. As we listened to the last faint prayer of the old canal and the crumbling of the bones of moribund palaces with their green growth of beard, suddenly the hungry automobiles roared beneath our windows.

'Come, my friends!' I said. 'Let us go! At last Mythology and the mystic cult of the ideal have been left behind. We are going to be present at the birth of the centaur and we shall soon see the first angels fly! We must break down the gates of life to test the bolts and the padlocks! Let us go! Here is the very first sunrise on earth! Nothing equals the splendour of its red sword which strikes for the first time in our millennial darkness.'

We went up to the snorting machines to caress their breasts. I lay along mine like a corpse on its bier, but I suddenly revived again beneath the steering wheel—a guillotine knife—which threatened my stomach. A great sweep of madness brought us sharply back to ourselves and drove us through the streets, steep and deep, like dried up torrents. Here and there unhappy lamps in the windows taught us to despise our mathematical eyes. 'Smell,' I exclaimed, 'smell is good enough for wild beasts!'

And we hunted, like young lions, death with its black fur dappled with pale crosses, who ran before us in the vast violet sky, palpable and living.

And yet we had no ideal Mistress stretching her form up to the clouds, nor yet a cruel Queen to whom to offer our corpses twisted into the shape of Byzantine rings! No reason to die unless it is the desire to be rid of the too great weight of our courage!

We drove on, crushing beneath our burning wheels, like shirt-collars under the iron, the watch dogs on the steps of the houses.

Death, tamed, went in front of me at each corner offering me his hand nicely, and sometimes lay on the ground with a noise of creaking jaws giving me velvet glances from the bottom of puddles.

'Let us leave good sense behind like a hideous husk and let us hurl ourselves, like truit spiced with pride, into the immense mouth and breast of the wind! Let us feed the unknown, not from despair, but simply to enrich the unfathomable reservoirs of the Absurd!'

As soon as I had said these words, I turned sharply back on my tracks with the mad intoxication of puppies biting their tails, and suddenly there were two cyclists disapproving of me and tottering in front of me like two persuasive but contradictory reasons. Their stupid swaying got in my way. What a bore! Pouah! I stopped short, and in disgust I hurled myself—vlan!—head over heels in a ditch.

Oh, maternal ditch, half full of muddy water! A factory

gutter! I savoured a mouthful of strengthening muck which recalled the black teat of my Sudanese nurse!

As I raised my body, mud-spattered and smelly, I felt the red-hot poker of joy deliciously pierce my heart. A crowd of fishermen and gouty naturalists crowded terrified around this marvel. With patient and tentative care they raised high enormous grappling irons to fish up my car, like a vast shark that had run aground. It rose slowly leaving in the ditch, like scales, its heavy coachwork of good sense and its upholstery of comfort.

We thought it was dead, my good shark, but I woke it with a single caress of its powerful back, and it was revived, running as fast as it could on its fins.

Then with my face covered in good factory mud, covered with metal scratches, useless sweat and celestial grime, amidst the complaint of the staid fishermen and the angry naturalists, we dictated our first will and testament to all the *living* men on earth.

Manifesto of Futurism

1. We want to sing the love of danger, the habit of energy and rashness.

2. The essential elements of our poetry will be courage, audacity and revolt.

3. Literature has up to now magnified pensive immobility, ecstasy and slumber. We want to exalt movements of aggression, feverish sleeplessness, the double march, the perilous leap, the slap and the blow with the fist.

4. We declare that the splendour of the world has been enriched by a new beauty: the beauty of speed. A racing automobile with its bonnet adorned with great tubes like serpents with explosive breath ... a roaring motor car which seems to run on machine-gun fire, is more beautiful than the Victory of Samothrace.

5. We want to sing the man at the wheel, the ideal axis of which crosses the earth, itself hurled along its orbit.

6. The poet must spend himself with warmth, glamour

and prodigality to increase the enthusiastic fervour of the primordial elements.

7. Beauty exists only in struggle. There is no masterpiece that has not an aggressive character. Poetry must be a violent assault on the forces of the unknown, to force them to bow before man.

8. We are on the extreme promontory of the centuries! What is the use of looking behind at the moment when we must open the mysterious shutters of the impossible? Time and Space died yesterday. We are already living in the absolute, since we have already created eternal, omnipresent speed.

9. We want to glorify war—the only cure for the world—militarism, patriotism, the destructive gesture of the anarchists, the beautiful ideas which kill, and contempt for woman.

10. We want to demolish museums and libraries, fight morality, feminism and all opportunist and utilitarian cowardice.

11. We will sing of great crowds agitated by work, pleasure and revolt; the multi-coloured and polyphonic surf of revolutions in modern capitals: the nocturnal vibration of the arsenals and the workshops beneath their violent electric moons: the gluttonous railway stations devouring smoking serpents; factories suspended from the clouds by the thread of their smoke; bridges with the leap of gymnasts flung across the diabolic cutlery of sunny rivers: adventurous steamers sniffing the horizon; great-breasted locomotives, puffing on the rails like enormous steel horses with long tubes for bridles, and the gliding flight of aeroplanes whose propellers sound like the flapping of a flag and the applause of enthusiastic crowds.

It is in Italy that we are issuing this manifesto of ruinous and incendiary violence, by which we today are founding Futurism, because we want to deliver Italy from its gangrene of professors, archaeologists, tourist guides and antiquaries.

Italy has been too long the great second-hand market. We want to get rid of the innumerable museums which cover it with innumerable cemeteries.

Museums, cemeteries! Truly identical in their sinister juxtaposition of bodies that do not know each other. Public dormitories where you sleep side by side for ever with beings you hate or do not know. Reciprocal ferocity of the painters and sculptors who murder each other in the same museum with blows of line and colour. To make a visit once a year, as one goes to see the graves of our dead once a year, that we could allow! We can even imagine placing flowers once a year at the feet of the Gioconda! But to take our sadness, our fragile courage and our anxiety to the museum every day, that we cannot admit! Do you want to poison yourselves? Do you want to rot?

What can you find in an old picture except the painful contortions of the artist trying to break uncrossable barriers which obstruct the full expression of his dream?

To admire an old picture is to pour our sensibility into a funeral urn instead of casting it forward with violent spurts of creation and action. Do you want to waste the best part of your strength in a useless admiration of the past, from which you will emerge exhausted, diminished, trampled on?

Indeed, daily visits to museums, libraries and academies (those cemeteries of wasted effort, calvaries of crucified dreams, registers of false starts!) is for artists what prolonged supervision by the parents is for intelligent young men, drunk with their own talent and ambition.

For the dying, for invalids and for prisoners it may be all right. It is, perhaps, some sort of balm for their wounds, the admirable past, at a moment when the future is denied them. But we will have none of it, we, the young, strong and living Futurists!

Let the good incendiaries with charred fingers come! Here they are! Heap up the fire to the shelves of the libraries! Divert the canals to flood the cellars of the museums! Let the glorious canvases swim ashore! Take the picks and hammers! Undermine the foundation of venerable towns!

The oldest among us are not yet thirty years old: we have therefore at least ten years to accomplish our task. When we are forty let younger and stronger men than we throw us in the wastepaper-basket like useless manuscripts! They will come against us from afar, leaping on the light cadence of their first poems, clutching the air with their predatory fingers and sniffing at the gates of the academies the good scent of our decaying spirits, already promised to the catacombs of the libraries.

But we shall not be there. They will find us at last one winter's night in the depths of the country in a sad hangar echoing with the notes of the monotonous rain, crouched near our trembling aeroplanes, warming our hands at the wretched fire which our books of today will make when they flame gaily beneath the glittering flight of their pictures.

They will crowd around us, panting with anguish and disappointment, and exasperated by our proud indefatigable courage, will hurl themselves forward to kill us, with all the more hatred as their hearts will be drunk with love and admiration for us. And strong healthy Injustice will shine radiantly from their eyes. For art can only be violence, cruelty and injustice.

The oldest among us are not yet thirty, and yet we have already wasted treasures, treasures of strength, love, courage and keen will, hastily, deliriously, without thinking, with all our might, till we are out of breath.

Look at us! We are not out of breath, our hearts are not in the least tired. For they are nourished by fire, hatred and speed! Does this surprise you? It is because you do not even remember having been alive! Standing on the world's summit, we launch once more our challenge to the stars!

Your objections? All right! I know them! Of course! We know just what our beautiful false intelligence affirms: 'We are only the sum and the prolongation of our ancestors,' it says. Perhaps! All right! What does it matter? But we will not listen! Take care not to repeat those infamous words! Instead, lift up your head!

Standing on the world's summit we launch once again our insolent challenge to the stars!

'OLD IDEAS WHICH ALWAYS GO HAND IN HAND AND MUST BE SEPARATED'

(From the newspaper *L'Ardito*, March 1919)

Up till now, politics have always subsisted on platitudes, or rather on ideas that went along stupidly hand-in-hand, joined in a fictitious relationship that, in fact, doesn't exist.

When someone says 'monarchy', we at once think of an army, war, the fatherland and patriotism. Nor is this unreasonable. But it's absurd, when we speak, for example, of an enthusiastic army, to be forced to think of a reactionary monarchy.

When you speak of nationalism, you immediately think of conservatism, a system of greedy imperialism, reactionary traditionalism, repressive police, militarism, a hereditary aristocracy, clericalism.

Associations of ideas that must be forcibly broken.

When you speak of democracy, you immediately think of the lack of any warlike spirit, humanitarianism, pacifism, pietism, quietism, abnegation, anti-colonialism, humility, internationalism, lack of racial pride and rejection of any idea of race.

Associations of ideas that must be forcibly broken.

When you speak of a healthy outdoor upbringing, dash, guts, boldness, physical strength, a mania for setting up records, you immediately think of an imperialist or clerical monarchy.

Associations of ideas that must be forcibly broken.

When you talk of justice, equality, freedom, the rights of the proletariat, of the peasants and of the under-privileged, the struggle against parasites, you immediately think of anti-patriotism, international pacifism, Marxism and collectivism.

Associations of ideas that must be forcibly broken.

The force of these platitudes which have been so absurdly joined together for ages was shown by the fact that one sentence of the first Futurist Manifesto published eleven years ago, glorifying both patriotism *and* the destructive action of lovers of freedom, seemed crazy or merely a joke to the political thinking of the time.

Everyone thought it was either absurd or ridiculous to associate for the first time the idea of freedom with that of the fatherland. Why wasn't the word patriotism accompanied this time by its good friend, reactionary and orderly monarchy?

Why was the idea of the destructive action of lovers of freedom not accompanied this time by its inseparable companion, anti-patriotism?

A vast bewilderment clouded the brains of the so-called 'political thinkers', fed on platitudes and ideologies culled from books and completely incapable of interpreting life, race, the masses or individuals.

But their bewilderment grew to giant proportions when, in the glorious month of May 1915, they suddenly saw that strange couple, the 'destructive action of lovers of freedom' and 'patriotism' once again making its turbulent appearance in the streets of Milan and Rome, under new names such as Mussolini, Corridoni, Corradini and Marinetti, all chanting, 'War or Revolution'.

And now today we can separate the idea of fatherland from that of clerical, imperialistic monarchy. We can join together the idea of the fatherland and bold progress, revolutionary democracy which rejects the police state.

But we must forcibly break up an idiotic association that is far more serious, those two ideas that go hand in hand in many Italian and other European papers nowadays: the League of Nations, and the appeasement of the desire for revenge of the defeated countries.

And that other pair of ideas: concessions to uncivilized and inferior nations, and the maintenance of peace.

Associations of ideas that must be broken.

In order to maintain the strength of the Entente during the immense conflagration, it was necessary to combine the idea of war with the idea of a victory in which there would be neither winners nor losers.

Vague thoughts of a compromise peace went hand in hand with the ferocious struggle to overthrow the enemy.

What hope could there be that, once this enemy was overthrown, he could be pacified without his harbouring a wild urge for revenge?

The idea of total victory was strangely combined with the thought of a Germany happy at being soundly thrashed. And the idea of a victorious Entente was strangely combined with the idea of an Entente almost mortified at the thought of having won.

Those who contradict us call it a swindle and even a European swindle. 'What?' they shout. 'So this conflagration won't bring us permanent peace? Quick, at all costs, let's set up the League of Nations to prevent the possibility of another war!' In their League of Nations, sitting round one single peace table, you would need to accommodate the winners, who had been attacked and had not wanted the war, the losers, countries which had unscrupulously plotted the war for their own gain, the neutrals who had pusillanimously remained on the side-lines, those newly created countries that are viable and those that are weak, together with a few countries which are decrepit and rotten to the core.

But it would also require every country to leave all its typical characteristics at the door of the conference room: the legitimate pride of the conqueror, the legitimate desire for revenge of the conquered, the healthy appetite of the flourishing newly created country, the deceit and stubbornness of the decrepit old ones and so on.

Ideologies are created, dominated and formed by life. Every political idea is a living organism. Political parties are almost always doomed to turn into splendid corpses.

The parties with a great past are the ones which now lack vitality. This is a Futurist law. Today, the republicans are reduced to an impotent doctrinaire attitude that is content to invoke the ghost of Mazzini. In fact Mazzini is as living as Cavour, whereas Cappa and Comandini[1] are dead, just as Salandra is dead.

Starting from these Futurist ideas of ours, the Futurist Volt[2] proves in detail how no tradition can be invoked nowadays, as this tradition is completely anti-national:

'Our great victory is an entirely *new* fact in the history of Italy. Faced by the monumental idiocy of the "sedulous apes" who clutter up the newspaper columns with suggestions for triumphal arches, Vendôme columns, eagles and carnival-style trophies dreamt up by archaeologists, it is important for us, today more than ever before, to repeat again and again that Italy's greatness has nothing to do with the greatness of earlier times. *We owe nothing to the past.* Alone amongst the European powers, Italy is a nation lacking national traditions. On the other hand, Italy is full of regional traditions that are a-national and even anti-national. Let us examine these unhappy traditions as seen in the various classes and social strata of Italian society:

'1. *Army.* This is too delicate a matter to be discussed today.

'2. *Clergy.* It may be disputed whether it is appropriate to rekindle the dissension between Church and state but this dissension in any case exists, at least covertly, and it is futile to deny it. The reason for this dissension lies, in fact, in the anti-national traditions that live on so vigorously in the organism of the Italian Church. It does contain some patriots, and it is to be hoped that they will increase, but to traditional clericalism they represent a revolutionary force.

'3. *Aristocracy.* The sons of the Italian aristocracy discharged their duty on the field of battle *to exactly the same extent* as did the sons of the people or the bourgeoisie, but, as a whole, it cannot be said that the aristocracy has taken the lead in our national war. From the unmannerly disparagement of some "priests' sons" to the suave obstructionism of

[1] Leaders of the Republican Party.

[2] Pseudonym of V. Fani Ciotti.

the aristocratic admirers of the demagogue of Dronero,[1] neutralism has made great inroads in the nobility. This comes from the absence of national traditions in the family trees of the most ancient Italian families. These traditions could not exist for the simple reason that as a united state, Italy has no past at all. For good or evil, we are a nation of *parvenus*. So those of the Italian aristocracy who have come over to the new regime, through their enthusiastic participation in our last war of independence, have had, for that very reason, to foreswear the Bourbon and pro-Austrian ghosts of their ancestors. And they have come to life.

'4. *Bourgeoisie*. What constitutes the chief claim to fame of the new ruling class of the bourgeoisie is the productive power of its work. But our recent flourishing industry and commerce is not in any way linked to the past. Italian industry has modelled itself on the example of foreign industry; no trace of the commercial activity of the medieval communes or of the glorious maritime republics now remains.

'The only traditional element remaining in our economic life is a negative one, a burden, a ball of lead tied to our feet. Hatred of change, routine, sedentary habits, horror of technical innovation, lack of initiative, fear of taking risks, petty-mindedness, being content to earn little with minimum effort: such are the things which Italian industry and commerce have inherited from our "great past". And it is the force of tradition that makes the peasant refuse to use the new industrial machines, the banker afraid to lend money to new industries and the industrialist reluctant to enlarge his field of operations. Anything of value that has been accomplished in the economic field has been a slap in the face for the so-called "sacred memories". Italy cannot become a great economic power unless she succeeds in ridding herself completely of her traditions.

'5. *Proletariat*. In most people's minds, popular defeatism is closely associated with the idea of revolution. Nothing is

[1] Giolitti.

more untrue. Defeatism is merely the product of ten centuries of national bondage. Amongst the Italian populace, especially in the country, there is an age-old anti-government, anti-militarist and anti-national tradition pre-dating socialism and which socialism merely exploited skilfully, as with the religious political movement of the *Sanfedisti* at the time, not very long ago, of the "war on brigandage".

'The spirit behind certain "leagues" in Romagna is substantially the same as that found in the Sicilian Mafia and the *Camorra* in Naples. Socialism has merely stuck its red label on a piece of damaged old goods. In any case, you only have to listen to certain miserable old defeatist songs that have somehow sprung up amongst the dregs of the people to realize that nothing new or daring, no revolutionary idealism, exists in such a state of mind.

'It is the state of mind of a primitive man, savage and full of fear, for whom the modern state merely represents the recruiting board and the extorter of taxes, a Moloch devouring men and property; he is the original brute beast, tied like a mole to his own wretched hole, torn by war from his domestic worries and the difficulties of his daily job and cast into a world of danger and adventure, an unknown world which will renew his spirit and make a man of him despite himself. The dull stubborn weight of tradition fights against this power of war, this real, great, spiritual revolution of the Italian people. The choice is ours! War has posed a dilemma between the past and the future. On the one hand, all the anti-national forces of the past grouped under the ambiguous banner of neutralism; on the other, Italy. The good grain and the tares which must be burnt. Life against death. Being Futurist means opting for life. The fight against parasitism is the fight against an anti-national tradition that is deeply rooted in the past. Because in Italy tradition is synonymous with defeat.'

CURZIO MALAPARTE
(1898–1957)

Malaparte, whose real name was Kurt Eric Suckert, was the son of an immigrant German technician. He is the only one of the writers included here who belonged to the generation of *squadrismo*, i.e. of those who were in their teens or early twenties at the end of the war. A romantic, cynical adventurer, rebellious but opportunist, a sophisticated admirer of simple brutality, Malaparte was in many ways the Fascist intellectual *par excellence*. In 1924–5 he became a spokesman for the extremist wing of the party. Later his unorthodoxy and irreverent malice earned him a short spell of confinement. His greatest success as a writer came after the Second World War, with his novels *Kaputt* (1944) and *La pelle* (1949).

Malaparte's ideological writings mirror the confusions of Fascism itself. He attempts to reconcile the activist and elitist philosophy of syndicalism with a reactionary regionalist populism. Malaparte followed the Garibaldian tradition in complaining of the passivity of the masses vis-à-vis the national cause, and yet he regards their resistance to the 'foreign' ideals of liberalism with sympathy. However, by separating the liberalism of the Risorgimento from nationalism, the contradiction could be overcome in appearance. The task of Malaparte's 'national revolution' was to educate the people to a sense of heroism and the necessity of suffering. The people themselves were incapable of achieving this: they had to be led and indeed driven. The 'national revolution' therefore had to be imposed from above, by Mussolini, the man who had lived through and finally rejected the experience of 'modernity', aided by 'an aristocracy of workers and intellectuals'.

The aims of Malaparte's 'national revolution' remained

for the most part obscure. The essential and characteristic idea or myth which he followed was that of the regeneration of the governing class through the absorption of new, combative, popular forces. However, Malaparte was also a sensationalist who craved for action; his romantic dynamism gave him a fascination for the destructive processes of revolution, not for its results.

MUSSOLINI AND NATIONAL SYNDICALISM

I

Mussolini is not a representative man but he reacts to the spirit of his times. He stands outside our race and he is not of our times. He does not belong to our national 'morality'. He is a proof of what our people can be but have not yet become. Like all our traditional heroes, Mussolini is physically and historically inimical to the Italians of our time. Did we not know that he was born at Predappio, had we no knowledge of his life, when and where he suffered and fought and dared, we should be unable to decide on his origins or his ancestry. He belongs to no climate or season. Like all our traditional heroes, he is different from the rest of the Italians, he is different from us. His 'morality' almost appears to be the fruit of a different historical climate. He seems to have been born in a hard and ungrateful land, harsh and dry, where, before learning to dominate man, men have learnt to dominate nature. His force is a specifically natural phenomenon, entirely physical, instinctive and human; his strength lies in his will-power, his tenacity and his harshness. Like every hero, he contains something primitive, simple and elemental, he is natural in the way that innocent and implacable tyrants are natural. His justice is of the body, not of the mind. Nevertheless, he is beyond all doubt a stoic.

If Mussolini were a 'representative man', which amounts to saying a mediocrity, had he really personified the spirit of the people and the times, he would certainly not have been able to organize and carry out the October revolution. Had he been an Italian like all the rest, he would not have been a revolutionary in what I would call the physical sense of the word. He would have submitted like everyone else to the humiliating mediocrity of our nation. He would have accepted everything, even the feeling of being an ordinary Italian: a hidden drama which few people experience. Nor must we think that his revolt against this spiritual mediocrity, against the normal sluggishness of our blood, against the historical climate of Italy today, took place without conflict. There is a tragic period in Mussolini's life of which he prefers not to speak in order not to relive his sufferings. I am speaking of the time when he realized that he had betrayed his own nature, that he had now become an Italian, an ordinary Italian, an Italian like all the rest; and he rebelled.

His true nature as a tyrant, opposed by physical and historical law to the ordinary nature of his fellow countrymen, was first revealed by his own extremely personal revolt in 1919.

From that first moment of his instinctive and unexpected revolt against the ordinary spirit of the nation, against the pretexts and opportunism which were the only things that Italians, rich and poor, understood by fate, Mussolini's historical function has been to give back to the nation the physical sense of heroism. The achievement of his revolution consists in this and this alone, not in any reversal of political values, the conquest of power or the submission of the masses or his patrons.

This was his second labour. As a modern hero, sick with unrest and bowed down with certain convictions, urged on more by the force of his natural qualities than by the course of events or the suasions of chance, continually oppressed by that obscure fear of time that is a sure sign of humanity in heroes, Mussolini found the justification for our final decadence in himself and his own fortunes and restless conscience. He suffered within himself the whole drama which is the age-old history of his people. He found within himself, in the restlessness and unhappiness of his own modernity, the reasons for our own irremediable antiquity: an heroic discovery. In his revolt and in his attack against us, taking his revenge on us by a tradition which we ourselves had forgotten and betrayed, he granted us the chance to suffer the deeply Christian experience of our 'rebirth'. He made manifest to us the law. Who would dare, as Sorel did, to compare him to one of our sixteenth-century *condottieri*? He is more like a man who has brought us back to Catholic law, a man of the Counter-Reformation, a soldier and a prophet, a knight and a martyr; an enemy of the modern Italy corrupted and fragmented by the heretical spirit of the Reformation; a restorer of authority, faith, dogma and heroism against the sceptical, critical, nationalistic and enlightened spirit of Western and Northern Europe; a defender of our instinctive and traditional liberty, rooted in history, and of our sense of hierarchy in nature, philosophy and public life, against those ultimate political forms of the Reformation, liberalism, democracy and socialism; an enemy of modern civilization, unsuited to our attitudes and irreconcilable with our legitimate traditions, and of present-day Italy, debased by her acceptance and assimilation of European ideas. He is rather the initiator of the revolt, already manifest, of the spirit of Italy which has always remained naturally ancient, despite pollution and compromise, against the modern Western, Nordic spirit; the initiator of the Italian revolution, an anti-modern, that is to say, an anti-European revolution. A Counter-Reformation.

He will need to be just and merciless towards us; at home he must show no respect or pity for those around him; he must be anti-bourgeois, anti-proletarian, anti-liberal, anti-European, anti-modern; and must not fear to make war on those of his own blood, before showing no mercy towards those outside. His war against us, and this revolt of his against our ordinary national attitudes which has been pursuing its course since March 1919, these are the elements of his inevitable function in Europe.

II

As a nation, we Italians have until recently shown ourselves unsuited to large-scale collective undertakings such as wars and revolutions. I should not have said 'unsuited' but 'averse to', because this has been the result of our instinctive dislike for facing and accepting collective suffering. Not indeed for lack of a sense of race or nation (which in Latin are one and the same thing) but because of our natural fear of suffering ...

... All revolutions spring from an heroic and pessimistic conception of life; they are the political fruit of a natural tendency towards desperation, we would almost be tempted to say, the political result of a natural desperation. The epicureanism of the Italians makes them physically unsuited to the revolutionary state of desperation. The happy events in the life of our nation have always been anti-revolutionary and the unfortunate ones always revolutionary. The Risorgimento was born at Novara; and Lissa, Custoza and Mentana did more to help than San Martino and Calatafimi, if we are to understand the Risorgimento as what it was, that is to say, as a revolution. The breach in the Porta Pia was, as everyone can see, a most happy event but an anti-revolutionary one, because far from completing the Italian revolution which had cost so much in blood and suffering for exactly fifty years it interrupted it. Socialism, depressing, anti-national and anti-revolutionary, entered through the breach in the Porta Pia. Similarly, everyone can see that the national revolutionary spirit of our people was reborn at Caporetto (here we are repeating an idea that is close to our heart, albeit painfully close and of ill repute), and that we won at Vittorio Veneto only because we had experienced the calvary of Caporetto.

Suffering is inseparable from life. The price of fame and freedom is blood, and suffering is needed to live proudly and with dignity in the midst of proud people. Anyone who fails to grasp this basic truth of human life is condemning himself to live like an animal. Anyone who teaches that suffering is hateful or preaches the law of paradise and not the law of hell is denying man's greatness, that is, everything that makes him human. An epicurean, paradise-loving mankind is anti-Christian and anti-human. Yet Dante left our impatient race of epicureans in order to accomplish his journey in the other world, and taught us that you must pass through pain and hell to reach heaven. But when the early socialists came dangling before our eyes the keys of their pragmatic Red heaven, our people had by then forgotten the value and meaning of myths and experience. With heads downcast, they followed those who preached the revolutionary necessity of sensual enjoyment, of indifference, of placid avoidance of suffering, those who preached that wine not blood was needed for revolutions: what depths of slavery! Hatred of the fatherland became hatred of the duty that it is incumbent on nations and societies to suffer. Pain is suffering love. Italy, like every other fatherland, demands blood and tears from him who would be worthy of it. Today, being Italian means having suffered; today as always. But perhaps (this is the meaning of the doctrine of socialism) it is better to renounce our natural qualities as Italians than to have to suffer.

We are Italians, not philanthropists; and as Fascists and syndicalists, that is to say, deeply revolutionary, we are anti-democratic because we are anti-humanitarian. The steadfast aversion to socialism felt by syndicalism in the first place and Fascism in the second springs from the physical, historical and political truth that suffering is a national and social duty and necessity. All revolutions are born out of suffering universally experienced and accepted. The religion of revolution is a religion of pain. Everyone knows what was and is the religion of socialism.

Anyone wishing to consider, as we are doing, the history of these last few years by taking into account the ethical experiences of socialism would see the fate that would have overtaken our people had the Italians not taught them the revolutionary function of suffering.

What would they not have done, to what depths would they not have sunk, rather than cause trouble on the threshing-floor or in the warehouse, in the shop or in the taverns, this people of ours, tough and splendid, in their work as in their leisure, in their grandeur or their wretchedness. And yet, once unleashed and forcibly compelled to risk their bellies and their food, they are capable of sacrifices and heroism unknown to peoples less accustomed to suffering. They would sooner have shut themselves up in a cellar rather than accomplish what is called a revolution, even after singing its praises and greeting it with 'The Red Flag'. We have seen all this recently. Revolt, confusion, trouble, these are frankly Italian words which form part of a whole tradition of *carrocci*[1] and sacked bakeries, Easter massacres[2] and Sicilian Vespers, of Republics in Romagna and chickens at sixpence a brace; but 'revolution' is a barbarous word, it looks well scrawled on walls but it is unpleasant when it may force you into the streets to set up barricades.

How happy we should feel, those of us who point out and prove the need for suffering, if we could simply indulge in irony or sarcasm and not be carried away by anger! But we are bitter and furious because we sincerely love this people of ours whom we have seen tearing at barbed wire entanglements with their bare hands or hurling themselves almost unarmed against machine-guns in the Dolomites or in the mud of the Carso. We love them with a love that is almost savage because we have seen proof that they would be capable of anything if they wished and proof of what they could become if they decided to stop squabbling about questions of grub or village politics and to face up unflinchingly to the problems that make them such an historic nation.

But here we must refrain from recalling the heroism of those four glorious years of martyrdom in order not to have to reveal the taste of sorrow and blood concealed beneath our words (what a people that could burn your victorious standards as you came back from Vittorio Veneto!), and in order not to make you think that our reproaches, too, spring from idiotic whimsy and impotent caprice, a nostalgic longing for grandeur, or because we are spoiling for a fight.

[1] Cars bearing the standards of the army of the Italian communes.

[2] Of French invaders in Verona at the end of the eighteenth century.

No! We do not want to indulge in regrets because we have a fierce and total belief in the national and social value of suffering which one day or other will inevitably drag the Italians out of their warm beds, their cafés, their shops, their political committees and municipal academies and drive them perforce towards their destiny, which most people call the future, and which history, steeped in blood, teaches us to call shame and denial of the past and of the present.

Our people must suffer, we must suffer; only deep and atrocious suffering, experienced by all, like that caused by famine, plague or civil war, can transform us from being parochial and gluttonous into a magnificent imperial people.

III

At the outbreak of the European war, the newly-fledged Italian syndicalist movement found itself unexpectedly having to fight two bodies that had momentarily joined forces: socialism, terribly afraid of war because of the bloodshed and sacrifices it demands; the bourgeoisie, which saw the tragedy as the beginning of the revolution which it wanted at all costs to avoid in order not to suffer the damage of a reversal of values. The socialists and bourgeois, actuated by the philistine spirit of Bourbonism which in forty years' domination of the political scene had smothered the national revolution that liberal democracy in Rome had already brought to a standstill in '70, were trying to gain the upper hand over the national revolutionary minority of syndicalists and republicans who in the name of Mazzini were sounding the old revolutionary tocsin of the communes against the foreigner.

The Red rabble was against the war, as always; they didn't want to suffer or put their blissful Saturday evenings at risk. As always they were against revolution: they were following their instincts or, more exactly, obeying the traditions of the house. For the last ten centuries they had never felt the physical need for a war, that is to say, for a revolution against the foreigner. They had had no share in the enthusiasm or suffering of the revolutions of '21, '34, '48, '59 or '60. Italy had come into being without their help, even against their wish; she had represented the magnificent enemy, the mother who was asking for all to forgive her for the sins of her son. The people had shed no tears or blood, or even been in despair for Italy, so powerful yet so frail, who was now at last calling on them to avenge themselves in her name. Who had ever spoken to our people of martyrdom or sacrifice or war? No one except, on one occasion, the bourgeoisie in 1848. But the memory of bloodshed had dried up; it had turned into a cause of hatred and shame, not of love or pride. After forty years of anti-revolutionary international socialism, the revolutionary bourgeoisie of the Risorgimento now seemed to be the enemy of the people inasmuch as the very idea of 'nation' was not a plebeian but a bourgeois one. The Red *canaille* hated the social class of the revolutionary bourgeoisie because historically and politically it represented essentially a national class. Class hatred, as we have already said, thus came to be justified as hatred of the idea of nation. The naturally anti-patriotic political attitude of our people is a legitimate, albeit insufficient, justification for the class struggle.

The Bourbon middle classes were—and were bound to be—allied with the plebs against war: in this way they were avenging themselves on the Risorgimento and showing their real historical and political *raison d'être*. As a class based on the state they could not fail to be suspicious of any recurrence of revolution. As early as 1914 they were able to foresee what has happened since; that is to say, their own decline in importance as a result of the inevitable diminution in their role in the state brought about by the war. All the same, this sort of alliance between the plebs and the bourgeoisie against revolution is not new nor should it arouse any particular surprise in someone who has studied the story of our past and can see its justification.

Since the second half of the eighteenth century, Italy has

known no other forms of government but those based on this sort of alliance. In recent times, it was Bourbon; this did not so much allow the maintenance of tyranny, as was perhaps intended, as the maintenance of a state of slavery. We have often been short of tyrants but we have never lacked slaves. Although this is ostensibly a justification of the unhappy plight of our society, it is primarily a pretext to protect our national pride which has always blamed tyranny, even non-existent tyranny, for all those unavoidable and necessary forms of slavery which we have not had sufficient willingness or ability to bear.

Thus at the beginning of the European war, the myth of syndicalist violence proved that it was part of the natural tradition of our history.

The particular nature of this violence revealed itself in its most historic form in so-called interventionism: 1821, 1914. For the syndicalists, war was felt to be necessary because it was a revolutionary necessity. Whereas the socialists saw the European war as anti-proletarian, brought about by economic causes, and the natural result of capitalism, the syndicalists saw it as anti-bourgeois, the result of history and the legitimate product of the revolutionary will of the proletariat, which it considered, as we said, as a class not in the economic and social sense but in the historical and national sense.

There are still many of us who do not understand that the people were anti-war not out of loyalty to the International or through pity, feelings which the Italians instinctively consider unnatural and barbarous, but because from earliest times they have lacked revolutionary qualities and have a very strong fear of suffering. The people were anti-war because they were anti-revolutionary. In this prologue to tragedy, a sort of curtain-raiser, socialism was merely a pretext for antagonism and served primarily as a justification for the chance which was being offered.

If we try to think of neutralism as a social phenomenon, a

Marxist form of class struggle, we are revealing our failure to understand the peculiar significance of our transference of the concept of class from the economic and social sphere into the historical and national one. Because interventionism is not, as many people think, to be contrasted with neutralism, as a bourgeois social phenomenon in contrast to a proletarian one: the struggle was between the old anti-revolutionary conception of the proletariat and the new syndicalist conception which saw the proletariat as taking over and continuing the revolutionary function of the bourgeoisie of 1821, degraded since 1870 by liberal democracy and socialism. The confrontation, as always, was between the two enemies: the Bourbon anti-revolutionary plebs and bourgeoisie against the national revolutionary plebs and bourgeoisie. The reason for certain alliances does not change with the times; this is a law based on painful facts of experience, especially for us Italians.

For the syndicalists, the proletariat should have had and has had the task of restoring, in Sorel's words, *quelque chose de son énergie* to the bourgeoisie, and of continuing the national revolution interrupted by '70. The transference of the concept of class from the economic and social to the historical and national sphere—to which we have referred several times already since it seems to us of fundamental importance—took place in the period between August 1914 and May 1915. The outward signs of that hidden transformation often appeared diverse and contradictory. But anyone analysing and measuring it at that time with the help of our new indigenous historical conception of Sorelian syndicalism would not have allowed himself to be deceived by the rhetoric and theatricality of events and acts; he would have recognized them for what they were, that is to say, as signs of the new and profound division of our people into two single antagonistic classes: the one national and revolutionary, seeking its justification in the history of the period stretching from 1821 to 1870, the other anti-national and anti-revolutionary, seeking justification in the degrading negative attitude of that most unfortunate period which stretches from 1870 to 1914.

As we have succeeded in demonstrating up till now, interventionism and neutralism appear logically to be what they in fact are, contingent aspects of the class struggle in the historical and national sense. The old division into classes, bourgeoisie and proletariat, in the economic and social sense seems, in fact, once again inadequate to explain our affairs. But rather than emphasize concepts that we have already expounded and in order not to burden our argument with too much detail we are anxious above all to show the part played by the revolutionary violence of national syndicalism in bringing about and developing the phenomenon of interventionism.

We are proud to be one of those who in 1914 lived through an historical revolutionary experience similar to the national martyrdom of 1821.

During the period of neutrality when we loudly proclaimed the revolutionary necessity of war in the streets and market-places, like voices crying in the wilderness, we realized that we were not initiating but continuing a splendid tradition of struggle and sacrifice. Our will ran counter to the spirit of the times: but we felt that the reasons for our strong feelings were based on race and history, that they were rooted in the physical laws of our historical and political world and would in themselves have justified the future greatness of our people. In contrast to what seemed the attitude of the majority of Italians, who were in favour of Italy's participation in a European war for rhetorical reasons, we completely spurned the rhetorical approach. Our justification went back no further than the beginnings of the last century; its traditions were not very old. Instinctively hostile as we were and still are to any motives based on nostalgia, we had no need to seek any justification or pretexts in the French Revolution. We were following our own instincts rather than obeying any reasons offered by the history of other peoples.

The market-place and the vociferous mob, the brawls and vicious partisan feelings provided the setting and personae of our national drama, age-old but still new. For us, Austria was a pretext for revolution and she represented only a part of our extraordinary hatred and our overflowing love. The motive behind the riots and anger, the disputes and disturbances which drove us out into the market-place during this period of neutrality, in opposition to the supporters of a conservative peace, was deeply revolutionary; for us it was not just a question of bringing Italy into the war but of starting the national revolution where it legitimately belonged, in the streets, from house to house, and then keeping it active by changing it into war against Austria. Amongst the neutralists, we saw not only supporters of a policy of peace and democracy but supporters of conservatism and the old order, and, as always, they were anti-national.

If one wants to view interventionism not merely in relation to the spirit and historical situation existing in 1914 but to the spirit and historical situation as it existed in 1821, one will see its revolutionary nature and how, as a physical historical phenomenon rather than as the result of politics, it arose independently of the state of things in Europe. We repeat: Austria was the occasion, the pretext; if we judge the revolutionary movement in 1914 from the point of view of what it meant rather than from the words it used, we can see that its ultimate aim was not war against Austria but that it arose as a continuation of the movement that had been stifled in 1870 and should have changed—and did change—into a national war and gone on to fulfil its proper historical function as a national revolution.

Like all revolutions, interventionism had its revolutionary army: the Garibaldi Legion in the Argonne. The function of this voluntary force was to turn chance into necessity. All rhetoric apart—our relations with the French have always been spoilt by rhetoric—the Garibaldi Legion in the Argonne fulfilled a most important role in determining the development of interventionism. Whereas in Italy the struggle between the two classes, conceived on the historical and national level, was being used as a pretext and completely falsified by opportunism to the point of reducing it to a struggle between individuals and parties, the new revolutionary elite, syndicalists and republicans in the vast majority of cases, was giving expression on foreign soil to the class struggle in the historical and national sense, significantly enough not far from the heights of Valmy. It was a surprising and unexpected return to legitimacy. So for the first time since 1870, the Italian revolution found itself once again resuming its legitimate role as a national war of liberation.

It is extremely significant that the Argonne Legionaries were the very same people who had been the first to oppose, in the streets and in the workshops, the anti-national socialists, who had put into effect the first syndicalist general strike and on that occasion had followed Filippo Corridoni almost up to the Mincio. Workers and students, bourgeois and proletarians, people of every skill and trade; iron-workers from Milan and Turin and Genoa, silk spinners and weavers from the districts of Como and Bergamo, button-makers from Treviglio, wool-workers from Biella, wine-growers from Gattinara, gold prospectors from the Valsesia, stone-quarriers and stone-cutters from the districts of Verona, Belluno and Friuli, day-labourers from the Romagna, harvesters from the Tavoliere, herdsmen and foresters from the Maremma and the Agro, miners from Elba, rice-growers from Lower Piedmont, cattle-men from the highlands of Modena; young men, restless and fearless, old republicans from the Marches of Ancona and the exarchate of Ravenna, Mazzini supporters from Massa and Grosseto, marsh dwellers pallid from malaria and rabid with the fierce blood of the ancient Etruscans, hard, pitiless Lombards, wrathful and warm-hearted Romagnoles: the fine flower of all those energetic generations that had kept intact within their souls the revolutionary violence of '21 and '49, all those of the Italians who had not forgotten the sufferings of past glories and past humiliation and had swarmed into France in order to be the army of the Italian Revolution.

No one will ever be able to forget how the Red revolutionaries fought and won in the Argonne, nor how they died. The blood shed in those early battles justified and made legitimate all the suffering and victories of our war, of the Carso and the Altopiano, of Caporetto and Vittorio Veneto. While the first revolutionary army was undergoing the triumphs of Valmy in France, the Mountain[1] was filling the streets of Italy with disorder and riot.

Today, those of us who had the honour to fight in the Argonne with the first followers of Corridoni cannot look back on those glorious days without pride. Shame upon us if we had been defeated! Shame upon us if we had been cowardly! In the desolate, sombre depths of those vast woods, we often looked into each other's eyes with suspicion, almost as enemies, for fear that one of us might offend against the honour of our blood; ready to draw our knives against anyone who hesitated for one single moment to accept the sacrifice. Shame upon us if we had not been magnificent and terrible! Shame upon us if the fierce and splendid manner of our dying had not filled with awe the whole world, always ready to laugh at us Italians.

When we descended towards Ste Menehould carrying on our shoulders our first dead, never to be forgotten, silently, in the rain, from one stretch of forest to the next, anyone who, aghast, saw us file by, would have thought that we had been fighting on the barricades. Our faces and our appearance suggested civil war: we moved like rebels and partisans, not like soldiers. Amongst our number there were those who had been at Dijon: yet the red shirt that showed beneath our blue jacket was still the one worn by the rebels of Calatafimi or Bezzecca. Even in our outward appearance we were avenging ourselves for our history. And amongst us, there were those who had more trust in the knife stuck in their belt, the proper weapon of every revolt, Vespers or private battle, than in the

[1] Reference to the extreme left of the French revolutionary assemblies.

rifle slung over his shoulder. We were still those very same people who had been the first to go down into the streets in Milan, Genoa or Turin to fight against the Bourbon rabble, the anti-revolutionary plebs and bourgeoisie; we were the very same who had been the first to burn the Red Flag of the counter-revolution in the market-place; the very same who had dared to proclaim the necessity of starting the revolution again in order to avenge all the shame and the victims of the last forty years and carry on, in a new, legitimate way, the glories of the Risorgimento.

Amongst us, together with the last Garibaldi supporters from Dijon, we had those same workers who had been the first to follow Corridoni through the streets of Milan under the banner and in the defence of the revolutionary rights of a new social class which had taken over the historical and national function of the bourgeoisie of 1821.

We Red Legionaries were all aware of our task and its significance; we were the First Army of the Second Italian Revolution, but not, you must note, as it seemed at first to the French and to many Italians – and still seems – a voluntary army that had rushed to France's aid in order to defend democracy and the brotherhood of Latins. It was an anti-democratic army, that is to say, a revolutionary one, whose members had left their country not out of love of France but because of their love of Italy; for them it was a painful but necessary exile; an aristocracy of workers and intellectuals, syndicalists and republicans, who were gathered together on a foreign soil in order to offer the sacrifice of their blood, to form and make ready the first nucleus of that revolutionary army which then recrossed the Alps, to the cry of 'War or Revolution' and gave the signal for the May rebellion.

On our return to Italy from the barricades of the Argonne, the Bourbon populace, the neutralist plebs and bourgeoisie came down into the market-place to attack us, just as they had once set up the gallows for the 'three hundred' of Pisacane.

Who can forget the passions of those times, the blows exchanged, the insults and the oaths? For many the events of those days have now only historical interest; they have remembered only the facts and not their meaning. Yet what a wind of tragedy blew through those by now trite scenes! In every Italian street, citizens of every confession, workers of every skill and trade, peasants and masters, bourgeois and proletarians, rose up to avenge themselves for forty years of national humiliation. The war-cry of the Argonne Legionaries, 'War or Revolution', set the market-places in uproar. The Mountain found its spokesmen in Filippo Corridoni and Mussolini. The leaders who spurred the people on, justifying by their own innocent yet relentless violence every change of decision or direction, and who transformed this new form of class struggle into a revolutionary war for national freedom, were the same as those who had snatched the proletariat from the safe precincts of the democratic-socialist counter-revolution and flung them into the arena in the name and for the honour of Italy, of tradition, of our blood, against the negativistic bourgeoisie and the foul-mouthed rabble; they were the same as had given back the bourgeoisie *quelque chose de son énergie* by means of the necessary, live experience of syndicalist violence; the same who had used the revolutionary exercise of the syndicalist general strikes to force the proletariat to become aware of itself as a new class with a legitimate function to restore national order.

The sounder elements of the people swarmed round the Red Shirts when they came back across the Alps after their first revolutionary experience in the Argonne, and added to the struggle the decisive weight of all the injustices they had suffered and their warm-hearted sense of justice bred on the shop-floor. Those who had preached national revolution against the foreigner and the anti-national bourgeois and socialists as being the sole legitimate form of class struggle were in the forefront of the interventionist workers during that period of the class struggle. Syndicalist action was thus logically transformed into revolutionary action; or rather not so much transformed into as shown for what it was. From the economic and social sphere, the revolutionary action of the syndicalists moved naturally over into the historical and national sphere. The leaders of the interventionist, that is of the revolutionary, movement were the same as those who had proclaimed the need to call upon the people, degraded by the depressing doctrines of conservative socialism, to play their part in the historical life of the nation; they were the same as had foreseen that the people were the sole heirs and legitimate continuation of the revolutionary function of the bourgeois of 1821, and had laid the foundations of the syndicalist action which one day was to – and did – become a revolutionary war for national freedom.

There are many who lived through those dramatic May days without realizing these changes, unaware of the fate controlling the events and the protagonists. We are quite happy to let the adepts of rhetoric follow their religion. There are some moods that we choose not to talk about, not even when it might perhaps be thought dangerous to keep silent. And so we are capable of denying ourselves the facile and agreeable pleasure of using bright colours and a vast canvas in depicting the events, the actions, the men and the crowds, the whole wild tumult of those days.

For us it is enough to show with what spirit a vast number of Italians went off to fight and die on the barricades in the Carso.

ALFREDO ROCCO
(1875–1935)

In youth Alfredo Rocco was for a time a socialist sympathizer; and he joined the Radicals before his final commitment to Nationalism. He acquired a very high reputation as a professor of commercial law. Rocco became the chief nationalist spokesman on economics, and his uncompromising protectionism earned him friends in industry. Corradini himself came under the influence of Rocco's more powerful intellect.

In 1925 Rocco became Minister of Justice, a post which he held till 1932. No other minister under Mussolini exercised comparable power for such a long period of time. He had the main part in drafting the most important laws of the regime. Rocco had advocated a rapprochement with the Church, but he was not altogether satisfied with the terms of the Concordat of 1929, which offended his absolutist views. In the last years of his life his influence was on the wane.

THE CRITICAL OBJECTIONS TO NATIONALISM

(Part 3 of *Che cosa è il nazionalismo e che cosa vogliono i nazionalisti* [1914])

FIRST OBJECTION: That nationalists are madmen who wish to reduce Italy to exhaustion by rearmament and push her into terrifying warlike ventures.

Those who raise this objection know only one part of the nationalist programme, which they exaggerate and distort to support their argument. It is true that nationalism wants to prepare for war because it considers that the expansion of the Italian race will inevitably lead to armed emigration, that is to say, to war, and it intends that any such unavoidable war or rather wars shall be crowned by victory. But nationalism does not want merely preparation for war. It wants to achieve—and this is the most important item on its agenda—a strengthening of society from within through the creation of national awareness and strong national discipline; it wishes in addition an increase in internal wealth by intensifying economic production; it wants improved economic and moral status for the working classes because this higher status is necessary to strengthen social cohesion, to increase the wealth of the nation and ensure that the nation is properly prepared for war. And as for the 'bellicose' nature attributed to nationalism, it is not true that nationalism wants war at any price. Nationalism wants to prepare the nation for the inevitable wars of the future: nationalism is merely showing foresight. It does not create war. It wishes merely to ensure that any war is won. As history shows, pacifism and socialism do not prevent war, they turn it into a disaster and lead to defeat. This is the difference between nationalism and pacifism. Pacifism prepares for defeat, nationalism for victory.

SECOND OBJECTION: Nationalists are pro-clerical.

This is a refrain we hear every day. The nationalists are unmoved by this because they well know that the accusation of clericalism is a form of political double-talk that the so-called democratic parties indulge in all the time. The whole essence and programme of nationalism give it the lie. How can a party be a clerical party when it puts the nation first, whereas it is well known that clericals put religion first? But one thing is true: the nationalists are not anti-clerical because, unlike the anti-clericals of today, they do not put their hatred of religion above the national interest. In a word, the nationalists are neither pro- nor anti-clerical, they are just nationalists and put the interests of the nation above both clericalism and anti-clericalism.

THIRD OBJECTION: The nationalists have no specific programme, because all parties desire the welfare of the nation and thus they are all nationalist.

This objection is based on a common confusion between patriotism and nationalism. Patriotism, which means chiefly attachment to our mother country, that is to say our land, is essentially defensive; it is a moderate, diffuse feeling that modestly holds back to let others by. It only makes its appearance on grand occasions; in the ordinary run of life it is relegated to the second or even third rank. Everything else takes precedence, anti-clericalism, democracy, socialism, middle-class conservatism, liberalism. Nationalism, however, means being attached to our nation and race, it is an assertion of our own race. Nationalism, especially in Italy, is thus essentially progressive and expansionist and, above all, an exclusive and exclusivist attitude. Nationalism puts the nation first, relates every activity to the national interest and subordinates everything to the prosperity and power of our race. Patriotism is the sauce in every dish whereas nationalism is a good substantial dish in itself. The characteristics of a party cannot be inferred from the secondary and subordinate items on its programmes; at that rate, even nationalism would be socialist because it too wants to improve the lot of the proletariat! In fact, however, nationalism must be inferred from the principal and predominant points of its programme and on this basis the only Italian national party is nationalism.

FOURTH OBJECTION: Italian nationalism is nothing but a copy of French nationalism.

We might well ask from what pulpit such an article of faith is being preached! Of course, Italian democracy is a copy of French democracy, a foolish copy when you think that in France democracy came to the fore when France had already achieved power and wealth as a nation and it was realized that once this overriding problem was solved attention could be given to others, whereas in Italy democracy has hampered the achievement of power and wealth as a nation! Of course Italian socialism is a copy of French and German socialism, and an equally foolish one because once the wealth of the nation was assured you could start thinking about distributing it, whereas in such a poor country as Italy, it was ludicrous to think of distributing wealth that had not yet been acquired. These are the effects of copying from other nations but they are not Italian nationalism.

In any case, there does not exist one single nationalism as there exists one single socialism. There are various sorts of nationalism. Just as nations and races are different, so the various attitudes of nations and races are different. For that reason alone, Italian nationalism differs from the French one. In France, a rich country but in political decline as a result of the impressive rate of depopulation, nationalism means regret for a vanished past that will never return, when the country was poor economically but rich in men and for that reason expansionist, progressive and energetic. And as at that time France was governed by an absolute monarchy in alliance with the Church, French nationalism is absolutist, clerical and anti-Semitic. In Italy, however, a poor but prolific country, nationalism does not mean regret for the past but confidence in the future. And since, when governed by an absolute monarchy in alliance with the Church, Italy was wretched and oppressed, Italian nationalism is neither absolutist nor clerical nor anti-Semitic. What is more, since the main problem for the French is to reinvigorate their race, French nationalism is turned inwards, whereas since our main problem is that of wealth and the expansion of the race, our nationalism is outward-looking and imperialistic. In sum, since France is a nation which has achieved power but lacks manpower, although more than adequately supplied with territories, French nationalism is conservative and defensive; whereas in Italy, a country short of territories but rich in manpower, nationalism is expansionist and aggressive. As you see, any similarity between these two forms of nationalism is purely one of name!

THE *POLITICA* MANIFESTO, DECEMBER 15TH, 1918

I

The future historian, who will be in a better position to judge the great events of these last four years than we who are actually witnessing and taking part in them, will not find it easy to grasp the contradiction that has dominated the whole war from beginning to end and is becoming steadily more obvious and serious; I mean the contradiction between the basic nature of this great conflict and the way in which it was conceived and understood by the vast majority of those who took part in it; between the reality of the war and its ideology.

The world conflict, started by the Austro-Hungarian ultimatum to Serbia on July 25th, 1914, and brought to its close by the victory of Italy when Austria surrendered to her on November 3rd, 1918, was undoubtedly a struggle between nations, races and empires, a grandiose and terrible episode in the eternal struggle for existence and mastery waged by the peoples of the world, but neither the first nor the last of such episodes. We need only go back to the origins and underlying reasons of the conflict in order to convince ourselves of this. The cause that determined the conflagration was the struggle between, on the one hand, Germanism, which already dominated the basin of the Danube where it exercised political and economic control over the diverse peoples under the Austro-Hungarian monarchy and was all set to extend its power eastwards, and, on the other, Slavism, already the major power in Asia and in the Balkans and threatening the German hegemony of the Danubian monarchy; it was this that led to the Austrian ultimatum of July 25th, 1914, the Russian intervention to protect the Slavs, and German solidarity with Austria-Hungary in preparing for war, diplomatically and militarily.

The fundamental reason for the opposition between Germany and England was the struggle between German imperialism, massive, ponderous and theoretical, lacking political and historical understanding, unfulfilled and thus aggressive, and British imperialism, nimble, practical, experienced, replete, and thus conservative and pacific. Similarly the age-old rivalry between the French and the Germans, culminating in the long period of war between France and Austria, when the Habsburg Empire was the main exponent of German power, and between France and Prussia (or France and Germany), when Prussia and the German Empire assumed the hegemony of the German world relinquished by Austria, is sufficient explanation of the nature and origins of French participation in the war.

The nature of Italy's intervention was more complex. The specific causes were the age-old conflicts between Italianism and Germanism, and Italianism and Slavism, which were bound inevitably to lead to Italy's opposing Austria-Hungary, which represented Germanism in the Alps and Slavism in the Adriatic; but its general cause was Italy's need to expand in the world, which was bound to lead her by an instinctive impulse to take part in the struggle which was to lay the foundations of a new balance of power.

Finally, even America's participation was effectively made necessary for national and imperial reasons, less immediate and less obvious but equally indisputable: the self-defence and future expansion of the great American empire, threatened by the preponderance of Germany, especially in South America, and the urge to intervene in world politics, above all in European politics, from a position of strength and to reverse the existing balance of power in that area.

Now these realities regarding the war, which were sufficiently plain at the beginning of the struggle, even in May 1915 at the time of the Italian intervention, were slowly being erased from people's minds as the war became more prolonged, complicated and arduous. This vast conflict, which was essentially an international struggle for existence, for world mastery and world hegemony, became increasingly, in the various speeches and writings and even in the official documents, a clash of political conceptions and doctrines, a struggle between democracy and autocracy, between the ideals of pacifism and militarism, between right and might, between the principles of nationhood and imperialism. Public opinion in the Entente became particularly incensed against imperialism, not only against German imperialism, which would have been a justifiable target for any non-German to attack because it was German, but against imperialism in general, forgetting that amongst the five nations forming the Entente, no less than four—England, America, France and Russia—were in fact vast empires that were fighting to survive and to expand! This conception reached its climax in the course of the discussions between the American and German Foreign Ministers after the Germans had asked for an armistice, during which at a given moment it seemed that the chief war aim had become the democratization of Germany, almost as if millions of men had laid down their lives for the last four years with the sole purpose of converting the enemy to a belief in these immortal principles!

This strange contrast between the reality of the war and its ideology sprang from many and complex causes. One primary influence was certainly the long-standing ideological weakness that had been growing for more than a century and had corrupted the political attitudes of the greatest nations. So in this emergency instinct reasserted itself and acted, while political awareness succumbed without a struggle. So nations which were showing themselves more and more willing and able to act and sacrifice themselves found themselves incapable of understanding the meaning, the validity or the principles underlying the history which they were themselves creating through their own suffering on such a noble and stupendous scale, since they had no other terms in which to think of it than those of contemporary democratic ideology, that is to say, of an ideology which is supremely anti-historical. The second influence was the position of the two powers, England and France, who at first were the leaders of world public opinion. Both were replete with empire and thus pacifistic and conservative, both had become involved in the conflict through force of circumstance and not of their own free will; a position, indeed, that perfectly matched the democratic ideology which from the international point of view was static and conservative *par excellence*. Later on, a further influence was the instinctively imperialistic mentality of the Americans who since they did not possess any political or intellectual ideology other than democracy were naturally inclined to export it to the rest of the world as a means of enhancing their world-wide prestige. There was also the short-sighted and oversimplified calculation based on political opportunism, which led the statesmen of the countries within the Entente to turn themselves into advocates of a democratic, anti-imperialistic and pacifistic war. In a word it was felt that, even in this war, the best way to obtain from the masses the individual sacrifices required for victory was to appeal to the individualistic feelings of the crowd, the feelings, in fact, from which democratic ideology derives its strength and validity. The persistent defeats suffered by the Entente powers were the final influence behind this pacifistic, anti-war myth of war. These defeats, seen as the living proof of the inferior strength of the Allies, gave rise to an instinctive appeal to something that might lead to victory apart from force; thus there arose the absurd conception of an anti-militaristic war, which is the same as saying an anti-war war because nations, like individuals, dislike nothing more strongly than those things which they are not able to do. For the same reasons today, we can see Germany becoming pacifist now that she has been beaten.

The ideology of democracy is, by definition, an ideology of defeat.

This mentality prolonged the war and made it more bitter and more bloody. For one thing, the pacifism of the various governments, Parliaments and anti-militaristic public opinion amongst the nations of the Entente was responsible for their total or relative lack of preparedness for war which made possible their enemies' initial successes (to be paid for so dearly throughout the whole war); which gave the Central Powers the time to crush and dismember Russia; which created amongst the Bulgarians and the Turks an illusion of superiority and decided their intervention. Therefore, whatever the apologists of weakness may claim, the truth is that, in this great clash of powers, might was not on the side of Germany and Austria but on the side of the Entente, assuming that it is true that 140 million men, in isolation, must be considered less strong than 1,000 million men with the resources of the whole world at their disposal. But this overwhelming strength of the Entente was badly used, for geographical, political and moral reasons, amongst which the prevailing humanitarian anti-war mentality must be given pride of place. This mentality meant that the people were not asked from the very beginning to make the bitter sacrifices essential for victory; and it prevented both the war from being waged with that relentless energy inherent in the very idea of war, and the forces that, for devious party or class interests, were undermining the will to fight within the country, from being swiftly crushed once and for all. This timid, uncertain, flabby, paralytic mentality cost England, France and Italy many hundreds of thousands in dead and many thousands of millions in money.

And unless a salutary reawakening takes place in public opinion in the West, this mentality will lead to further harm and further peril for the countries of the Entente. Their defeated enemies have already begun to make use of it as the most effective means of escaping the consequences of defeat. Powerless to continue to fight with weapons, they will fight to the last in the field of diplomacy, using Wilsonian arguments in order to deprive the victors of what they have won on the field of battle. This danger is hanging over the heads of all the nations of the Entente: England, whose age-old maritime supremacy is jeopardized by the principle of the freedom of the seas; and France, who is about to have as neighbour a German state of eighty million people. But above all, danger is menacing Italy who, as a result of the wiles of its age-old enemies, formerly Austrian but now called Tyroleans and Yugoslavs, and perhaps even more as a result of the short-sighted policy of her allies, finds that the fruits of her heroic efforts, her unparalleled sacrifices and her indomitable perseverance are being called into question. And they are being called into question precisely in the name of that democratic, anti-imperialistic and egalitarian ideology which her overt enemies and faithless friends are using as their most formidable and decisive weapon to cause her discomfiture.

Finally, we must not ignore the debilitating effect of the faint-hearted and flabby democratic attitude towards the virus of Bolshevism. Being founded entirely on the disruptive effects of individualism, which undermined the modern world as a result of the collapse of the Middle Ages, democratic ideology is expressly designed to produce in any society where it flourishes an almost complete absence of the will to fight the anarchy of Bolshevism, which is nothing more nor less than the ultimate expression of the wildest and most unbridled individualism. And, in reality, at every time and place, democraticism and its impotent verbosity have unwittingly but inevitably opened the road to anarchy; it is not by chance that, even in these days, Lenin was preceded by Kerensky.

II

We must resist and react against the spread of such a mentality.

Fortunately, the instinct of self-preservation among the great Entente nations, when they saw the very fruits of their victory threatened, aroused an active and practical reaction. Public opinion in England has already made it manifestly clear that no one, whether friend or foe, will be allowed in the name of the 'freedom of the seas' to question the British Empire's maritime supremacy. In France, hostility towards 'democratized' Germany continues to be no less considerable than it was against the old absolutist and feudal Germany: and the 'principle of nationality' is neatly sidestepped when it is a question of stopping Germany from annexing the ten million Germans in Austria. In Italy, the bigoted upholders of the principle of nationality and the high priests of abnegation have had to hold their tongues when faced by the universal outburst of indignation against the attempt by the Yugoslavs to perpetuate, in the name of this principle of nationality, foreign domination of the other coast of the Adriatic which belongs to us by a tradition that goes back a thousand years, as well as by its geographical position, its genius and culture; and above all because it is indispensable for our security and our expansion.

This movement must be accelerated and extended to form an organized system of ideas and deliberate intention. And to achieve this we need to recognize and overcome mental structures that have their roots in the remote Middle Ages.

Democratic ideology, though directly derived from the intellectual movement usually described as 'the philosophy of the French Revolution', has in fact far more distant origins and as a social and political conception must be linked to the trends of thought that produced and accompanied the Protestant Reformation in Germany, whence it spread to England in the seventeenth century and to America in the eighteenth, and then to France who imposed it on Europe by the force and prestige of her victorious armies. This eminently individualistic and anti-state ideology is thus the result of the thousand-year-old individualism of the Germanic tribes. This individualism, after vainly battering for centuries against the admirable political state organization of Rome, ended by submerging it not by force of arms but by long and persistently disruptive action within the structure of the empire itself, already undermined by the formidably corrosive force of primitive Christianity. After the collapse of the Roman Empire through the joint effort of these two forces, in the general social and political disruption that then followed for many centuries to which we have given the name of Middle Ages, there came to the fore the individualistic, anti-social and anti-state attitude, an attitude that the political reforms achieved by the action of the great national states have not yet had time successfully to counteract; it is this attitude that is largely responsible for the fact that the old medieval mentality, individualistic and thus universalistic, disruptive and thus anti-state, has re-emerged and is flourishing in the guise of the new liberal and democratic ideological formulas.

Nor should we be surprised by this persistent and successful revival of disruptive individualism, for if gregariousness is fundamental to mankind and indeed one of the essential aspects of the preservation of the species, the instinct for preservation and the welfare of the individual is equally fundamental. Only, whereas in the natural order of things the two feelings harmonize and the first of them inevitably prevails, in some human societies it not infrequently happens that concern for the welfare of the individual comes to predominate to the detriment of the preservation of the species. This is a phenomenon that indicates and exists in a period of decadence and leads to the disappearance of societies and races; that in the demographic sphere produces a deliberate reduction in the birth-rate and in the size of the population; that at the economic level makes for large estates and leads the peasantry to desert the countryside in favour of the town; that at the military level makes people unwilling to fight and accept military service; that at the national level leads to the disorganization of the state and to demagogy; and that at the international political level creates empty humanitarianism and universalism so that the national instinct of preservation and expansion vanishes into thin air, thereby abandoning its essential function.

We have not yet reached that stage. But we were launched

on that path at the time of the outbreak of the Great War which, having been provoked by Germany as a result of a miscalculation, probably saved the Western powers, England, France and Italy, from the imminent danger of decadence. The long, tough and bloody ordeal has certainly, in fact, called forth within the Western societies themselves new powers of resistance to oppose any further degeneration through individualistic attitudes, by reawakening a sense of sociality and the instinct of preservation of the species.

The task of our review is to transform this obscure and instinctive feeling into a deliberately conscious doctrine. It is, therefore, essentially a spiritual and intellectual task and much more concerned with creating in the public a state of mind and attitude opposed to the teachings of liberal-democratic ideology than with advocating changes in institutions or political regimes. We are in fact convinced that where political and social reality is concerned, form counts for nothing and the spirit for everything. There are examples of nations which, technically, are governed by authoritarian regimes but in which the disruptive spirit of individualism and ultra-democratic culture have so overwhelmed the organization of the state as to paralyse it and make it powerless. This was the case in Tsarist Russia, which carried within itself all the seeds of Bolshevik anarchy. On the other hand, there are examples of nations whose institutions are democratic in the sense that supreme power, at least when it comes to designating the head of state, lies in the votes of half plus one of their citizens but whose spirit is so well disciplined and organic and whose awareness of their historical aims is so mature as to make it possible for policies to be followed which are, in practice, the negation of democratic ideology. Such is the case in the United States, where the awareness of America's imperial mission is so deep-rooted and widespread as to permit of policies inspired by the most far-reaching and far-sighted imperialism that history can recall.

III

For this task of spiritual reformation that we are proposing, it is above all necessary to restore the idea of the relationship between society and the individual. Society is not, as it appears in the political philosophy taught by demo-liberals, a mere sum of individuals which can be resolved into its separate elements, but is a real organism with an existence and a purpose quite distinct from those of its particular members. In the unending series of generations of individuals, society has a continuous existence over the centuries. And its purpose is to contribute, in accordance with its own genius and powers, to the development of world civilization. Because, contrary to the medieval idea, expressed in the theories of the philosophy of the revolution, of one universal human society, the human race does not constitute one, single vast society of mankind including all the inhabitants of the terrestrial globe but is divided into numerous societies, each of which is a distinct organism with its own life and goals, as is proved not only by history but by the biological and moral laws governing social life.

These laws are the exact opposite of those bandied about by liberal-democratic ideology. The latter wants, in the name of the equality of all mankind, to abolish all social hierarchies within society and in foreign affairs to establish perpetual peace and the United States of the World; in other words, it tends towards disorganization, that is to say, towards the disruption of traditional societies, the only existing social reality, in order to replace them by a hypothetical society which is at present outside reality and will shortly be beyond the range of possibility; and it will be beyond the range of possibility precisely because if you abolish the distinctions between the various human societies, their mutual competitiveness and conflicts, you not only destroy the life of each particular society but even the life of mankind itself, which is in fact produced by their active interreaction. Conflict is in fact the basic law of life of all social organisms, as it is of all biological ones; societies are formed, gain strength and move forwards through conflict; the healthiest and most vital of them assert themselves against the weakest and less well adapted through conflict; the natural evolution of nations and races takes place through conflict. And so to refute the democratic formula: the equality of the individual leads to the abolition of all social hierarchies and thus to internal disorganization; equality among all nations leads to perpetual peace and external immobility. Instead, we substitute our formula: disciplined control of inequality and thus hierarchy and organization within the state; free competition and struggle in external relationships between nations, in order that, as a result of their inequality, those nations should assert themselves who are best prepared for and best adapted to the function that devolves on every powerful and capable nation in the evolution of civilization.

So all the forms of conflict are directed outwards, from the bloodless conflict of economic and political competition to the violence of the armed conflict that in extreme cases represents the *ultima ratio* to which every nation has the right and duty to have recourse; internally, however, peace will be assured by discipline, good order and a hierarchical system. Thus the cause of peace will be served in the only way compatible with life and the development of society. In fact, as a society gradually achieves strength and cohesion and turns towards expansion to increase the area of its power and extend the struggle outwards to a wider field, the area that is at peace will grow; the best way to guarantee peace is continually to increase the area under the control of one single social organization, with one single type of law and order and one single authority.

The rise of the state is a result of and is subject to this ineluctable law of the struggle for existence; the state cannot, as liberal-democratic ideologists would have it, be considered except as part of society, since it is identified sometimes with the organs of sovereignty, at others with the political class from which these latter are drawn, and at yet other times even with the individuals who in turn exercise this sovereignty; but the state is, on the other hand, nothing but society itself in so far as it is organized under one supreme power; it is thus the necessary historical form of the life of society, which is of indefinite length, as distinct from the ephemeral value of the individual. This is why our conception of the state is organic, dynamic and historical, whereas the liberal-democratic conception is mechanical, static and anti-historical. This is why it is our conception only that is able to provide their logical and necessary place for all the institutions and phenomena in which the individual can reveal himself to us in his function as the instrument and organ of the purposes of the state, amongst which war takes precedence since it requires the individual to make the supreme sacrifice. Thus, too, for example, the idea of liberty, which appears in liberal theory as an unlimited natural right of the individual vis-à-vis the state, in fact cannot be based on anything but the will of the state itself which grants it to him, because the state is primarily and most directly interested in ensuring that the individual is provided with the opportunity for the organic development of his own personality. And so, too, the democratic and individualistic principle of the sovereignty of the masses, popular sovereignty, is opposed by the concept of government by the most able, that is to say, those who by tradition, culture and social class are in a position to rise above the contingencies and interests of their own generation and to discern and realize the broad historical interests of the state.

Everyone, therefore, rulers and ruled, those in more exacting positions of authority as well as subordinates, are active organs of the state. Service to the state is thus everyone's duty but at the same time in everyone's interest. The stronger and more powerful a state, the higher and richer the life of its inhabitants: *civis Romanus sum.*

However, the relationship between one state and other states is radically different. This is not a relationship of subordination or co-ordination but a relationship based on competition and struggle. Every state wishes to achieve its own ends and has to achieve them with its own forces. The force which each state has at its disposal thus represents the limit of the aims which it can contemplate and pursue. The law of international justice works according to this formula: to each according to his power. We use the words force and power in their fullest and most comprehensive sense to include not only material forces, population, wealth, armaments, but also spiritual forces of self-sacrifice, internal solidarity, discipline, intellectual superiority in the sciences, the arts and technology; and, above all, the ability to understand the hearts and minds of other nations, a sense of proportion, the ability to choose the right moment, the quality of self-knowledge and self-criticism, all of which add up to political understanding, first and highest gift of peoples destined to empire, the gift that the Romans possessed to a supreme degree, that the British have today to a very high degree, and the lack of which caused the downfall of the power of the Germanic peoples in the Great World War.

So the first duty and essential function of the state is to be strong in every field. For the contradiction between right and might which democratic ideology was pleased to establish does not exist. It does not exist in internal affairs, where right means self-interest as controlled by organized law and order, that is to say, by the power of the state, so that power consequently seems to us an essential element of right. It does not exist in the international field where, in fact, right is nothing more than the interest of any state that possesses sufficient material and spiritual power to impose it. Even here might is an essential part of right, only that might no longer springs from a source independent of the interest, but is the might of the state whose own interest is concerned. And it is natural that this should be so, because if, where internal relationships are concerned, there is a superior body—the state—that acts as intermediary between individuals so as to establish justice between them, in international relations each state must seek justice on its own account since there is no body higher than the state that could dispense justice to the state, nor is it possible to conceive of any such body.

This idea of the state as a force (which as a result of the current general state of ignorance is seen as a German-Prussian idea) is plainly a Latin and Italian one. It is directly linked with the intellectual tradition of Rome and was refurbished by Machiavelli's political philosophy, by Vico's philosophy of history and by historians and economists from the south at the beginning of the nineteenth century, whose criticism of the philosophy of the French Revolution is either too little known or forgotten. Just because the Germans, when they tried to apply it, failed to understand it fully in theory and then applied it wrongly in practice, we should not repudiate it, having forgotten it as a result of the influence of other foreign ideologies. On the contrary, it is the Italians' duty to reclaim it as part of our national heritage, in its genuine form, and translate it into action with that political wisdom that over the centuries has always been part of the genius of our race.

IV

Similarly, according to the theory of indefinite progress—another feature of democratic ideology—one of the laws of history is the inevitable and steady evolution of society from more restricted to more extensive forms. This leads to the optimistic and happy consequence that since social organizations are always increasing in size, they will finally reach the point of forming a state comprising the whole of mankind. There, too, we are faced by a hypothesis that can have no claim to be taken seriously. The experience of history shows that periods of vast organized states are followed by others where sovereignty has been completely whittled away; thus in the Middle Ages we see an empire of immense proportion that broke up into a host of tiny bodies, in which, as in ancient Greek towns, the city state again predominates. So the origin of every state shows us that no social organization can be extended to other such organizations except by absorption, that is, by conquest; or by association, that is, by alliance; but always with war as the decisive factor, either as the result of winning a war or of the need to defend oneself against a common enemy. We have never heard of any state being formed as a result of the preaching of any theoretician or out of a love of symmetry. So the only foreseeable possibility for the reunification of mankind into one single organization is some possible future interplanetary struggle between the inhabitants of the earth and those of Mars or Venus.

History teaches us a very different lesson. And this lesson is that certain forms of political organization predominate amongst the most advanced nations in each period. Thus in the Greek world and in the Middle Ages, the city state prevailed; in modern times, it is the national state, and at the present time empire is already the predominant form.

Until not long ago, the nation appeared as the largest and most perfect form of social organization, perfect because it was homogeneous, that is to say, composed of groups which, by reason of their similar origins and even more their unity of traditions, customs, language, religion, the considerable geographical unity of their territory, their community of needs and interests, have, with time, achieved the awareness of forming one single social organism, the nation. For centuries it was the national states—Spain, France and England—whose force and prosperity far exceeded those of the others. Those nations such as Italy and Germany who had not succeeded in forming themselves into states remained in a position of political, economic and moral inferiority and stagnation. On the other hand, all attempts to enlarge the state beyond the national boundaries failed one after the other; the Spanish colonial empire collapsed, as did those of the Portuguese and Dutch; even the British Empire was placed in jeopardy by the secession of the American colonies. In the middle of the nineteenth century, the national state was triumphant everywhere; the last remnants of non-national states, Austria and Turkey, seemed destined to perish without hope of salvation. Nor did this development stop until the historical phenomenon of national reconstruction moved into its final phase with the Great War.

But while this phase was coming into being, there were already signs of a new world order. The grandiose phenomenon of British colonization was laying the foundations of the vast British Empire, extending over an area of nearly 13 million square miles and containing some 500 million inhabitants. Russia, which had barely formed a nation in the eighteenth century, was starting its rapid and remarkable expansion eastwards and in its turn was founding a very large empire of well over 8½ million square miles and 200 million inhabitants. The United States of America which, by its vast size and diversity of race, was already on its way to becoming an empire, began increasingly to move towards a position of hegemony over the whole American continent; this movement ended with the war against Spain, the seizure of the Panama Canal and the expedition against Mexico. Even France had found the way to revive her fortunes after the defeat in 1870 by increasing and refurbishing her colonial empire which, within a few decades, grew to such a considerable size that it formed an area of over 4,300,000 square miles with 50 million inhabitants. But it was left to the World War to conclude the national phase, by bringing about the fall of Austria and Turkey and, at the same time, to inaugurate decisively and on a vast scale the stage of imperial development. So we see that this war which was fought under the banner of 'nationality' versus 'imperialism' represents in fact a violent crisis as a result of which an *imperial* type of civilization, an *imperial* balance of power is succeeding to a national civilization and balance of power. This evolution which had been taking place over the last century is now reaching completion under our very eyes: it is a democratic development, of course – if only in the sense that the peoples of the world are themselves becoming the protagonists in the world drama – but an imperialist development also.

The British Empire has come through the war with her internal unity strengthened by the prominent and active part played by all her great colonies in their joint defence; with her territory greatly enlarged by the acquisition of vast regions such as Mesopotamia, Arabia, the greater part of the former German colonies and the entire residue of the Ottoman Empire which now comes automatically under British hegemony; and finally with her moral prestige and influence increased by the ascendency which she has acquired over the whole Muslim world through her possession of the Caliphate. Even though without any formal territorial gains, the United States has been enabled by the war to lay an unshakeable foundation on which to build a vast and powerful empire. The whole of Central and South America now offers it an unlimited field of influence, over which political control is guaranteed by the Monroe Doctrine and economic control by its immense industrial power. By its intervention in European affairs, it has assumed the role of arbiter throughout Europe and, as Europe is the centre of world policy, throughout the whole world. Japan, which had launched out on its imperial mission by conquering Korea and Port Arthur, is now proudly completing it by asserting its preeminent position in the Chinese Empire by annexing Manchuria and establishing a foothold in Siberia. France, more limited in scope, is still doggedly strengthening and enlarging her own empire, by annexing the European territories that will give her absolute superiority in the production of steel in the Old World; enlarging her magnificent African empire by taking over the German colonies that form an organic whole with her own; looking towards Siberia; and all in all, bringing under the French tricolour, including the metropolis and the colonies, a population of 100 million inhabitants. Despite its setbacks and the mad folly of Bolshevism, Russia still remains a great empire which sooner or later will end up by discovering its own path and continue to exercise its weight in world affairs. Germany has pursued a series of ambitious dreams to acquire vast empires, first of all planning to dominate the Danube basin, the Balkans and Turkey in Asia, from Berlin to the Persian Gulf, then to take over the British and French Empires, then to conquer almost the whole of Russia in Europe; and though she has for the moment seen these dreams shattered, she continues to remain such a large and expansive power that it is impossible for her to fail to take up once again, sooner or later, her imperial ambitions in the world. We can thus see how a war which, in the words of an eminent Italian statesman, was to have marked the downfall of imperialism, has left the world split up into five formidable empires.

In view of this, any Italian who does not lack national consciousness and who has not had the naivety to allow himself to be overcome by the clever anti-imperialistic propaganda which foreign imperialisms are so fond of using to disguise their designs, any such Italian must be justifiably concerned when he sees that amongst the great powers who were victorious in the war, only one is in danger of having fought without acquiring an empire, namely Italy. Italy is in danger, in a word, once again, as at the end of the fifteenth century, of finding herself left behind in the political evolution of the new order in Europe and the world. And if she does not react in time against her traditional superstition, the principle of nationality, which, although useful at one stage of her formation as a nation, could now turn into a dead weight in face of new historical necessities, she is in danger of finding herself overwhelmed by the stronger and much larger states which are now being formed.

This will not happen if, like all the large nations of the world, Italy comes to realize the truth even further accentuated by the war: that for ineluctable historical, political, demographic, economic and social reasons, the open competition between imperialist powers has become an iron law which no nation can afford to overlook and still survive, and that each nation must plan and adapt and organize its whole life, energy and structure to meet this necessity.

This basic truth is the sole measure by which to judge all

political values. As a result foreign policy is the pivot round which all other policies revolve: internal policy, which must restore the idea and authority of the state as an organized will to exert power and to ensure the firm cohesion and discipline of the nation; military policy, which must provide the preparation and training in the use of direct force in support of foreign policy; economic policy, which must foster, develop and protect its production and trade, defend them in the home market and help them to win foreign markets, thus providing a guarantee of independence as well as an instrument of expansion; social policy, which must replace class struggle and international solidarity by class solidarity in the international struggle, for which the most perfect instrument seems to be, at this moment of time, the syndicate; cultural policy, which must make the nation aware of its own genius and its heritage and of the need to defend them and ensure their victory in the civilization of the world; religious policy, which, while positively and actively defending the sovereignty of the state and renouncing the dispassionate agnosticism of the old-fashioned doctrinaire liberals, must recreate once more the spiritual unity of the nation and transform it into a cohesive force at home and an expansionist force abroad – an essential task for Italy which, now that the outworn disagreement between Church and state has been settled, cannot and must not forget or neglect the favoured position that it holds by being Italian within the organized spiritual and traditional power of the Roman Catholic Church, that is to say, the institution that still enjoys the most universal prestige and possesses the greatest potential of universal expansion. All these policies must contribute to the most fundamental and important policy of all, foreign policy; they must provide the various facets or rather the momentum for the organization and training of the nation in this world-wide struggle for empire.

This truth must be defended and reaffirmed in Italy who, having arrived on the scene of international competition last amongst the nations, in a state of spiritual disarray, has a more urgent and vital need than any other to find a worthier, more adequate place in the balance of power and prosperity, where she has hitherto been cabined and confined within narrow limits and forced to send millions of her sons abroad as exiles in bondage to the foreigner.

Yet everything urges Italy to fulfil her imperial mission: the traditions of Rome, Venice and Genoa; the political genius of her race which has always made her a consummate mistress in the art of governing nations; her geographical position which, while joining her to the mainland of Europe, allows her to dominate from the centre the whole of the Mediterranean basin, where today the heart of three continents is once more beginning to throb.

This is where Italy's duty and mission lie. As history proves, every time that life has flowed back into our land of destiny, creating an ethnic, political unity and a strong organized power, the iron hand of circumstance has drawn her outward beyond her boundaries towards that sea that bathes three continents, outwards towards their shores, in response to her natural historical vocation, stronger than any opposing power or will.

THE SYNDICATES AND THE CRISIS WITHIN THE STATE

(Speech inaugurating the academic year 1920–21, given at the University of Padua, November 15th, 1920)

I

There is a crisis within the state; day by day, the state is dissolving into a mass of small particles, parties, associations, groups and syndicates that are binding it in chains and paralysing and stifling its activity: one by one, with increasing speed, the state is losing its attributes of sovereignty. This is the fact which we hear repeated all around us and which each of us interprets in his own way, some deploring it, others delighted by it. The principle of self-defence, whether of individuals or groups, which is paramount in all primitive and disorganized societies, is making a triumphant return. The conflict of interests between groups and classes is now being settled by the use of private force alone: I mean physical force, based on weapons and strong arms, and the winner is not the one who is right but the one who has the advantage of boldness or weight of numbers. The struggle between the various parties and factions has now openly become an armed struggle; in this struggle they are not only using the vote or propaganda, but the most modern instruments of war, and not infrequently the outcome of many electoral battles is dependent on the material forces which the contending parties are able to bring to bear. The state stands by impassively watching these conflicts which involve countless violations of public and private rights. This neutrality which, in liberal doctrine, was intended to allow free play for economic law in the clash of interests between the classes is now being interpreted as allowing the state to abandon its essential function of guardian of public order and agent of justice. This is not all. A number of the functions appertaining to the state are being taken over by private bodies. Air and sea transport are controlled by private associations and they can ban exports to certain specified countries, dislocate troop movements and the free passage of others responsible for the national forces; but above all they are able, by unilateral action, to impose their own economic and legal relationship with the state. At present, it is no longer merely a matter of self-defence between individuals and groups, but between individuals and the state and between groups and the state. The latter has not only abandoned any idea of controlling the relationships between private persons and other bodies, but is becoming powerless to control the relationship between itself and those persons and bodies. The only criterion for such control is the force at the disposal of individuals and groups. The remuneration of employees of the state is no longer governed by the law of supply and demand, which has been upset like so many others by the collapse of the liberal economy, nor by the amount or usefulness of the work, but by the material force of the group to which the worker belongs. Thus we find the highest paid are not those who show most ability or whose work is most useful to society, but those who belong to the largest organizations and have the best political and physical means to enforce their claims.

This is no recent crisis: it goes back to the early years of this century ... It cannot be denied that the syndicalist movement has played an important part in this progressive collapse of the authority of the state. But the present crisis has deeper and more widespread causes and syndicalism, while hastening and aggravating it, is only one of its aspects and consequences.

II

Since the state is merely society as organized under one sovereign power, the history of the state is the history of the various societies of mankind and thus the history of civilization itself. History shows us the lives of the different societies evolving in more or less extended cycles but substantially the same within these phases of their development; so we see the birth of the state, we see it become organized, gain strength and prosperity and then become disorganized, decline and perish, just as any biological organism is born, develops, grows old and dies. Now the life of every social body is an unceasing struggle between the principle of organization represented by the state and the principle of disintegration, represented by individuals and groups, which tend to disrupt it and thus lead to its decline and fall. When the state is in the ascendant, society develops and prospers; when individuals and groups gain the upper hand, it disintegrates and dies. We must not imagine that the history of mankind evolves in one continuous cycle. The theory of indefinite progress, whereby mankind would tend steadily to improve and achieve increasingly higher forms of life, is not only false and contradicted by the facts, which show us that periods of splendid civilization are regularly followed by dark ages of barbarism, but it is not true either, generally speaking, that the development of mankind can be portrayed as unilinear. On the contrary, as was suggested by the intuitive genius of Giovanni Battista Vico, history unfolds in cycles that are distinct but similar and recurring. This is natural: the story of mankind is nothing but the history of the various social organizations which have succeeded each other over the centuries for thousands of years and each of them has, like every other organism, a life which begins at birth and ends in death, passing through youth, maturity and old age. So it is no wonder if history repeats itself because life repeats itself in identical stages in the various social bodies of which it is successively composed.

Now contemporary societies present characteristics similar to those which have distinguished the societies which preceded them over the last few thousands of years. The fierce and never-ending battle against the centrifugal forces of disruption continues to be fought, as always, in order to enable a society to come into being, organize itself and develop. This relentless battle, that the Roman state waged for centuries and won, until new disruptive factors brought about its collapse during the concluding centuries of the empire, has continued to be fought by modern societies for almost the last thousand years, with varying degrees of success. After painfully emerging from the immense social and political chaos that followed the downfall of the Roman Empire, which we call the Middle Ages (a period of universal disruption that itself lasted for well-nigh ten centuries), modern social organizations still contain the seeds of disintegration, lingering on from the Middle Ages, which they have not yet been able to eliminate. When you think that France, the first of the European states to become strong and united and a state which has always been and perhaps still is today the most soundly constituted of them all, was still struggling against the relicts of feudal power as late as the seventeenth century and was torn by civil strife, we need not be surprised if the effect of these age-old forces of disruption can still be felt in Italy, which emerged from medieval chaos virtually a mere sixty years ago.

Today we are witnessing in fear and trembling the onslaught of the new forces of disruption against the sovereignty of the state and we fail to remember other, perhaps more formidable, crises which the modern state has successfully overcome. We do not remember the mighty struggle against the Church which lasted for two whole centuries and ended with an alliance between the two that barely disguised the Church's defeat. We do not remember the century-long battle against feudalism, another formidable force of disruption, which had carried over from the Middle Ages and was still being waged at the end of the seventeenth century. We do not remember the struggle against the minor groups that emerged in the course of the anarchy of the Middle Ages, the communes and corporations, ending in their absorption into the state and their incorporation into its structure. We do not remember the struggle against the attempt to achieve independent power by families and individuals, against their claims to take the law into their own hands, against private feuds and privately organized forces, against criminal behaviour.

The truth is that, even today, fifteen centuries later, we are still feeling the effects of the social and political disintegration following upon the collapse of the Roman Empire. After more than fifteen hundred years, the debris of this broken colossus still bears down on us with all its weight. The modern state had reached the peak of its power and achieved its greatest internal strength and unity at the beginning of the eighteenth century. By that time, it had forced the Church into submission and asserted its legal authority over it in the deferential and obsequious form of a protective alliance; it had forced feudalism into submission by giving the feudal lords official positions in the government, the army and the administration in exchange for their loss of sovereign power; it had forced the communes and corporations into submission by turning them into official state bodies and by using them as instruments of its economic and fiscal policies. But at the very moment when the state was reaching the zenith of its power, another attack by the forces of disruption was under way. This time it was no longer the organizations which had emerged during the anarchy of the Middle Ages that were moving into the attack: it was not the feudal families or the Church, not the communes or the corporations. These movements had at last become exhausted and ceased to be a danger to the state. This attack came from the amorphous and disorganized mass of the people under the leadership of an intelligent and cultivated class that had achieved wealth by means of commerce and industry: the middle class. This time the rebellion was not being launched under the banner of the old organizations, it was being carried out in the name of the individuals; it was not the minor bodies within the state but its cells which were revolting against the body itself. The eighteenth-century reaction against the state was thus an individualistic reaction. Its intellectual foundations were provided by the exponents of the philosophy of natural law and by the Encyclopaedists, and it came to a head politically in the explosion of the French Revolution. The state had to withstand a rude assault but its powers of organization and absorption once again enabled it to survive. Under the pressure of the needs of a foreign war and of national defence, after a brief period of disruption and anarchy, the power and unity of the state reasserted itself. The re-establishment of power began under the dictatorship of the Committee of Public Safety during the Terror and was brought to a magnificent conclusion by the powerful military and administrative organization of the Napoleonic Empire.

However, once peace had returned after twenty-three years of bloody conflict and the dictatorship had come to an end, the disruptive spirit of individualism once more reared its ugly head. Under the gentle guise of liberal idealism, it insinuated itself everywhere and in particular it permeated the cultivated class of the bourgeoisie which had completely replaced the old nobility as the ruling class in the state. This diffusion of the liberal idea of non-interference by the state and its withdrawal from the most important problems of social life, which even maintained that as a mark of respect towards the rights of the individual the state should virtually abandon any defence against its enemies, undermined the authority of the state. From that time onwards, the claims of individualism knew no bounds. The masses of individuals wanted to govern the state and govern it in accordance with their own individual interests. The state, a living organism with a continuous existence over the centuries that extends beyond successive generations and as such the guardian of the immanent historical interests of the species, was turned into a monopoly to serve the individual interests of each separate generation. In countries where there was a long tradition of state government and lively political awareness, the damage caused by the self-government of the masses was without doubt not excessive; but it was very serious indeed in those countries in which the pursuit of individual advantage was not limited by any higher consciousness of, or feeling for, the general historical interests of society.

III

The main cause of the present weakness of the state is, therefore, the spread of individualistic and anti-state attitudes. In my opinion, it would be unfair to blame this on the syndicates, the more so as the excesses and erroneous policies of the syndicates, whose repercussions on the structure of the state are so greatly to be deplored, are themselves due to those liberal doctrines which have, in theory and in practice, been lauded to the skies for decades as infallible political dogmas, especially by the conservatives themselves. This is understandable. Whilst the state, following upon the collapse of the Roman Empire and the ensuing disintegration of the Middle Ages, had steadily asserted itself in a series of struggles over the centuries and gradually brought to a successful conclusion its energetic endeavours to dam the political forces that were corrupting and dismantling it, liberalism paralysed the state or rendered it powerless to resist the disruption caused by individuals and by groups. The disruptive, individualistic, anti-state attitudes of the Middle Ages emerged once again in the guise of liberalism and brought to a standstill the process of unification and consolidation of the state which, after an uncertain start, had been gaining momentum over the last few centuries.

Now there is no doubt that one of the most serious consequences of liberal agnosticism was the emergence of syndicalism, a syndicalism that was at once violent, subversive and opposed to the state. This agnosticism, which by blatantly ignoring religion and bringing about, more or less overtly, the separation of Church and state, had impeded the absorption of the Church into the state and allowed the Church, officially ignored, in fact to regain the upper hand that it had lost centuries before – this liberal agnosticism then, tried to ignore the class struggle, class interests and organization into classes by turning a blind eye to them as being of no concern to the state. There were indeed times when agnosticism of this kind succeeded in achieving a kind of consummate mastery of the art of government.

But the liberal state allowed syndicalism to become a powerful and hostile force, not only because it ignored essential problems of society, but also because its conception of society was mechanistic, atomistic and egalitarian. By its conception of the state as the sum of equal individuals, an amorphous undifferentiated grey mass, liberalism, from the moment it began to practise politics, destroyed those ancient and venerable professional organizations, the guilds and corporations of arts and crafts which, since their emergence outside state control had been absorbed, disciplined and completely assimilated by the state. On the night of August 4th, 1789, the French National Assembly decreed the abolition of the corporations and in the subsequent law of August 14th–17th, 1791, expressly banned citizens exercising the same art, craft or profession from holding meetings, in order, so the law ran, to protect their so-called common interests. In Italy, this ban was quickly lifted but no legal recognition was ever granted and they continued to be completely ignored.

Yet professional organization or syndicalism, as it is normally known, or corporativism, to use the more traditional Italian word, is a natural and irrepressible phenomenon to be found in every age. It existed in Greece as well as in Rome, and in the Middle Ages as in modern times. The development of large industry, a specifically contemporary phenomenon, could only increase its importance. If, indeed, by syndicalism we mean the tendency of those engaged in similar undertakings, arts or professions, to form associations in order to protect their joint interests, it is natural that in view of the enormous growth in the number of entrepreneurs or technical directors or workers in industry, and of the inordinate increase in the value of their production, this imposing array of men with all their interests should have resolutely embarked on the syndicalist movement.

Today, we have, in fact, two forms of syndicalism, one for employers and the other for workers. The employers' syndicalism, which takes the form of trusts or cartels, depends on modern trends of production which are tending all the time towards increasingly large industrial concerns and thus towards industrial concentration. In little more than a century, we have moved from the artisan to the small firm, from there to large firms, to groups of firms, to syndicates of entrepreneurs.

But more impressive and increasingly dangerous is the development of workers' syndicates. Under the artisan system and in small family concerns, continuous contact existed between the owner and the worker and collaboration was friendly and easy; but once these had, so to speak, vanished, large firms employing hosts of workers stepped in and replaced handwork by machine labour, by creating vast factories in which the manual worker had to accomplish merely a few very simple mechanical operations requiring a minimum amount of professional skill. There no longer existed a close collaboration between manager and workman but a steadily increasing gap between the entrepreneur who directed the concern, with his team of engineers and technicians, and the mass of workers brutalized by their tiring and unskilled work. Those highly trained workers who used to transmit the secrets of their skills from father to son as a result of years of difficult apprenticeship now almost completely disappeared and were very difficult to replace. Instead, the workshops filled up with hordes of untrained peasants who migrated to the cities and went into industry without ever acquiring the indispensable skills. In such circumstances, the worker was completely at the mercy of management: in a free enterprise system, the continual influx of workers into industry and the simple nature of industrial techniques made for the maximum demand for employment and the minimum supply of the same, and therefore a low level of wages. This was the time when Ricardo was elaborating his pessimistic theory of a natural wage and Ferdinand de Lassalle was expressing his no less pessimistic 'brazen law of wages'.

Thus in the early decades of the nineteenth century, the free play of economic laws produced really difficult conditions for the workers. The liberal state, faithful to its dogma of non-intervention, let things follow their natural course and the wretched life of the manual worker spread discontent and a spirit of rebellion amongst the masses. At the time, completely in accordance with the idea of non-interference by the state, the workers were allowed to organize the class struggle and prepare, in other words, to obtain by their own endeavours, the justice that was being denied them by the apathy of the state. So liberalism became the most powerful factor in the emergence and spread of socialism which gathered together within itself the scattered forces of the workers, provided them with a discipline and led them on to fight for their own particular interests. They began with the strike, a weapon which in principle still maintained a semblance of legality inasmuch as it claimed to remain within the framework of the liberal economic system as a means of restricting the supply of labour and thus to achieve an increase in wages. But this was an initial passing stage of the battle. The next stage was dominated by the increasing political importance achieved by the mass of workers as a result of the progressive widening of the right to vote which was fostered by liberal democratic individualism. There came the time when the liberal democratic state found itself in such a position of weakness vis-à-vis the syndicalist movement that the struggle which had hitherto been legal and economic became a physical and violent one, without the state's having either the strength or the wish to interfere. So in the last thirty years we have seen the revival of self-defence as it existed in the Middle Ages, at first in a mild and later in an increasingly violent form. Today we have reached the position that, since the state is weak and permissive, there is a state of war of everyone against everyone else, a war fought with every material and moral force, a bloody and destructive war. The Middle Ages have returned in all their horror and misery.

In all times and places, the emergence of a system of self-defence goes together with a revival of the spirit of association. When the state is weak and each individual has to seek justice for himself, it is only natural for individuals to tend to form groups in order to be in a better position to defend themselves and gain their cause. This is how the corporative guilds arose in the Middle Ages. This is how the syndicates arose in the modern world. The two cases are completely parallel. Nevertheless, since medieval corporativism belonged to the period of the reorganization of society at the beginning of the movement which eventually halted the widespread disintegration of the late Middle Ages, it was incomparably more constructive in character than present-day syndicalism, which instead belongs to a period of incipient disintegration. Thus, for example, whereas in the corporations, all the elements of production were allied with each other and worked in complete harmony to protect their joint enterprise and to increase production, in modern syndicates, the employers and workers are separated and the main purpose of the group is no longer collaboration in the interests of all but the struggle to protect particular interests. But the most revealing difference between the two types of organization is this: whereas the corporations very soon moved into the orbit of the state, modern syndicates are now completely outside the state and frequently opposed to it.

Thus the indifference shown by the liberal state, true to its optimistic creed that freedom cures all the ills which it causes, has encouraged syndicalism to degenerate so seriously that, over and above its natural and legitimate economic aims, a whole political doctrine has been constructed with the ultimate aim of replacing the state by syndicates, entrusting them not only with the management of firms, with complete powers of control, but also, through confederation, with the responsibility for protecting all interests in general. And that is not enough. By an obvious distortion of its purpose, the syndicalist movement has gone over from the realm of private industry into that of public enterprise and even into the jealously guarded field of public administration and the civil service, thus giving rise to administrative syndicalism which has dealt the final and most serious blow to the authority of the state and eventually caused the complete disorganization of the public services.

IV

... Any idea of abolishing the syndicalist movement is inconceivable. It is a phenomenon of so far-reaching an extent in the life of our times as to be irrepressible, and, on the other hand, it must be judged for itself and not in its aberrations. The solution is thus to remove the causes of its aberrations and consequently to put an end to the passive attitude which the state, blinkered by its preconceived and completely outworn liberalistic ideas, has hitherto shown towards it. The state must return to its traditions, interrupted by the triumph of liberal ideology, and treat the modern syndicates exactly as it treated the medieval corporations. It must absorb them and make them part of the state. To achieve this it is not sufficient merely to recognize them. A far more fundamental change in attitude is required. On the one hand, syndicates must be recognized as essential and on the other they must be placed firmly beneath the control of the state, which must lay down their precise functions and ensure that their role of watchdog and guardian should be held within fixed limits, in the form of independence without excessive licence. But above all, it is necessary to change them from aggressive bodies defending particular interests into a means of collaboration to achieve common aims. The workers' syndicates and the employers' syndicates must join together within each industry to form one single mixed syndicate, organized, of course, into two or preferably even three sections, since it would be right and proper for management, the engineers, technicians and factory managers, to be specifically represented. But joint action by the syndicate must be unified by an appropriate body, a syndicate committee or board of directors, in order to achieve the many common aims.

Various important results would thus be achieved. First and foremost, this mixed syndicate, as a self-governing entity, could be entrusted with certain functions appertaining to the state, such as the protection of workers, public assistance and professional training. Secondly—and this is a particularly important point—through these reconstituted syndicates the state would at last possess the technical bodies to enable it properly to fulfil the various functions in the economy which necessity has forced upon it but which it has hitherto always exercised most incompetently.

It is true that many people believe that the state is radically unsuited to exercise any economic activity. And the total failure of almost every concern run by the state would seem to lend weight to that conclusion. I am less pessimistic. I believe that it is not the state in general that is unsuited in this way but the *liberal* state which has tried to take over functions for which it was technically unprepared and for which it lacked the suitable competent bodies. The main cause of the downfall of all state industries is the arrogant incompetence of the bureaucrats who were placed in charge of them. This truth is borne out by the fact that there are some state enterprises, for example tobacco, which, having succeeded over the years, after countless mistakes, in creating competent bodies, have achieved results appreciated and acknowledged by all.

The syndicates, including as they do within their ranks the most competent authorities in every branch of economic activity, are obviously the most appropriate bodies to make this expertise available to the state, that is, to provide the state, once it has undergone its fundamental reform, with the technical organization which it at present lacks.

Finally, the mixed syndicate can act as a friendly arbitrator and provide an effective means of conciliation in any disputes that may arise between its members. But the final judgment of such disputes, acting with the force of law, must be delegated to special state tribunals. This has a double implication. First, it absolutely precludes any of those forms of self-defence of class interests still remaining as relics of long-outmoded legal attitudes, and which disguise old social ills, left-overs from the struggles of the Middle Ages under another name: strikes, lock-outs, obstructionism, boycotts. This ban would finally complete, in the field of class conflicts, the development which has long since been reached where individual conflicts are concerned: that is to say, we should move from the primitive system of private defence, appropriate to periods of barbarism, to the principle of state justice, which is appropriate to more advanced societies. In the second place, this ban implies that we should abandon the rigid dogma which is given the lie every day by the facts, that wages and systems of labour are dominated by the law of supply and demand, and instead adopt the concept of a fair wage, which our lawyers would very soon manage to elaborate and set out in precise legal form. This change might not be very difficult when we realize that nowadays the fixing of wage levels has become purely a matter of force, achieved not by the free interplay of economic laws but by the material pressure of the interested party ...

If the state is to be able to discipline the syndicates, ban strikes and enforce the decisions reached by its tribunals, you may object that this requires powers that it does not possess. The elements that have overwhelmed it, such as organized syndicates and the parties, will always prevent the state from becoming any stronger and regaining the powers which it has been relinquishing over the last century or so. Consequently, we shall find ourselves in a vicious circle which it is impossible to break. I am not so pessimistic. In the modern state, the power of the syndicates and parties is considerable but the force of public opinion is also considerable and the latter is tired of the undeclared war that each group is waging against all the other members of the state in order to further, in a blind and selfish manner, its own particular interests. The conviction is becoming more and more widespread that the only way to improve the situation of everyone is to reinforce the authority of the state as supreme guardian of the interests of all.

At present, all that is needed is for a few energetic men with authority, supported by the public, to dare to break the circle in which the state is being smothered by particular interests and enforce the power of the state over the syndicates as well. On the other hand, as has always been the case in the struggle against particular interests, the state can temper its claims to re-establish its authority by offering concessions: legal recognition, economic aid, the organization of political representation for the syndicates, which would amount to assimilating them into the state; i.e. much more (and far more satisfactorily) than the miserable policy of surrender towards which, in its steady decline, the liberal state has been heading in recent years. But first and foremost it is necessary for the latter to give up the democratic-liberal mentality which is solely responsible for the way in which syndicalism, harmless in itself, has taken on the threatening, destructive aspect of which everyone rightly complains. To do this, we must be quite clear on one thing. The existence of syndicates is not a bad thing. What is bad is that they should constitute a super-state.

Despite the grave state of affairs and the social and political crisis which is causing concern to each and every one of us, I have faith in the future of the state. The state is not something different from or superior to society, it is society itself as a organized body, that is to say, in so far as it exists and has life and being, because organization is life. Having faith in the future of the state thus means having faith in the future of civilized society and in the future of civilization. It is inconceivable that modern industrial civilization can last for ever. Other perhaps superior civilizations, the Graeco-Roman, the Egyptian, the Assyrian-Babylonian, have collapsed in the past and ours, too, will inevitably collapse because there is nothing permanent under the sun. But if we think that those civilizations lasted thousands of years and ours is hardly at the beginning of its cycle, because it emerged in the fifteenth and sixteenth centuries, at the end of the anarchy of the Middle Ages and at the rebirth of the arts and the sciences, then we cannot imagine that our present one is fated to perish within a few centuries. For civilization would certainly perish if the state, as the supreme guardian of internal peace, were to fall apart and perish. So therefore we must have faith that the state will take up once again its essential task of guaranteeing, as it must, peace within the country. Then and then alone will modern civilization have overcome the terrible crisis which today threatens its very existence.

THE LAW ON THE DEFENCE OF THE STATE

(Report introducing the Bill in the Chamber of Deputies, November 9th, 1926)

... In the face of the new wave of aggression, which has led to no less than four attempts on the life of the head of state within a period of less than a year, it is plain that energetic precautionary measures must be taken. In the situation that has arisen in Italy today any delay would be criminal. Current legislation has proved inadequate, not only to prevent crime but also to satisfy public opinion by swift and salutary punishment of crimes already committed. There are many clear indications that if there is no effective intervention by the state to prevent and repress crime, the public will spontaneously take the law into its own hands to the grave detriment of the majesty of the law and the sovereignty of the state.

Nor is it possible to wait for a complete reform of the legal codes because, however rapidly we may proceed, some few months must elapse before we can finish drawing up new criminal laws and procedure. Nor, indeed, in such a grave emergency, would normal legislation be adequate, however much it may be amended. We must strike not only hard but fast so that both prevention of crime in general and its punishment can be achieved with maximum efficiency. Such an aim can be met only by exceptional legislation in accordance with an old tradition of the Italian state going back to the early days of her unification.

After 1860, a situation arose in Italy similar in some respects to the one existing today; groups of inveterate opponents of the new regime who had taken refuge outside the state frontiers were plotting and conspiring to cause acts of brigandage. And as a result, the men in charge of the government of the day, although professing themselves liberals, did not shrink from obtaining the approval of

Parliament for the Pica law which provided the most effective instrument in achieving victory for the young state over the Bourbon reactionaries. Similarly, we believe that, faced by the anti-Fascist reaction which is rearing its head at present in the form of criminal activity, we have to take urgent and exceptionally severe precautionary measures ...

I

The main innovation contained in this proposed law is the introduction of the death penalty for attempts on the lives of the king, the queen, the crown prince and the head of the government, as well as for certain grave crimes against the security of the state.

The temporary and exceptional nature of this proposed law would make it unnecessary to enter into a detailed critical examination of the vexed question of capital punishment. But since in fact this proposed law anticipates on this point a reform in the criminal code which the government intends to introduce into the new code, I shall need briefly to sum up the reasons why we have been led to reconsider the problem that liberal-democratic thought in Italy imagined had henceforth been settled once and for all.

There is no doubt that from an abstract philosophical viewpoint, liberal-democratic individualism leads to the rejection of capital punishment. In the individualistic conception of the state, the individual is an end in himself, and society and the state are the means; consequently, it is natural that the individual, as an end, cannot at the same time be a means, as Immanuel Kant plainly explains. Now since the death penalty involves the complete abolition of the personality, the individual is being considered purely and simply as an instrument or means to realize the following social aims: the protection of society against the delinquent, general deterrence and the appeasing of public opinion. It is true enough that in every form of punishment, including imprisonment, a similar sort of reversal occurs to a greater or lesser degree; but in capital punishment, this reversal is complete. If you accept the liberals' premise, the conclusion is irrefutable and this explains the trend amongst liberal theorists towards abolishing the death penalty. We use the word trend because, faced by the iron law of necessity, even liberal criminologists have, to a very great extent, cried halt. Hence the anomaly that the death penalty continues to be accepted by the legal systems of the vast majority of free countries and has the support of the opinion of very many criminal lawyers who are strong believers in liberal ideology ... The strange fate of individualistic philosophy in having posed the principles that would logically lead to the abolition of the death penalty whilst nevertheless long continuing to advocate it in theory and in practice is revealed even in the vicissitudes of criminal legislation under the French Revolution, which proclaimed the immortal principles of the philosophy of individualism in the declaration of the rights of man and the citizen. Marat and Robespierre were leading advocates of the abolition of capital punishment yet they later sent thousands of men to the guillotine and the two penal codes of the Revolution, one dated 3 Brumaire in Year IV, and the other the *Code Napoléon* of 1810, still retained the death penalty to a large extent.

This contradiction between theory and practice is the best possible proof that capital punishment reflects political and social necessities that cannot be disregarded. But in our view it also reflects exactly the conception of the relationship between the individual and the state, which is not at all the one propounded by individualistic philosophers. In fact it is untrue that the individual is the sole end in life and in society. It is, on the other hand, true that society, seen as the body which contains within itself the sum of a never-ending series of generations, and the state, which is its organized legal expression, have their own ends and exist for this purpose; whereas the individual is merely a transient and infinitesimal fraction of the social body to whose ends his own actions and own existence must be subordinated.

In this more accurate conception of society and the state, Kant's statement that since the individual is an end he cannot be adopted as a means is shown to be obviously erroneous. No! The individual is precisely the means to social ends which extend far beyond his own span. It is consequently no wonder that, if necessary, individual aims should be sacrificed to the immanent ends of the state; and consequently, should the need arise, for overriding reasons of defence of the state and of society, to inflict solemn and exemplary punishment and appease the justifiable indignation of the public conscience, thus avoiding bloodthirsty reprisals and grave disorder, it is perfectly legitimate to compel the individual to suffer the supreme sacrifice by the use of the death penalty. The repugnance that some people feel for this sacrifice is all the less justified in that no one doubts the legitimacy of another far larger and weightier sacrifice imposed by the state on its citizen: fighting and dying for one's country. If such a sacrifice is imposed on hundreds of thousands of honest citizens, why should anyone have doubts as to the legal and moral possibility of inflicting a similar sacrifice on the most wretched delinquents?

This is also the doctrine of the Roman Catholic Church ...

... There is no doubt, therefore, that from an abstract philosophical viewpoint, capital punishment may be considered as something perfectly legitimate once it has been shown to be necessary.

This is the nub of the matter: the death penalty is legitimate when it is necessary. Now there is no doubt that for the most serious crimes, those that shock public opinion most deeply and endanger the peace of society, the death penalty is by far the most effective, indeed, the only effective punishment.

Amongst the various functions of punishment by the law, the chief ones are certainly that of the prevention of crime in general, by means of threat and example; and that of retribution, which is also generally preventive in a certain sense because the satisfaction which the public feels at the sight of the punishment prevents acts of vengeance and reprisal, a very serious cause of disorder and the occasion for yet further crimes. From this angle, no punishment is as effective as the death penalty, none is more deterrent, either as a threat or at the moment of execution; no punishment better appeases the suffering caused to the feelings of the relatives or friends of the victim or more completely satisfies public indignation. But even the role of individual prevention which punishment undoubtedly fulfils, is represented, we would say almost to the point of perfection, by the death penalty, since no punishment is more successful as an instrument of elimination.

It is, of course, true that the death penalty makes it impossible for the criminal to repent and be rehabilitated, but we do not believe that these are the essential purposes of punishment; these are, in fact, secondary and additional aims that, indeed, would not be applicable in the sectors covered by capital punishment, which are precisely those of the most atrocious crimes and most perverse criminals, for whom any thought of repentance or rehabilitation is obviously futile. But the need for capital punishment can be deduced not only from its undeniable effectiveness. It can also be deduced from the fact that at a particular moment in history, the public conscience demands it as being necessary. When this happens only the supreme penalty is capable of satisfying the feelings of the people and of avoiding extra-legal reactions to crime. This is, in fact, the case at the present moment of time, as is demonstrated by the experience of this past year.

If we look at the question from this angle, all the objections that have been raised by the arguments of the abolitionists fall to the ground. These objections were clearly and lucidly summed up in the Zanardelli report on the proposals for the present Penal Code. They were the following:

1. While the death penalty is a barbarous and revolting punishment in the minds of the public, it has no deterrent effect. Executions, far from being terrifying, solemn, salutary

and exemplary, always turn out to be immoral and disgusting spectacles, liable to arouse bloodthirsty instincts in the crowd which attends them out of morbid curiosity ...

3. The death penalty not only has the effect of eliminating a criminal, it also permanently removes a human being, capable of rehabilitation, and is thus in contradiction to the reformatory aims of punishment.

4. The death penalty is without redress and the pronouncements of justice, which is always fallible, should never be without redress.

None of these objections is decisive. In fact:

1. As for the so-called barbarous nature of the death penalty, the reply could be made, first of all, that when the defence of the state requires it, there is no means or precaution that can be set aside merely because it may appear cruel from the point of view of the individual: we drew attention to the example of war. Now in such matters, it is not the point of view of the individual that must count, but that of society; anyway, even from the point of view of the individual, it is not true that the death penalty is more cruel than some other punishments that are accepted without demur, such as convict prisons and close confinement ...

3. The argument deriving from the fact that the death penalty, by destroying the human personality, renders any rehabilitation of the criminal impossible is based on the false supposition that rehabilitation is an essential part of punishment. This is an individualistic conception that ignores the eminently social nature of punishment and thus its primary functions of deterrence and retribution.

4. We are left with the argument which is probably the most impressive, namely that we condemn with no possible redress. But even that is not a decisive argument. Error is unfortunately an integral part of human nature and if fear of being mistaken were to inhibit action, the life of both individuals and society would be completely paralysed. Mistakes made by doctors and surgeons which result in the death of the patient are far more numerous than judicial

errors, although no one has ever thought of abolishing medicine or surgery. In any case, not only capital punishment but all punishment is in itself without redress, because there are consequences of sentences which no redress can succeed in obliterating.

THE FORMATION AND FUNCTIONS OF THE CORPORATIONS

(Report introducing the Bill in the Chamber of Deputies January 16th, 1934)

... The idea of the corporations has long-standing precedents in Italy. It appeared even before the Great War in two political trends that started separately and gradually drew closer to each other until they merged first during the period of neutrality and then during the hostilities: nationalism and syndicalism. As the first became progressively social, in the simple sense of the word, and the latter progressively more national, they found a natural point of contact in the idea of a national syndicalism, from which the idea of the corporation was bound to emerge. Then, following the rise of Fascism after the war, the idea of the corporation began not only to become more widespread and more closely defined but to move firmly from the realm of ideas into that of deeds, above all through the work of Fascist syndicalism. We must not forget that the Fascist syndicates organized themselves into corporations not only in name but in spirit.

After the revolution of October 1922 the corporative spirit of the Fascist syndicalist organizations asserted itself with increasing effect. The agreements reached in the Palazzo Vidoni on October 2nd, 1925, represented the culmination of this movement. The time was thus ripe for more far-reaching experiments in the field of legislation and organization.

The law of April 3rd, 1926, governing collective labour relations and the norms for its application as laid down on July 1st were of fundamental importance in the development of corporativism. In this legislation, the corporative idea became no longer merely a concept, a trend or intellectual tendency, but took concrete form in precise and clearly outlined legal institutions.

True, the immediate purpose of the 1926 legislation was to eliminate self-defence on the part of classes or groups, to organize classes and groups within the orbit and under the supervision of the state and to settle labour disputes peacefully by legal means. After eleven years of the Fascist regime, now that the attitudes of employers and workers have changed, in part as a result of the new institutions, these problems which Fascism has solved may even be considered as no longer relevant. The truth is that at that time they were both grave and urgent and they continue to be grave and urgent in those countries left untouched by Fascist ideas. Anyhow, it was a signal triumph, both then and now, and it represents one of Fascism's important titles to fame.

But the 1926 laws foresaw quite clearly that the economic innovations of Fascism could not be considered complete with the disciplining of labour relations. Not only had the problem of the distribution of wealth to be solved without recourse to liberal anarchy or socialist tyranny but there was also the problem of production. And the work of controlling, organizing and improving production could not be entrusted only to the syndicates but had perforce to be undertaken by a new body bringing all the factors of production together under state direction and control: from the very beginning, this body was called a corporation ...

... The time is now indeed ripe for the further development of corporative institutions: that is, for an autonomous and independent organization of corporations and for a more exact definition of their powers and activities in the field of production.

The systems hitherto operating to regulate the production of wealth have already been subjected to adequate critical examination and this criticism does not therefore need to be repeated. Liberal economics and socialist economics have been condemned by the facts: the failure of both is no longer a matter for argument. Anyone wishing to explore the causes, development and various manifestations of this failure need only reread Benito Mussolini's vigorous summaries of the matter, above all in his masterly speeches in the Consiglio Nazionale delle Corporazioni and in the Senate. Liberal economics, which expected that production could be governed by the undisturbed interplay of free competition and the laws of supply and demand, have proved a failure, as have the attempted experiments of socialist economists who, by subordinating production to distribution, eliminated from the process of production the extremely powerful impulse of personal interest, abolished any desire to save and prevented the formation of capital, with the double result that production was hampered by red tape and rendered fruitless. So, according to the results achieved hitherto, the only remaining live economic force is that of Fascism, which has overtaken liberal and socialist economic ideas in the field of distribution as well as of production.

From the point of view of distribution, it organizes the factors of production under state control, governs their interrelations through the system of collective contract and settles any disputes by the decision of the labour tribunal. From the point of view of production, the Fascist economic system recognizes the need for an organization capable of co-ordinating the efforts of all elements, improving productivity and forming the productive activity of the nation into one united whole. But Fascism does not believe that such an organization can be formed as a result of the free interplay of economic forces nor does it believe either that it can be achieved by the state's taking over the task of production; it has no trust in the illusions of either the liberals or the socialists. In their place, Fascism wants to make use of the expertise and interests of these various categories of producers and entrust them with the primary task of organizing production. But it wants the state to act as watch-dog to supervise this task which is so essential for the whole nation.

So a Fascist economy is not an economy of association nor merely a directed or controlled economy, it is above all an organized one. It is organized by the efforts of the producers themselves, with the state to direct and control them from above. In this sense we can speak of a Fascist economy as the self-government of the various categories of producers. The expression is a telling one, albeit not quite exact, because these categories of producers are not governing themselves, but governing production, which is also in their interest, even though it is above all a collective interest. And this is why control of production by these organized classes of producers can take place only under the overall guidance and control of the state.

The key body in this new Fascist economy is the corporation in which the various categories of producers, employers and workers are all represented and which is certainly the best fitted to regulate production, not in the interest of any one producer but in order to achieve the highest output, which is in the interests of all the producers but above all in the national interest.

So the state will be making use of individual expertise and self-interest in the higher interests of the nation.

For this reason the so-called self-government of the various groups of producers can perfectly easily be reconciled with state intervention. The self-interest of the producers is not in fact an end but a means, an instrument employed by the state to achieve its own ends, as the representative of the whole collectivity.

This is why the corporations are and must remain state bodies; this does not mean that the state takes over production, any more, incidentally, than it means that the corporations take it over either. Except in special cases where the state takes over directly for important political reasons, as laid down in the Labour Charter, production remains in private hands. The corporations are merely entrusted with the overall control, organization and improvement of production; although state bodies, they are autonomous and composed of representatives of the groups that are themselves responsible for production. The modern corporation is thus very different from the medieval corporation or guild. The latter was indeed a completely self-governing body of producers but it regulated production only in their own selfish interests. The guild existed outside the state and sometimes in opposition to it and it was natural that, being thus enclosed in the narrow circle of its own interests, it ended by stifling productive activity and arousing the hatred of the mass of consumers, thus bringing about its own demise which was greeted with universal acclaim. The Fascist corporation on the contrary regulates production through the producers, not only in their interest but primarily in the interests of all concerned, under the effective guidance of the state. The modern corporation is thus not organized outside but within the state, as a state body. This is certainly how it will act, by utilizing the technical expertise and the individual drive of the producers in order to improve and increase production and make it more profitable, thereby increasing the wealth of the nation.

The Fascist corporation is thus an innovation when compared with the medieval guild; it is also different from the other attempts that have been made outside Italy, since the Fascist experiment started, to utilize the expertise of producers in order to further production. It differs profoundly from the *mixed syndicates*, in which the balance between the various productive factors is impossible to maintain and the union of employers and workers is effected in such a way as to give rise to confusion and mistrust.

The corporation on the other hand is solidly based on the system of specialized syndicates. Corporativism presupposes the existence of syndicalism and embodies it. Meanwhile, it is now possible to bring the corporative system into being inasmuch as, by reason of the law of April 3rd, 1926, the various categories of syndicate have been specifically laid down and they are now aware of their role.

At this point, it is fair to acknowledge the great merits of those higher syndicalist organizations known as *confederations*. The large confederations will now certainly have to adapt themselves to the new circumstances of the corporations, but no one can overlook their past merits. The first is that of having given life and soul to the idea of the specialized syndicates, of having inspired in them a spirit both national and Fascist and of having made them conscious of their mission, not only at the individual but also at the social and political level. Their second merit is the great contribution they have made in strengthening the Italian economy during the period of stabilization by adapting costs and wages to the new value of the lira …

The spirit of the law is contained in everything that we have been privileged to explain in our account of the history of the Fascist corporation and in our examination of its economic and legal characteristics. We have faith in the future of the Fascist economy and this means that we have faith in the future of the corporations …

throughout [illegible] their importance. The first is that of having given life and spirit to the idea of the syndicates, of having [illegible] and [illegible] of having made them conscious of their mission [illegible] of the [illegible] political field. Their second merit is the great contribution they have made in strengthening the Italian economy during the period of stabilization by adapting [illegible] wages to the new value of the lira.

The spirit of the law is contained [illegible] everything that we have been privileged to explain [illegible] of the Fascist Corporation [illegible] in our examination of its economic and legal characteristics [illegible] future of the Fascist economy and the [illegible] that we have [illegible] in the future of the corporative [illegible].

GIOVANNI GENTILE
(1875–1944)

Gentile was the chief collaborator of Croce in the review *La Critica*, founded by the latter in 1903. Before the war he was not actively involved in politics, except in the debates on the organization of education. It was only in the critical year of 1917 that he began to write regularly on political themes. He had few or no contacts with Fascism before he joined Mussolini's first Cabinet as Minister of Education. Some months later he resigned from the Liberal party, on the grounds that Fascism was now the true liberalism. During his time as Minister of Education he carried out a major reform of the whole educational system.

Although he ceased to be a minister in 1924, between 1925 and 1929 he was very active as a propagandist for the new regime. He drew up the 'Manifesto of the Fascist intellectuals', an inferior piece of writing to which Croce made a withering reply, and he became president of the Fascist Institute of Culture.

After 1932 he became progressively more isolated, largely as a result of the Conciliation. He opposed the anti-semitic legislation of 1938, and for a time his position within Fascism became very precarious. However, in 1943, after launching an unsuccessful appeal for national unity, he threw in his lot with the Salò republic. He was assassinated in 1944, probably by the Communist partisans, although it is possible that the murder was instead the work of Fascist extremists who feared him as an influence for moderation.

FROM *THE ORIGINS AND DOCTRINE OF FASCISM* (1934)

IX. *The totalitarian nature of Fascist doctrine*

Our study of the history of the spiritual and political crisis in Italy and its solution has already introduced us to the concepts of Fascism. This is not the place to talk about its work in the sphere of government, legislation or administration since for the moment we wish rather to throw light on the ideas underlying this action, which in the last five years has achieved a profound transformation in the laws, organization and institutions of the state, and thus to clarify the essence of Fascism.

What we have said makes clear the complex nature of the movement and nothing is more instructive in enabling us to understand it than, in fact, the consideration of Mazzini with which we began. His conception was certainly a political one but political in that overall sense which is indistinguishable from morality, religion or any other conception of life and which thus cannot be considered as existing on its own, separated and standing apart from these other fundamental ideas and interests of mankind. Mazzini's politics represent what he believes as a moral, religious and philosophical being. If you try to separate, within his beliefs and his teaching, what is of purely political significance from his religious or metaphysical convictions, his moral intuition or his ethical demands, you will no longer be able to realize the great historical importance of his beliefs and his teaching or the reasons why he fascinated and attracted so many minds and disturbed the dreams of so many statesmen and so many guardians of law and order. Any analysis that does not always presuppose the oneness of things leads not to clarification but to the destruction of the ideas that have had the greatest effect on history: a proof that men cannot be considered in fragments but only as one and indivisible.

So we have established the first point in defining Fascism: the totalitarian nature of its doctrine which is concerned not only with the political order and management of a nation but with its will, thought and feelings.

X. *Thought and Action*

Second point: Fascist doctrine is not a philosophy in the ordinary sense of the word and even less a religion. Nor is it even a fully elaborated and definite political doctrine which can be expressed in a series of formulas. The truth is that the meaning of Fascism cannot be measured in terms of the special theses that it adopts from time to time, in theory or in practice. As we said, at the beginning it did not put forward any precise, well-determined doctrine. Frequently, after having tried to define a goal that it hoped to achieve, an idea that it wanted to realize or a path which it intended to follow, it did not hesitate, after trial and error, to change its course and reject the goal or the idea as inadequate or repugnant to its own principles. It always refused to commit itself with regard to the future. It frequently announced reforms when the announcement was politically opportune but without feeling any obligation for that reason to carry them out. The Duce's real decisions have always been those which were not only formulated but implemented. For that reason he boasts of his 'timing' and ability to make decisions and act at the right moment, when all the conditions and reasons which make action possible and opportune are fully ripe. In the Fascist movement it is he who gives the most rigorous meaning to Mazzini's maxim of 'thought and action', bringing the two terms together in such a way as to make them coincide perfectly and attaching no value whatsoever to any thought that has not already been translated into or expressed in action. This is the source of all the arguments concerning anti-intellectualism, one of the themes which arises most frequently in Fascist discussions. It is an argument—and I must emphasize this point—which is specifically related to Mazzini's thought, since intellectualism is thought divorced from action, science divorced from life, brain divorced from heart, theory divorced from practice: it is the attitude adopted by the idle prattler and the sceptic, the incomplete man who hides behind the maxim that words are not deeds; by the builder of Utopias which will not have to face the harsh facts of reality; by poets, scientists or philosophers who shut themselves up in their imagination or their intelligence and do not use their eyes to look at the world in which they are living and in which they too share the fundamental interests of the rest of mankind, who provide the material for their imagination and their intelligence; by all the representatives of the old Italy of the past, who were the target of Mazzini's virulent denunciation.

Anti-intellectualism does not mean—as the more stupid Fascists imagine when they chuckle with joy every time they think themselves authorized by the Duce to jeer at science and philosophy—it does not mean that thought is in fact denied all validity, any more than it is denied to those higher forms of culture in which thought comes into its own. Spiritual reality is a synthesis whose unity and value is shown as thought which is also action. But many elements combine to form this final unified synthesis; they must combine and they must do so consciously; without these elements, the synthesis would be an empty one functioning in a vacuum. These elements include every form of spiritual activity, all of which thus possess the same value as that of the synthesis, of which they form an essential part. You do not rout an army which is threatening the frontiers of the fatherland by the use of trigonometry; but without trigonometry you cannot direct the fire of your artillery. The argument is directed against men whose spiritual life is devoted solely to the exercise of abstract intellectual activities remote from the realities of life in which every man must feel his existence to be firmly rooted, and hence against certain attitudes adopted by such men in exercising their spiritual activities, against certain conclusions which they assume to be definitive whereas in fact they are merely steps to higher conclusions, more concrete and more human. But the real target, the real enemy, is the historically typical mentality of the cultivated classes of Italy, namely the attitude of the man who was for centuries called *the man of letters*. This was not only an author or lover of literature, but any writer at all, even a scientist or philosopher, who concerned himself with liberal studies in a disinterested and unprofessional way; any academic, learned or erudite man, convinced on principle that he should not take part in politics or deal in business matters, is thereby reduced to a cypher in the practical world. The man of letters is a bastard product of our Renaissance whom Fascism rightly holds in disrepute as a bad citizen and intends to weed out completely from our soil.

This sort of anti-intellectualism is not the enemy of culture but of bad culture, of that culture which does not educate and form a man but deforms him, turns him into a pedant and makes him a Don Ferrante or an intellectual aesthete; that is to say, an egoist or a man morally and therefore politically indifferent: a man who remains aloof from the fray even when his own country is involved, even when interests are in jeopardy which ought to prevail, although their success might mark the victory of a group or a considerable body of people and the defeat of another group or equally considerable body. For mankind progresses only through division, and progress is achieved through the clash and victory of one side over another; and woe unto him who refuses to take sides and will not commit himself in the struggle and stands apart and considers it his duty to remain a spectator waiting for the conflict to be decided and then, once it is over, reaps the fruits of victory. The intellectual considers it the height of wisdom to attain to this state of apathy in which all the pros and cons are understood and all passion dies in his breast and he shuns the streets where people are fighting, suffering and dying and stands watching in safety from his window. *Suavi mari magno*, etc. But this is the epicurean ideal. And the whole history of mankind belies epicureanism. It may be a troubled history, full of trial and tribulation, but this is the history which has given birth to all that is dear to us, on which and by which we live and have our being.

Through its dislike for intellectualism, Fascism has no desire to spend its time drawing up abstract theories, not because it does not accept theories but because, in its efforts to reform and further Italian life and culture, constructing theories is no part of its role. On the other hand, when we say that Fascism is not a system or a doctrine, it must not be thought that it is mere abstraction, a blind working-to-rule or an indefinable instinct. Indeed, if by system or philosophy we mean—as we must mean whenever we intend to talk about something living—a universal principle as it unfolds in action, a principle with the power of revealing its richness, the range of consequences and applications of which it is capable, stage by stage and almost from one day to the next, then Fascism is a perfect system and its development is based on the soundest of principles and most rigorous logic; and, from its Duce down to the humblest foot soldier, those who feel within themselves the truth and vitality of this principle are working unceasingly to develop it, sometimes striding steadfastly straight towards the goal, at other times building up and pulling down, advancing and going back to the beginning because the attempt has failed to match the principle and has deviated from its logical development.

In this sense, that is as an open system capable of dynamic development, there is a philosophy contained in every great thought, whether it be the essence of a political or social revolution or a religious reformation or a moral or literary critical movement. In this sense Mazzini is a philosopher as well as Manzoni, Pascal as well as Goethe, Leopardi as well as Byron or Shelley; none of them belongs properly to the history of philosophy but they all adhere to a philosophy or philosophical trend and oppose all those which diverge from or contradict them. If this were not the case, we should have no means to define and evaluate Fascism. You may prefer to define it as a method rather than as a system, since by system we normally understand a closed doctrine worked out in a fixed pattern of theories laid down in propositions or theories to which nothing can be added or from which nothing can be taken. In that sense, which is implicit in every philosophical or religious doctrine that gives rise to schools or sects, adepts and heretics, there is nothing more foreign to Fascism than any claim to being a system or philosophy.

XI. *The core of the system*

Third point. Fascism is not a speculative system but has its centre of gravity in politics and political matters. Having started as a conception of the state, with the purpose of solving the political problems that had reached a pitch of exasperation as a result of the unbridled passions of the uninformed masses after the war, Fascism has taken to the arena as a method of politics. But the fact of tackling and solving political problems leads Fascism by its very nature – and this means by its very method – to consider cultural problems of morality, religion and philosophy, in a word to develop and prove its essentially totalitarian nature. It is thus appropriate to draw attention first to the political form of its principles, the development of which constitutes the content of Fascism, not however forgetting to point out that its spiritual origins lie in a deeper intuition of life, which is the source of its political principles.

With this caveat, we can summarize the political doctrine of Fascism briefly thus: this doctrine does not exhaust the content of Fascism but is none the less its outstanding and, speaking generally, its most interesting part or rather form.

XII. *The doctrine of the state*

Fascist politics revolve entirely round the concept of the national state. This concept has points of contact with the nationalist doctrine, so many, indeed, as to have made it possible, in practice, to weld the nationalist and Fascist parties into one single programme, which none the less has its own characteristics. And these cannot be passed over without ignoring what is its real and most characteristic feature. Comparisons are always invidious and the one that I have alluded to will now certainly hardly appear otherwise; despite this, I shall venture to pursue it in view of the light which it can throw on the essence of Fascism.

Both doctrines make the state the basis of every value and every right possessed by the individuals who belong to it. For both of them, the state is not a result but a principle. But nationalism reverses the view of the relationship between the state and the individual held by individualistic liberalism and even socialism, and since it conceives the state as a principle, it sees the individual as a result, something that has in the state antecedents which limit and determine him, limiting his freedom or restricting him to a particular territory in which he is born and has to live and die. For Fascism however, the state and the individual are one and the same thing, or rather are inseparable terms of an essential synthesis.

The nationalists in fact base the state on the concept of 'nation', an entity which, according to them, transcends the individual will and personality, because it is conceived as existing objectively, independently of the consciousness of its individuals, existing even if the latter do nothing to make it exist or to create it. The nationalists' 'nation' is, in a word, something which exists not by virtue of the spirit but as a given fact of nature, either because the elements that give it being, such as the land or the race, depend on nature itself or else because they must be considered as human creations: language, religion, history. Because even these human elements contribute to the formation of the national entity, inasmuch as they are already in being and the individual finds himself face to face with them, since they pre-exist him, from the moment he begins to act as a moral being; they are therefore on the same plane as the land and the race. This naturalistic attitude is a weakness of the spiritualistic tendency of the nationalists' conception and lends it a certain harshness and illiberality—a retrogade and crude conservatism which was its least attractive aspect and one which, prior to Fascism, with which it was later to be assimilated and amalgamated, aroused distrust and dislike even amongst the politicians whose political tendencies made them sympathetic to the majority of the nationalists' premises; meanwhile it favoured certain mystico-religious attitudes which were one of the most effective reasons for the enthusiastic and idealistic support for nationalism by young men and intellectuals unused to political reflection.

This naturalism was particularly and obviously visible in the loyal support shown by the nationalists for the monarchy. For them, monarchy was an *a priori* assumption, inasmuch as the Italian state was born at the same time as and by virtue of its monarchy and inasmuch as the historical basis that today forms the foundation of Italian nationhood, as realized in the Kingdom of Italy, includes the monarchy, the history of which is ultimately and inextricably bound up with the history of the people. There are the Alps and the Apennines, Sicily and Dalmatia, there is the epic of the Thousand and the House of Savoy. Remove any one of these elements and you no longer have the 'nation'. Support the latter, as you must, and that means supporting all these elements, experiencing them as inseparable from your own personality as an Italian. It is not your consciousness which, by recognizing and experiencing this bond or relationship, creates it and gives it perforce its appropriate moral value but the bond or relationship itself which pre-exists and determines the consciousness which thus has to support it, and in a way, submit to it.

On the other hand, while Fascism was seeking its way, keenly aware of the troubled and acutely unsatisfactory state of Italian politics at the time and unable to understand why the monarchy could not take vigorous and energetic steps to put the nation on the path already foreshadowed by the generous sacrifices of the war and the honourable terms of the subsequent victory (and thus was unable to see the roots that the monarchy might have and still possess in the consciousness of the Italians of what was called the Italy of Vittorio Veneto), it did not hesitate to admit to having a markedly republican bias. But later on, above all when Victor Emmanuel rejected the state of siege which the last Ministry of the old regime proposed to adopt against the Fascist revolution and, as in 1915, preferred to settle the crisis existing between the old and the new Italy by handing over power to the latter, thereby firmly breaking with the normal practice of parliamentarism which had been responsible for this tremendous crisis, this openly admitted bias did not prevent Mussolini from taking the oath of loyalty to the king and making a definitive break, in all good faith and logic, with these Republican tendencies. This means that, in contrast to the nationalists, Fascism does not see the monarchy as something inherited from the past and thus to be respected as a *fait accompli*, especially when it is beneficial, but as a living spiritual present and future which our minds turn to as our own ideal and lovingly admire as part of our aspirations, our needs, our very nature.

Monarchy, like everything resulting from the state, like the state itself, is not ahead of or outside us. The state is within ourselves; it reigns and lives, and must always live and grow and increase and rise up in dignity and in its consciousness of itself and of its noble duties and the high purposes to which it is called, as part of our will, our thoughts and passions. The individual develops and so does the state; individual character grows in strength and within the individual the structure, the force and the efficiency of the state grows strong as well. And its seas and coasts and mountains become more solid and compact, as if they were ideas and feelings; because everything in nature can become divided and dispersed if it so pleases us, or at least if it does not displease us; and everything is united and indivisible if we feel that its oneness is necessary. And past history with its memories and traditions, its vaunted and glorious deeds, builds up and takes root in us by means of our fervid interest and the remembrance within our own souls, which make it their own and control and defend it with their support and vigilant awareness. And we savour the tongue of our fathers and make it our own and it lives again in us when we learn it with care and appreciate it in its living power of expression. And everything that seemed already in being, a sort of heirloom, becomes transformed into our own personal conquest, a never-ending act of creation liable to disappear the moment our attention were to falter, since we are its begetters.

XIII. *The Fascist State as a Democratic State*

So the Fascist state, unlike the nationalist state, is a purely spiritual creation. And it is a national state because, from the Fascist standpoint, the nation itself is realized in the spirit and is not a mere presupposition. The nation is never complete and neither is the state, which is the nation itself expressed in concrete political form. The state is always becoming. It is, in its entirety, within our own hands. Hence our immeasurably great responsibility.

But this state, which achieves its reality in the very consciousness and will of the individual and is not a force imposing its authority from above, cannot have the same relationship with the mass of the people as the nationalists assumed. The latter, who made state and nation coincide and considered the nation as an already existing entity that did not need to be created but merely acknowledged, had need of a ruling class, primarily intellectual in character, which would experience this entity that had first to be acknowledged, understood, appreciated and glorified. Moreover, the authority of the state was not a consequence but an assumption. It could not depend on the people; indeed, the people depended on the state, and on the authority that they were obliged to recognize as a necessary condition of their lives, outside which they would sooner or later have realized, even on their own, that life was impossible. The nationalist state was for this reason an aristocratic state, deriving its strength from its origins and thus able to prevail over the masses. The Fascist state, on the other hand, is a popular state, and in this sense, the democratic state *par excellence*. As we have seen, the relationship between the state and not merely *some* citizens but *every* citizen with the right to describe himself as such is so close that the state exists inasmuch as and to the extent that it is given existence by its citizens. Thus its formation is a factor of individual consciousness and so of the consciousness of the masses; its power is composed of their power. Hence the necessity for the party and all the propaganda and educational institutions based on the political and moral ideas of Fascism which it uses to ensure that the thoughts and wishes of the Duce become the thoughts and wishes of the masses. This gives rise to the immense problem to which Fascism feels committed: the problem of bringing the whole people, from their tenderest years, into the framework of the party and its institutions. A formidable problem, the solution of which is creating infinite difficulties, either because it is well-nigh impossible to adapt the great masses of the people to the demands of an elite party with a forward-looking morality, when they can only be educated and reformed slowly over the centuries; or else because of the dichotomy between governmental and party action, a dichotomy difficult to avoid, despite every effort and single-minded discipline, when a party organization expands almost to the same size as the state; or else because of the danger incurred by every progressive and creative power when the individuals are all caught up in the cogs of a mechanism which, however powerful and single-minded its central inspiration, is bound to enfeeble and destroy freedom of movement and independent action as you move from the centre outwards.

XIV. *The Corporative State*

From this characteristic of the Fascist state there springs, however, the great social and constitutional reform which

Fascism is realizing by creating a corporative syndicalist regime and working to replace the liberal state by the corporative state. Fascism has in fact taken over from syndicalism the idea of syndicates as an educative moral force, but since the antithesis between state and syndicate must be overcome, it has endeavoured to develop a system whereby this function should be attributed to syndicates grouped together into corporations subject to state discipline and indeed reflecting within themselves the same organization as the state. Since the latter wants to make contact with the individual, in order to realize itself as an expression of his will, it does not approach him as the abstract political individual, which old-fashioned liberalism conceived as a purely indifferent atom, but instead approaches him in the only possible way, in his concrete reality as a specialized force of production who, by reason of his speciality, is led to associate himself with all the other individuals in the same category and belonging to the same unitary economic group provided by the nation. By clinging as closely as possible to the concrete reality of the individual as he really is, the syndicate enables him to achieve his proper dignity, either through the self-awareness which he gradually acquires or else by the rights which he is required to exercise regarding the general interests of the nation which will itself arise out of the harmonious whole formed by the syndicates ...

The corporative state aims at achieving that immanence of the state within the individual without which there is no strength, which is the very essence of the state and of individual freedom; and it provides that ethical and religious value which Fascism feels so deeply and which the Duce, its mouthpiece, has taken every opportunity to proclaim, in theory and practice, with the utmost solemnity.

XV. *Liberty, Ethics and Religion*

Once the Duce of Fascism put forward and discussed the theme of 'force or consensus?', reaching the conclusion that the two terms are inseparable and that the one requires the other and cannot exist without it. This means that the authority of the state and the liberty of the citizen form an unbroken and unbreakable circle in which authority presupposes freedom and vice versa. For freedom resides only in the state and the state represents authority; but the state is not an abstraction, an entity descended from heaven, living in the air above the heads of its citizens; on the contrary, it forms one single personality with the individual citizen whom it must thus recognize and help, knowing that it exists in so far as it makes its own existence.

In fact, Fascism does not oppose liberalism as an authoritarian system opposing a system based on liberty, but as a system based on real, concrete liberty opposed to a system of false, abstract liberty. For liberalism begins by breaking the circle mentioned above, and sets the individual against the state and liberty against authority. It wants a liberty which limits the state, thereby resigning itself to the inevitable evil of a state which limits freedom. Such foolish abstract ideas had indeed already been the subject of criticism within liberalism itself; in the nineteenth century there were plenty of noteworthy liberals who advocated the need for a strong state in the interests of liberty itself. But it is one of Fascism's merits that it has set its face vigorously and courageously against current liberal prejudice and has stated loud and clear that that sort of freedom benefits neither a nation nor its individual members. Moreover, inasmuch as the corporative state tends to realize a closer and more substantial unity or circle of authority and liberty by means of a more honest and realistic system of representation, the new state is more liberal than the old one.

But in that circle, which can only be realized within the sphere of the individual conscience developing historically through the association of productive forces and the historical tradition of moral and intellectual conquests, the state would be unable to achieve the concreteness which it seeks and needs if, within that sphere, it did not invest the conscience in its entirety as an unconditional and unlimited sovereign force. Otherwise, the state in its own inner essence would remain suspended in a vacuum. Nothing can live or be of value in the spirit except what takes hold of the whole spirit, leaving nothing over. For that reason the authority of the state refuses to compromise or come to terms or share its sphere of influence with any other moral or religious principles that might interfere in the consciousness. The vigour and the authority of the state exist when its authority is unconditional and infinite, within the consciousness. The consciousness that gives reality to the state is total consciousness, containing all the elements from which it is derived. Morality and religion, essential elements for every consciousness, are therefore bound to be present in this consciousness, but must necessarily be subordinated to the law and authority of the state, and be indissolubly absorbed into them.

The man whose will is, at its deepest level, the will of the state, as a synthesis of the two terms of authority and freedom, each of which acts on the other and determines its development, is the man who can through this will also resolve his own religious and moral problems as they occur. Were it deprived of such influences and values, the state would again become something mechanical and as a result lose the values which it claims to represent politically.

This explains the exquisitely political character of the relationship between the Church and the Fascist state. The Italian Fascist state, desirous, for the above-mentioned reasons, of forming one single unit with the mass of the Italians, must be either religious or else Catholic. It cannot fail to be religious because the absolute nature which it attributes to its own value and authority cannot be conceived except in relation to a Divine Absolute. There is only one religion based on and indeed rooted in the mass of the Italian people and meaningful for them, on which they can graft this religious feeling of the absolute nature of the will of the country; unless, rather than developing what lies within the consciousness, a stupid attempt were made to introduce into it a moral criterion from outside. And you cannot be a Catholic except within the Church and under its discipline. So the Fascist state must recognize the religious authority of the Church; this is a political necessity, for political recognition, in order to realize the state itself. The ecclesiastical policy of the Italian state must solve the problem of ensuring that its sovereignty remains internal and absolute even vis-à-vis the Church, without offending either the Italians' Catholic consciousness or the Church to which this consciousness owes allegiance.

This, too, is a difficult problem since the transcendental conception on which the Catholic Church is based contradicts the immanent political conception of Fascism; and Fascism, I must reiterate, far from being a negation of liberalism and democracy, as people say—and as its leaders, for political reasons, are often justified in repeating—is, in fact, or strives to be, the most perfect form of liberalism and democracy as defined by Mazzini, to whose doctrine it has reverted.

So this, at least, is the path and the way. A long and arduous path. The Italian people have set out with a faith and a passion which has seized hold of the soul of the people in a way unprecedented in their history. They are on the march, obedient and disciplined as never before, without hesitation or discussion, with their eyes fixed on the man of heroic mould who possesses all the outstanding and admirable gifts of the great leaders of peoples. He strides ahead, crowned by a halo of myth, as if a man chosen by God, tireless and infallible, the instrument elected by Providence to create a new civilization.

And in this civilization all men see what is contingent and specifically Italian and what is of permanent and universal validity.

BIBLIOGRAPHY

General

In English

B. Croce, *History of Italy 1871–1915*, trans. C. M. Ady (Oxford, 1929).

A. J. Gregor, *The Ideology of Fascism* (New York: Free Press, 1969: London: Collier-Macmillan, 1969).

A. Hamilton, *The Appeal of Fascism: a study of intellectuals and Fascism* (London: Anthony Blond, 1971).

E. Nolte, *Three Faces of Fascism* (London: Weidenfeld & Nicolson, 1965). The best study of the nature of Fascist ideology. The section on Italy contains an excellent analysis of Mussolini's Marxism, but is less convincing, to my mind, on later developments.

J. A. Thayer, *Italy and the Great War. Politics and Culture 1870–1915* (University of Wisconsin Press, 1964). A lively and learned, if not always reliable, study.

In Italian

F. Gaeta, *Nazionalismo italiano* (Naples: Edizioni Scientifiche Italiana). 1965.

M. Isnenghi, *Il mito della grande guerra* (Bari: Laterza, 1971).

N. Valeri, *Da Giolitti a Mussolini: momenti della crisi del liberalismo* (Florence: Parenti, 1956). Contains a brilliant study of the change in cultural attitudes and how it affected politics.

P. Vita-Finzi, *Le delusioni della libertà* (Florence: Vallecchi, 1961). Short studies of the anti-democratic thinkers of the Giolittian period.

On Individual Authors

D'ANNUNZIO: An interesting Marxist analysis is given by C. Salinari, *Miti e coscienza del decadentismo italiano* (Milan: Editore Riuniti, 1960).

GENTILE: H. S. Harris, *The Social Philosophy of Giovanni Gentile* (University of Illinois Press, 1960). A thorough and serious study, though occasionally inclined to white-wash Gentile's relationship to Fascism.

MARINETTI: There is an excellent essay by James Joll in his *Intellectuals in Politics* (London: Weidenfeld & Nicolson, 1960).

PARETO: The literature on Pareto is vast. Apart from S. E. Finer's introduction to the selection of *Sociological Writings* (London: Pall Mall Press, 1966), see Raymond Aron, 'Vilfredo Pareto' in Raymond Aron, *Main Currents of Sociological Thought*, trans. R. Howard and H. Weaver (London: Weidenfeld & Nicolson, 1965; Penguin Books, 1968). See also F. Borkenau, *Pareto* (New York: John Wiley & Sons, 1936; London: Chapman & Hall, 1946); and J. Burnham, *The Machiavellians* (London: Putnam & Co., 1943). In Italian, N. Bobbio, *Saggi sulla scienza politica in Italia* (Bari: Laterza, 1969) gives the most balanced assessment.

ROCCO: There is a brilliant study by P. Ungari, *Alfredo Rocco e l'ideologia giuridica del Fascismo* (Brescia: Morcelliana, 1963).